Dear Reader:

The book you are about to read is the latest bestseller from the St. Martin's True Crime Library, the imprint *The New York Times* calls "the leader in true crime!" The True Crime Library offers you fascinating accounts of the latest, most sensational crimes that have captured the national attention. St. Martin's is the publisher of John Glatt's riveting and horrifying SECRETS IN THE CELLAR, which shines a light on the man who shocked the world when it was revealed that he had kept his daughter locked in his hidden basement for 24 years. In the Edgar-nominated WRITTEN IN BLOOD, Diane Fanning looks at Michael Petersen, a Marine-turned-novelist found guilty of beating his wife to death and pushing her down the stairs of their home—only to reveal another similar death from his past. In the book you now hold, MY SWEET ANGEL, John Glatt provides a gripping account of a "perfect" mother who was anything but.

St. Martin's True Crime Library gives you the stories behind the headlines. Our authors take you right to the scene of the crime and into the minds of the most notorious murderers to show you what really makes them tick. St. Martin's True Crime Library paperbacks are better than the most terrifying thriller, because it's all true! The next time you want a crackling good read, make sure it's got the St. Martin's True Crime Library logo on the spine—you'll be up all night!

Charles E. Spicer, Jr.
Executive Editor, St. Martin's True Crime Library

ALSO BY JOHN GLATT

MY SWEET ANGEL

THE TRUE STORY OF LACEY SPEARS, THE SEEMINGLY PERFECT

MOTHER WHO MURDERED HER SON IN COLD BLOOD

JOHN GLATT

St. Martin's Paperbacks

This is a work of fiction. All of the characters, organizations, and events portrayed in this novel are either products of the author's imagination or are used fictitiously.

MY SWEET ANGEL

Copyright © 2016 by John Glatt.

For information address St. Martin's Press, 175 Fifth Avenue, New York, NY 10010.

ISBN: 978-1-250-13634-3

Our books may be purchased in bulk for promotional, educational, or business use. Please contact your local bookseller or the Macmillan Corporate and Premium Sales Department at 1-800-221-7945, extension 5442, or by e-mail at MacmillanSpecialMarkets@macmillan.com.

Printed in the United States of America

St. Martin's Press edition / October 2016
St. Martin's Paperbacks edition / October 2017

St. Martin's Paperbacks are published by St. Martin's Press, 175 Fifth Avenue, New York, NY 10010.

10 9 8 7 6 5 4 3

For Jerome Freund

1924–2015

ACKNOWLEDGMENTS

On a sunny morning in early June 2015, I caught the train to Bedford Hills Correctional Facility in upstate New York. After many weeks of negotiations, I was on my way to visit inmate Lacey Spears, who had been a resident of the maximum-security women's prison for the previous three months, serving twenty years to life for the "depraved indifference" murder of her beautiful five-year-old son, Garnett.

I had spent eighteen months researching every inch of Lacey's life, as well as sitting through her entire trial, so I was curious to finally meet her in person. Despite much anticipation that she would take the stand to explain how massive amounts of salt had gotten into Garnett's body and killed him, she had decided at the last minute not to testify.

Outside the prison I was met by one of her attorneys, Stephen Riebling, who had helped arrange the visit and would be my guide through the thick layers of security. When we finally reached the visiting room, complete with soda machines and pictures on the walls, several other inmates were already there with their families.

After several minutes, Lacey entered, wearing a light-pink short-sleeve shirt and trousers, her long hair tied severely back. As she sat down across the long table from me, I was surprised at how petite she is. She immediately informed me that she had read eight of my true crime books in preparation for our meeting.

I first asked her how she was faring in the prison's general population after her case had received such heavy media coverage and had made her the poster child for Munchausen syndrome by proxy.

"It's been brutal," she admitted, adding that the other inmates constantly mocked her behind her back with taunts of "baby killer" and "mother of the year."

"But I know it's not who I am," she explained defiantly.

For the next several hours, Lacey spoke about her life and her love of Garnett, emphasizing she would never have done anything to harm him. Articulate and fluent, she appeared eager to talk, often elaborating well beyond my questions. She vehemently protested her innocence, complaining that she had been railroaded by police and was in fact *the* victim in this tragic case. She blamed doctors and nurses at the two hospitals that treated Garnett in his final days, saying they had made "mistakes" and were solely responsible for his death.

"I think about Garnett all the time," she told me emotionally, "and I'll always love him."

Throughout our interview, Lacey expressed confidence that justice would prevail, that she would soon be back home with her family and getting on with life.

"I will fight to get out of here and go home," she said.

Lacey also totally refuted any suggestion that she suffers from Munchausen syndrome by proxy, which had been suggested by many, including Judge Robert Neary at her sentencing.

"I couldn't believe what he said," she told me angrily. "He's had no training as a psychiatrist."

This book is the result of extensive interviews with Lacey's friends and acquaintances over the years, many of whom wished to remain anonymous.

Most of all I'd like to thank the three main case investigators, Detective Daniel Carfi of the Westchester County Police and detectives Kirk Budnick and Gregory Dunn of the Town of Ramapo Police Department. Their unstinting help was invaluable, and they were always there to answer my questions about this complex case spanning four states.

Thanks also to Lacey's tenacious defense team of David Sachs and Stephen Riebling, for their invaluable help and for facilitating my meeting with Lacey Spears, and to Rebecca Spears for talking to me. I know how difficult it must have been for her.

I am especially grateful to Chris Hill, who told me over an emotional lunch in Decatur, Alabama, about his brief affair with Lacey, which had resulted in Garnett.

I would also like to thank Ricardo Alv, Ginger Dabbs-Anderson, Seth Burkett, Shawn Cohen, Rania Cottingham, Lucian Chalfen, Ramapo Police Detective Lieutenant Mark Emma, Dr. Marc Feldman, Nellie Grossenbacher, Lee Higgins, Kathy Hunt, Laura Jarosch, Ian Lamb, Shawna and Jeannine Lynch, Christine O'Brien, Amy and Michael Pollick, Mallory McWhorter, Kenwood Paulen, Will Payne, Kimberly Philipson, Melissa Ramos, Barry Spear, Juani Tantillo, Tonya Wallenstein, and Robert Wolf.

As always I am deeply indebted to Charles Spicer and April Osborn at St. Martin's Press for the wonderful job they always do. Much gratitude also to Jane Dystel and

Miriam Goderich of Dystel & Goderich Literary Management for their unstinting encouragement and support.

I'd also like to thank my wife, Gail, Jerry and Emily Freund; Debbie, Douglas and Taylor Baldwin; Gurcher, Danny, Cari and Allie Trachtenberg; Annette Witheridge, Virginia Randall, Katherine O'Connell, Roger Hitts, Big Bob Gibson, and Ena Bissell.

MY SWEET ANGEL

PROLOGUE

A little after 2:00 on a slow Friday afternoon, Oona Younger's cell phone rang. It was a brief call that will haunt her for the rest of her life.

"It's happening again!" Lacey Spears yelled down the phone. "Garnett's having more seizures! I *have* to get him to the hospital!"

Lacey's adorable five-year-old son had been home from school for a week with a high fever. Several times already he had been rushed to the emergency room for seizures, so Oona knew it could be a matter of life and death.

"She was frantic," remembered Oona. "She kept screaming, 'Get Judy's car! Get Judy's car!'"

Since the twenty-six-year-old single mother and Garnett had first arrived at the Fellowship Community, Oona had taken them under her wing. Now, fifteen months later, in January 2014, she considered them family.

"She was the daughter that I never had," said Oona, forty-nine, "and Garnett was like an extra son."

Married, with a grown-up son, Oona had lived almost ten years in the secluded Fellowship Community in Rockland County, New York. Founded half a century ago, the nonprofit farming cooperative's seventy adults and children follow the spiritual science teachings of Austrian philosopher Rudolf Steiner. There is an eldercare home, crafts studios, and a large working farm with cows, sheep, and chickens.

Forty-six-year-old former businessman Matt Uppenbrink, who now runs the Fellowship, first met Lacey and Garnett through a mutual friend in Clearwater, Florida. With his encouragement, the widowed young mother had applied to join the Fellowship so that Garnett could attend its prestigious Green Meadow Waldorf School. After several interviews and a reference check, they had been welcomed into the community.

Lacey and Garnett had arrived in early November 2012, soon after Hurricane Sandy had ravaged the small cluster of Fellowship buildings. They moved into the Uppenbrinks' house until an apartment was available.

From the beginning, Lacey Spears had made a big impression on everyone with her tragic life story. She would emotionally recount how Garnett's father, Blake, a policeman, had been killed in a car crash. There had also been several miscarriages before and after Garnett, a very sick baby who had been in and out of hospitals since birth.

He was a failure-to-thrive child, she would explain, who had to be fed nightly through a gastrostomy tube that had been surgically implanted in his abdomen when he was nine months old. He also suffered from celiac disease and Crohn's disease, and his esophagus was just a quarter of the size it should be.

"[She said] he wouldn't eat and would be hungry," said

Oona, "and he'd go for hours and days sometimes without food."

There was much sympathy and goodwill for Lacey in the caring Fellowship, which soon opened its heart to her. She was admired as a devoted mother whose entire life revolved around her son and coping with his continual illnesses.

Lacey was also a holistic evangelist, frequently preaching on Facebook against Western medicine and child vaccinations. She poured the mixture into a feeding bag attached to a special machine hanging from an IV pole in her front room. It would go directly into Garnett's stomach via the G-tube.

Although sympathetic to Garnett's eating problem, Oona noticed that, whenever she took him out to eat at a local diner, he happily devoured hamburgers and fries or anything else put in front of him. And he always asked for more.

After Lacey's hysterical call, Oona grabbed the keys to her friend Judy's car, driving at high speed to Lacey's apartment. She had been expecting Lacey and Garnett to be waiting outside so they could go straight to the emergency room. But when she pulled into the driveway, there was no sign of them.

"So I sat there in the car for a moment," said Oona, "thinking she would come out running with Garnett. I was anxious . . . because I thought he needed to get to the hospital right away."

Finally, after sounding the car horn several times, Oona went inside to see if Lacey needed help. She entered through the front door, which was unlocked, and walked downstairs into the living room. There in the center of the room was Lacey, standing over Garnett, who was face-down on a couch, moaning in pain and breathing rapidly.

He was hooked up to the feeding machine, which was attached to an IV pole with a clear plastic bag full of milky-colored liquid hanging from it.

"What really surprised me was the color of the liquid inside the feeding bag," Oona would say later, "because Lacey always said she would add greens and healthy vegetables to the formula, but there was nothing green about what was inside that bag. It was creamy white."

Oona also wondered why Lacey seemed in no hurry to leave, as the feeding machine pumped the white liquid directly into Garnett's stomach.

"She was very, very calm," recalled Oona, "but on the phone she had been frantic. I kept saying, 'Let's go! Let's go! We need to get going.' Then I went over to Garnett . . . and I stroked his back. He squirmed and made some moaning noises."

Finally, about ten minutes after Oona had arrived, Lacey began leisurely packing up some bags to bring to the hospital. Oona went back outside to wait in the car.

Several minutes later, after unhooking Garnett from the feeding machine and putting one of the machine's connector tubes in her pocket, Lacey emerged. She placed the boy, who was still "lethargic and moaning," in the backseat of the car.

Oona offered to drive them to Nyack Hospital so Lacey could ride in the backseat with her sick son, but Lacey refused.

"She insisted on driving herself," said Oona. "Then she dropped me off."

The following afternoon, Oona visited Lacey and Garnett in Nyack Hospital. She was delighted to see that Garnett's condition had vastly improved, and he seemed back to normal. After playing with him for a couple of hours,

Oona left, feeling happy that the little boy would soon be home.

Early Sunday evening, Lacey called with bad news. Garnett was now critically ill and about to be airlifted across the Hudson River to the Westchester Medical Center because it was the only area hospital with a pediatric intensive care unit (PICU). Lacey explained that his sodium level had suddenly soared from 144 to a life-threatening 182 and that he'd been having more seizures.

"I told her I would come right over," said Oona. "I drove [straight] there."

It was snowing heavily when Oona arrived at Westchester Medical Center. She was just in time to see the paramedics carry an intubated Garnett out of the helicopter, on a stretcher, and into the intensive care unit.

"He was very grave," she remembered. "I went up to [Lacey] and said, 'I'm sorry. How are you?' She smiled."

A few minutes later, while Garnett was being set up in a hospital room, Oona accompanied Lacey to a conference room for a meeting with Dr. Carey Goltzman, the director of the Westchester Medical Center's Maria Fareri Children's Hospital.

Goltzman questioned Lacey about Garnett's medical history, attempting to understand why the boy's sodium had suddenly risen to such a dangerous level. But Oona felt Lacey seemed strangely evasive, unable to remember details of Garnett's various sicknesses and the hospital stays she had so often spoken about.

Then the doctor asked when Lacey had last fed her son through his G-tube. To Oona's astonishment, Lacey replied that she had not used it in over a week.

When Oona tried to interrupt to remind Lacey that she had seen her using it to feed Garnett just two days earlier, Lacey suddenly spun around, shooting her an icy look that took Oona's breath away. Oona was so shocked that she just stood up and left the room to compose herself.

"[Lacey] gave me the most evil face you could imagine," Oona would later tell detectives.

PART ONE

1

PLAYING WITH DOLLS

Lacey Elizabeth Spears was born on October 16, 1987, at Castle Air Force Base in Atwater, California. She was the youngest of Terry and Tina Spears's three children. The eldest, Rebecca Ann, was born in 1984, and her brother, Daniel Joseph, arrived eighteen months later.

When Lacey was six weeks old the air force base closed, and Terry Spears quit his job as an aircraft mechanic to move his family to Decatur, Alabama.

"We were all born on the air force base," said Rebecca Spears. "It was closing, so we moved to Alabama, where my grandparents had a home."

Located on the banks of the Tennessee River in north-central Alabama, Decatur is one of the poorest towns in America, with a median family income of just over $37,000. With a population below fifty-five thousand, it lies in the heart of the Bible Belt, with literally a church on every street corner. The town's sole claim to fame was making *Guinness World Records* for the highest number of churches per capita in the world. Indeed, the phrase "Have a Blessed Day" is part of Decatur's vernacular.

The Spears family settled down in the ranch home of Tina's parents, Paul and Peggy Florence, on leafy Cedar Lake Road. Terry found a job as a welder, and Tina stayed at home, looking after their three children.

Lacey's paternal uncle, Richard Lawrence, would later remember Terry and Tina as not a close couple. Growing up, he said, his niece Lacey was always "at odds" with her father, and Tina was a "cold and unaffectionate mother."

Both Lacey's parents had severe health issues. Tina, who was twenty-two years old when Lacey was born, suffered from type 1 diabetes for most of her life. Terry had celiac disease and Crohn's disease and was slightly deaf. But he worked hard to support the family.

From infancy, Lacey loved playing with dolls. She found comfort in her growing collection of American Girl dolls, which she washed, dressed, and fussed over, pretending they were her children.

"Lacey always loved to play house," said Rebecca, "and we would take care of the dolls together."

At the age of five, Lacey joined the kindergarten class at Frances Nungester Elementary School on Tammy Street, less than half a mile from her house. She soon became best friends with Mallory McWhorter, and for the next several years they were inseparable.

"Lacey was my very best friend in kindergarten," said Mallory. "She was very outgoing and fun. I remember in school playing dress-up with dolls, and playing house."

Although Lacey regularly played over at Mallory's house one street away, Mallory was never allowed to go over to the Spears's house.

"My mom had a funny feeling about her family," Mallory recalled. "She was scared for me to go over there."

The one time Mallory persuaded her mother to allow her to go over to the Spears's house, it ended badly. They were in Lacey's bedroom, playing house, when Mallory picked up one of Lacey's dolls, and, Mallory recalls, Lacey tried to strangle her.

"I was scared," said Mallory. "It was a bad situation. Boom! She just put her hands around my neck."

When her mother collected her, Mallory says she was shocked to see bruising on her daughter's neck.

"There were handprints around my neck," said Mallory. "I told my mom we were just playing, but she took it as 'something's up with that family.'"

In third grade, Lacey become close friends with Jessica Kyle. The first time they met they got into a fight after Jessica accused Lacey of "hogging" the monkey bars.

"And I spit on her glasses," said Jessica. "Our teacher made us make up, and ever since, we've been best friends."

Both girls liked dolls, although Jessica remembers Lacey being far more attached to hers than Jessica ever was.

"We'd act like we were the babies' mothers," said Jessica. "We would take care of them as if they were our own kids. But [Lacey] took it to a more extreme level than I did. She'd take [the doll] everywhere. It was something that gave her comfort."

When Lacey was in fifth grade her grandfather died, and her grandmother, Peggy Florence, moved to Clearwater, Florida, to live with her son Toby, affectionately known as Uncle Bo. Lacey was devastated, as she had been very close to her grandfather.

During the next few years, the three Spears children

often visited Clearwater, staying at Uncle Bo's house. Lacey loved the beach weather and dreamed of one day living there.

"We were all very close to Bo," said Rebecca. "He was a fun-loving guy who liked to live on the edge a little bit."

Uncle Bo taught Lacey how to fish and scuba dive and would take her for thrilling rides in his sports car.

"He was a daredevil," said Rebecca, "and always exciting to be around."

They also spent time on the Spears's family farm in Scottsville, Kentucky, which had been in Terry's family for hundreds of years. At one time, his family had been so prominent in Scottsville that a road had been named in their honor.

"Spears Road was named after us," said Rebecca, "because pretty much everyone that lived on that road had the last name of Spears."

Over the years, much of the large sprawling cattle farm had been sold off, with just a small part of it remaining in the family.

Two of Lacey's aunts lived a few miles from the farm, and during school vacations the family would stay with them. Occasionally, another uncle would join them, bringing his kids in a large RV, and they'd all go camping on the farm.

"We always loved going there," recalled Rebecca. "We liked playing with our cousins on the dairy farm. We'd have marshmallow roasts and go jumping on their trampoline."

Every afternoon, Lacey would volunteer to milk the cows.

"She liked to go and help do the milking," said Rebecca. "It was a fun experience."

* * *

In 1998, Lacey Spears started at Brookhaven Middle School, often sleeping over at Jessica Kyle's house. On her twelfth birthday, Lacey told Jessica that it was time to stop playing with dolls and to grow up.

Lacey was a good student and seemed eager to please her teachers, always handing her work in early. She was a popular girl and was given the nickname "Lacey Bug."

Late one night, Lacey arrived at the Kyle house in a terrible state. She told Jessica's mother, Lisa Kyle, that she had been molested by a relative and was too afraid to go home. Lisa was so concerned for Lacey's welfare that she immediately reported it to the Alabama Department of Human Resources (DHR). But there is no record of any subsequent investigation.

For the next several weeks, Lacey moved into the Kyle house and even started calling Lisa Kyle "Mom." Jessica would later tell police that Lacey had claimed that she had been sexually assaulted by relatives and was scared as a child.

Lacey also complained of abuse to her parents' neighbors, who frequently provided sanctuary for her over the next few years.

"Lacey would sneak out of her house sometimes and come over to them, because she was scared," said Rania Cottingham, who knew the neighbors' daughter and would later become close friends with Lacey in high school. "She would complain of sexual abuse, and they would just try and take her to church and be there for her without directly intervening."

But Rebecca Spears maintains that she has no knowledge of her younger sister ever being molested.

"We had a happy childhood," she said. "As far as I know, that's not true. I don't know why people would say that or think that, in all honesty."

* * *

In early 2002, fourteen-year-old Lacey Spears became a regular at Parkview Baptist Church, joining the softball team. At the weekly practices, she befriended Paula Sandlin, who was then forty-seven. Over the next few months, Sandlin would drive Lacey to and from practices and games, becoming "uncomfortable" when Lacey started calling her "Mom."

She also was disturbed by the fanciful stories Lacey told her, which became increasingly far-fetched as the weeks went on.

"If she didn't get a certain reaction," Sandlin said, "she would move to a bigger lie."

One time, Lacey limped into church wearing an ankle brace, saying she had fallen down and injured herself while cheerleading. Soon afterwards, her story changed. Now she was suffering from anorexia and had collapsed in the street from lack of food.

When she claimed not to have eaten for three days, somebody challenged her, saying she had seen her eating a hot dog the day before. Lacey conceded that was true, but that was all she had eaten.

Whitney Riley Pena, who was in Lacey's class at Brookhaven, remembered Lacey having many issues and seeing a therapist for an eating disorder.

That summer, Lacey told friends she was pregnant. Paula Sandlin was suspicious and asked what she planned to do, since she was about to start high school.

"I didn't believe her," Sandlin would later tell *Journal News* reporter Shawn Cohen. "She didn't look pregnant. But I didn't want to call her a liar, in case there was some bit of truth to it."

A few days later Lacey announced that she had had an abortion at the Carraway Methodist Medical Center in Birmingham, Alabama. But when someone pointed out that the medical center did not perform abortions, Lacey changed her story. She now said she had had it done in Florida.

In August, 2002, Lacey Spears started her freshman year at Decatur High School, a year below her siblings Rebecca and Daniel. Two months shy of her fifteenth birthday, Lacey was petite and strikingly thin, with her long sandy-colored hair tied back and a wide toothy smile.

Decatur High School's stated mission is to educate students in "academic and social skills for them to succeed as . . . compassionate members of a global society."

Lacey soon threw herself into school activities, joining the school choir and the drama club. She also joined the Decatur High School branch of Family, Career and Community Leaders of America, where Rebecca was treasurer. For the next several years Lacey would be active in the nationally recognized group dedicated to developing personal growth and leadership through family. She also belonged to the school's Future Business Leaders of America.

Mallory McWhorter, who had not seen Lacey since first grade, when they had been sent to different primary schools, was now reunited with her. The two girls resumed their old friendship, but Mallory saw a distinctive change in Lacey. She now craved the attention and approval of her teachers, and seemed to feed off it.

"She was a goody-goody," explained Mallory. "She was teacher's pet and a people pleaser. She turned her papers in on time and pleased all the teachers with big grades."

Lacey's constant need to be admired by her teachers did not endear her to her classmates.

"She wasn't very popular in high school," explained Mallory. "She wasn't like a beauty queen or anything like that, so the teachers praised her because she's perfect. And that was her way of getting attention."

Soon after starting at Decatur High, Lacey drifted apart from Jessica Kyle, who had become a self-confessed "nerd" and "band geek."

Lacey now met a whole new group of friends. When April Chambers (not her real name) first met Lacey in ninth grade, she found her very standoffish.

"Lacey wasn't outgoing," said April. "She had her own group of friends, but they were really close-knit. There were a lot of strange things that I heard about her in high school."

Kara Couch got to know Lacey in math class and began an enduring friendship. She would later tell police that, in high school, Lacey secretly "fooled around with diet pills, water pills, and Adderall."

Lacey confided in Kara, telling her how unhappy she was at home and that she could not communicate with her mother and sister. She claimed her father had undergone a liver transplant and talked about a family member who had molested her.

During her sophomore year, Lacey joined Decatur High School's forensics and public debating team. The team, which was part of the National Forensic League honor society, was highly rated, and Lacey was one of its stars.

Through the forensics team, Lacey became close friends with Rania Cottingham. They often spent weekends traveling together to out-of-town debate competitions.

"I loved her," said Rania. "She was as sweet as could be. I mean, she was really cool."

Rania remembers how Lacey could hold forth on any subject, from abortion to prayer in schools, spending hours preparing for every competition.

"Lacey liked to strive for perfection," recalled Rania.

"She'd memorize speeches and go over and over them until she got it perfect. And she was great at it."

Lacey also worked hard to be a good student, and several teachers took a special interest in her.

"She made good grades," said Rania. "She was very close to a couple of our teachers."

But, all through high school, Rania never saw Lacey date anyone.

"It never got brought up," said Rania, "and nobody ever saw her with [a boy]. So if she did, it was secret."

Lacey constantly complained to Rania about her family, saying they fought all the time. She, too, heard Lacey's claims of sexual abuse, as had most of their classmates.

All through high school, Lacey spoke about her dreams of having children.

"We all knew that she wanted to be a mom," said Mallory. "She made that very clear. She would verbalize it to you. We had a girl pregnant in our class, and Lacey brought in kids' clothes. And she was like, 'This is what my kid's going to wear.'"

In the Decatur High School's 2005 *Golden Memories* yearbook, Terry Spears took out a special one-page ad for Lacey, who was then a junior, including several pictures of a grinning Lacey and her sister, Rebecca.

"Wherever life may take you," read the message to her, "we hope you continue to bless us as you always have . . . Never lose the wonderful smile we have grown to love. Love Mom, Dad, Beck, & Dan."

To make extra money, Lacey Spears found a part-time job at Jack's burger place, where her mother, sister, and brother had all worked at one time or another. There she became friendly with a fellow cashier named Autumn Hunt, who was very impressed with her.

"If you needed help, you'd call on Lacey," said Autumn. "If you needed a ride, somebody to cover your shift, she'd do it for you."

During their time together at Jack's, Autumn remembers Lacey briefly dating another employee, named Rich Wright, before they split up.

Writer Mike Pollick, a Jack's regular, was often served by Lacey.

"She was striking," Pollick remembered. "She waited on me, and she would always be around the restaurant. She just had this wide-eyed look. A scared-rabbit type."

Lacey also started doing volunteer work at the Parkview Baptist Church nursery. She looked after the infants and began paying special attention to a one-year-old boy named Charlie. The boy's mother eventually complained to the nursery, saying Lacey made her nervous and she no longer wanted Lacey to look after her son.

2

THE CHILD CARER

On May 26, 2006, eighteen-year-old Lacey Spears graduated from Decatur High School. Her parting message in the 2006 *Golden Memories* yearbook quoted iconic feminist writer Anaïs Nin: "Each friend represents a world in us, a world possibly not born until they arrive, and it is only by this meeting that a new world is born."

Soon after graduating, Lacey moved into a two-bedroom apartment with her sister, Rebecca. It was on the second floor of Cedar Key Apartments on Cedar Lake Road, just a few hundred yards away from their parents' house.

"I'd been away to college," said Rebecca, "and then I came home and got used to my independence . . . So it worked out real well to share an apartment."

Lacey quit her job at Jack's and started working at Kid's Club day care in Decatur, to help pay her share of the $525-per-month rent. Rebecca worked at another local day care center, across town.

"She loved her job," said Rebecca, "and she liked hanging out with her friends to go out to eat or to a movie."

Lacey impressed everybody at Kid's Club with her boundless enthusiasm, happily caring for up to five babies at a time. She was soon opening the center at 5:30 A.M. and closing up at 6:00 P.M.

Lacey also tried to recruit some of her Decatur High School friends to join Kid's Club.

"She tried to get me a job there," said Rania Cottingham. "She told me to go down there, but I didn't ever go and apply."

That summer, Lacey went on several dates with Blake Robinson, a handsome young policeman from the Morgan County Sheriff's Office. He only saw Lacey three times, later telling detectives that they never had sex because he was a strict Southern Baptist.

The last time he ever saw her was waiting on line in a store. For no apparent reason, Lacey started berating him and stormed out.

"They went out very briefly," said Rebecca, who met Blake once. "He was a policeman and really nice and quiet. She never gave me a reason [why] they broke up."

That October, Lacey enrolled in a nursing course at Calhoun College, telling friends she wanted to become a nurse. In one class, she met a young single mother named Christy Burnham, whom she had known in elementary school. Soon Lacey was driving Christy to and from classes at Calhoun, meeting Christy's ten-month-old son, Camryn.

"I had Camryn when I was seventeen. A mixed-race baby," Burnham told writer Shawn Cohen. "I was still involved with the daddy. [Lacey] would let me use her car to go see the kid's father. And Lacey would watch Camryn."

Because Christy's mother, Patricia, did not approve of Camryn's father, Christy often would sneak out to visit him while Lacey babysat Camryn.

Lacey soon became "obsessed" with the baby boy, spending as much time as she could with him. She was always volunteering to look after Camryn without being paid, buying him diapers, a car seat, and a crib out of her own pocket. She seemed to resent handing Camryn back to his mother after babysitting him.

Whenever Lacey took Camryn out in public, she acted like she was his mother. One day, when Christy was out with her son, someone asked if she was watching Lacey's baby.

"I was like, 'That's not Lacey's baby,'" said Christy. "'That's Camryn. That's *my* baby.' She was telling people that it was her son. And I thought that was weird."

During the six months that Lacey looked after Camryn, he began suffering chronic ear infections, frequently requiring medical attention.

"We were back and forth to the doctor," recalled Burnham. "If I would keep him, they'd go away. And then, as she had him, he would have ear infections again."

One Saturday morning in spring 2007, Lacey collected Camryn for the weekend and then disappeared. When she had not brought him back by Sunday night, Christy started getting worried. She called all her friends, but no one had seen them.

Finally, on Monday, Christy tracked Lacey down and ordered her to bring Camryn home immediately.

"I was going to beat her ass, literally," said Burnham. "And my mom was like, 'Just let it go. Let it go.' So when she brought my child back, I was like, 'You're never going to watch him again.'"

Then Lacey broke down in tears, begging her to let her see the little boy again.

"She was crying," said Burnham, "telling me not to take Camryn away from her."

In August 2006, Lacey Spears became fixated on another child: a beautiful cherubic six-month-old boy named Jonathon Strain. She had worked with his nineteen-year-old mother, Autumn Hunt, at Jack's, and when Lacey offered Autumn her "family discount" at Kid's Club, Autumn gratefully accepted.

"I needed somewhere to look after Jonathon, and she said I should bring him there," said Autumn. "I was working, and I was at school and didn't finish until 7:00 P.M. The center closed at 6:00 P.M., but she looked after him for an extra hour."

Soon, Lacey was taking JonJon, as she now called him, back to her apartment after day care for a few hours. Then Autumn would collect him after finishing work. Lacey never asked Autumn for any money, even buying JonJon formula, diapers, and dozens of toys.

"I completely trusted her," said Autumn. "People thought we were sisters . . . and I just went with that."

Soon Lacey was seeing more of JonJon than his mother was, wanting to be with the curly-haired blond boy all the time.

"Lacey kept him quite a bit as his mother worked," said Rebecca, who often saw him over at their apartment. "JonJon was a happy little boy. He was just real sweet to be around."

When Autumn wanted to spend weekends with her long-distance boyfriend, Lacey was only too happy to look after JonJon.

"If I decided to stay out of town Sunday night," said Autumn, "she'd say, 'Fine.'"

It would be almost a year before Autumn would discover that Lacey Spears had been posting hundreds of photographs of herself and JonJon on her MySpace page, suggesting she was his mother.

"I love him so," Lacey captioned one picture of Jon-Jon at around seven months old. On another one she wrote, "Sweet Baby JonJon."

Over the next two years Lacey posted photographs of JonJon on MySpace almost daily.

"She wanted to keep Jonathon all the time," said his grandmother, Kathy Hunt, who often collected him from Lacey's apartment. "She had all the toys and everything that a child would need—baby wipes, baby food. I was wondering how she could afford it."

Later, Kathy would discover that Lacey had been taking JonJon to several local churches for Sunday services, pretending to be his mom to get charity supplies that were handed out to needy mothers.

On November 2, 2007, Lacey took JonJon with her to watch a Decatur Red Raiders football game. There, she met her old school friend Mallory McWhorter, who asked about JonJon.

"She told me it was her kid," said Mallory. "But later, when I started asking about him, she said it was her sister's kid. And I knew her sister did not have a kid. So that was kind of like a red flag."

Soon after Lacey Spears started babysitting Jonathon Strain, he began suffering from chronic ear infections, often requiring medical attention.

"His ears would actually leak pus," said his grandmother, Kathy Hunt. "He developed a hole in his eardrum."

The doctors who treated JonJon never raised any suspicions, and no one suspected anything untoward.

"He had ear infections all the time," said Kathy. "He had over twenty-one ear infections while Lacey was around. It was a mystery."

In late 2007, Shawna Lynch began bringing her eighteen-month-old son, McKelly, and his older brother, Zack, to Kid's Club. It was there that she first met Lacey Spears, who was caring for them.

"We became friends at Kid's Club," said Shawna. "Lacey was very quiet. Really shy, until we started talking . . . and she came out of her shell a little bit."

One day Lacey asked if she could take McKelly home to spend the night with her.

"She had baby JonJon at the time," Shawna remembered. "And she just asked if she could keep him one night, as she was really attached to him. I really didn't think anything of it, because we were friends and had gone out a couple of times. So I said, 'Sure, you can take him home with you. Not a problem.'"

Soon Lacey was taking care of McKelly, whom she called "Kel-Kel," most weekends, at her apartment, where he and JonJon would play and sleep over. Shawna, who never paid Lacey, often visited her Cedar Key apartment to drop off McKelly and was very impressed by what she saw.

"Lacey portrayed herself as a child-care provider," explained Shawna. "Her apartment was like baby heaven, with all kinds of baby toys. It was like it was set up for kids, and baby safety [equipment] was everywhere."

Initially, Lacey portrayed herself as JonJon's mother, but she changed her story after Shawna eventually met Autumn Hunt.

"She told me that JonJon was her baby," said Shawna, "but Autumn was saying it was *her* baby. Then Lacey told me that Autumn was her stepsister, so my assumption was that they were half sisters."

And, just like JonJon, McKelly began suffering from mysterious ear infections soon after Lacey began babysitting him.

"JonJon had severe issues with ear infections, and so did McKelly," said McKelly's grandmother, Jeannine Lynch. "It got to the point where their ears would just pus, and it was nasty."

In November, 2007, Kid's Club closed down, and Lacey found work at another Decatur day care center, Childcare Network. By now she had dropped out of her nursing course at Calhoun College and regularly looked after JonJon, McKelly, and his brother, Zack, in her cramped two-room apartment. Over the next few months, Shawna Lynch found herself spending more and more time with Lacey.

"We were super close," explained Shawna. "I mean, it was to the point to where I pushed my family to the side because me and her were so close."

Soon Lacey began talking about being molested by a relative and how she was powerless to stop it.

"She began calling me in the middle of the night," said Shawna, "and she was crying. She would say, '[He's] just left, and he hurt me.' Then she would come over and sleep at my house, because she was too scared to go home."

Eventually Shawna gave Lacey keys to her house, so Lacey could come over and watch her children whenever Shawna needed help.

One day Lacey informed Shawna that she was pregnant, saying her relative was the father. A few weeks later Lacey proudly showed off her "baby bump," which Shawna duly photographed.

"Lacey was tiny, so you could see any weight gain," said Shawna. "And there was a roundness about her stomach."

Lacey also started talking about her fiancé, Blake, telling Shawna he had been killed in a traffic accident. She described the young policeman as her high school sweetheart and soul mate.

"One day she even took me to the place where they had supposedly lived," said Shawna. "But I thought it was strange she never had any pictures of him up at her house."

Shawna's mother-in-law, Jeannine Lynch, became concerned with Lacey's apparent obsession with her grandson McKelly and confronted her one day when she arrived to collect him.

"I wanted to get to know who she was," said Jeannine, who is a Christian counselor at her church. "I needed to locate her heart."

Jeannine began by asking about her childhood, and she thought Lacey's answers were "clinical."

"There were no clues whatever," said Jeannine, "that she was not a happy child."

Then she asked Lacey if she believed in Jesus Christ. Lacey said she did and was a church regular, but then she became evasive and aloof.

"She was shutting down," remembered Jeannine, "so I wasn't going to push her. I could see there was something deep in there . . . that there was a darkness."

Concerned about the negative effect Lacey was having on their family, Jeannine and her son, Aaron, staged an intervention, demanding that Shawna distance herself from Lacey.

"My son saw some red flags, too," said Jeannine, "so it was at my advice that Shawna put Lacey to the test, so she could get a better perspective."

When Lacey next arrived to collect McKelly, Shawna, Aaron, and Jeannine sat her down and asked for their house key back. Shawna explained she needed space away from Lacey, for the sake of her marriage.

"I said, 'Listen, I can't do this anymore,'" recalled Shawna. "'I feel like you're coming between my family, and my marriage is rocky because of you.' It broke my heart, and I was bawling like a baby."

Then Lacey started screaming at Shawna, accusing her of betrayal and hurling abuse.

"She just freaked out," said Shawna. "She was mad. She was cursing . . . I saw a side of her that I've never seen before."

Then Lacey stormed out of Shawna's house, and for the next few months they only communicated through Facebook.

Soon afterwards, Lacey flew to Clearwater, Florida, to visit her grandmother and Uncle Bo. When she returned to Decatur several months later, she was no longer pregnant. Shawna heard through friends that she had "lost" the baby and buried it in Florida.

"It was kind of weird," said Shawna. "So I don't know if she miscarried or even if there was a baby in there to begin with. But it looked to me as if she was pregnant."

3

CHRIS HILL

Soon after returning from Florida, Lacey caught the attention of Chris Hill, who lived on the ground floor of the Cedar Key Apartments. The stocky, balding twenty-three-year-old with a goatee would often pass Lacey in the hallway.

"She was just kind of strange," he recalled, "and kept to herself."

Hill, a garage door installer, would see Lacey arrive home with JonJon, going upstairs to her apartment.

"She was always taking care of him," said Hill, "day in and day out."

He and his friends often drank cocktails in the parking lot, poking fun at Lacey.

"We called her 'the Predator,'" he said, "as she always appeared so cold and distant. We would just mess with her."

One night in early February 2008, Lacey came down to Hill's apartment, asking for help assembling a new baby bassinet cradle she had bought for JonJon.

"So I went upstairs and put it together," said Hill, "and one thing led to another. We did the business."

Lacey spent the night in his bed, and the next morning they exchanged cell phone numbers.

"So we just started texting back and forth," he said. "She said she liked me and wanted things to go a little further. And I said, 'Sure, you're cute. I like your personality.'"

Lacey started going downstairs on dates, watching movies and having sex. But she would never stay the night, always making an excuse and going back upstairs.

"It was kind of a strange relationship," explained Hill. "She wasn't very affectionate."

During sex, Lacey never brought up the subject of contraceptives, and Hill never mentioned it.

"I was a dumb-ass," he admitted. "I drank a lot in those days and she didn't. Maybe if I hadn't, I wouldn't have made this mistake."

On the rare occasions Lacey would invite him up to her apartment, he felt awkward. It was full of toys, and Rebecca and JonJon would always be there.

"I went up there sometimes," he said, "but I felt uncomfortable being around her sister because she seemed not to approve of me. I felt more comfortable being in my zone."

Although Lacey loved looking after JonJon and other small children, she would totally ignore Hill's five-year-old son, Colton, whenever he visited.

"She acted like he didn't exist," said Hill, "and wouldn't take care of him like she did the other children. I don't know what that's about."

On February 14, 2008, JonJon turned one, and Lacey celebrated with a new album on MySpace, entitled

"Classic—Jonathon 1 Year Old." She posted 366 photos of her posing with her "Sweet Baby JonJon."

"Hey Mommy Lacey," she captioned one. "What Are You Doing Mommy Lacey," she wrote on another. Other captions included "JonJon I love You," "My World My Everything," and "He Completes Me."

One of Lacey's MySpace friends saw her album, asking if JonJon was hers.

"Yes, he is," Lacey replied. "That's the love of my life. He was born Feb. 14."

A few days later, Autumn Hunt learned that Lacey was claiming to be her son's mother. Initially, she thought it was a misunderstanding, but then she went online and was livid.

"It was more of a shock than anything," Autumn told the *Journal News* reporter Shawn Cohen. "I felt like it was . . . a cry for attention. Being a teen mom brings you a lot of attention."

But Autumn still allowed JonJon to spend nights over at Lacey's apartment.

In March, Shawna Lynch and her husband, Aaron, went on a double date with Lacey and Chris Hill. Shawna and Lacey were now back on speaking terms, although McKelly no longer visited Lacey's apartment.

"We just decided we'd all go out one night," said Shawna. "We went to a restaurant to eat, and that was it."

Hill said he and Lacey rarely went out on dates because she always wanted to stay home.

"She was just a stick-to-herself kind of person," he explained. "All she cared about was kids."

Several times a week, Lacey would go downstairs to Hill's apartment. He would cook her a meal and then they would have sex.

"She'd come down when it was convenient," he said,

"and hang out for a little while. She was a very finicky-type person. She wouldn't eat much of anything. I would make meals and she'd go, 'Oh, I don't like that. I like chicken.' She would say it like a little baby."

Chris Hill had heard from Shawna about Lacey's claims of being raped by various members of her family. One night he asked her if it was true.

"I said, 'I'm not going to think any differently of you,'" said Hill. "'Did this really happen?' She said, 'I don't want to talk about it.' That's all she said. She tried to shut the situation down."

Hill described their lovemaking as cold and passionless.

"She'd spend the night," he said, "but then she'd go back to her place, which I thought was kind of weird if you're a couple. She was just there. I called it 'neighbors with benefits.' But I didn't have anybody, so she filled in that void."

Late one night, Lacey texted Hill, inviting him up for sex. A few minutes later, when he knocked on her door, there was no answer.

"I could see her shadow through the peephole," he remembered, "and I heard footsteps. I just kept knocking. I said, 'Hello, Lacey, is that you? You just told me to come up here.' She never said anything, and her shadow moved away from the peephole."

Frustrated, he went back down to his apartment, sending her a barrage of texts, asking what was wrong. Lacey never responded.

Several times, Lacey mentioned that she used to date a policeman named Blake, but she refused to elaborate.

"She kept it short," Hill said. "She never told me what they did together. She just said her last boyfriend was Blake."

* * *

In early March, Lacey Spears became pregnant and was delighted. She texted Autumn Hunt that she had had twenty-three pregnancy tests before finding out she really was pregnant. She told friends that the father was the "older bald fat guy" who already had a kid and lived downstairs.

Chris Hill claims that, after telling him the news, Lacey suggested they get married.

"She wanted to have a family," said Hill. "And I said, 'Yes, I'm for that. I don't want to have another child out of wedlock.'"

But years later Lacey's sister would maintain it was the other way around.

"[Chris] asked her to marry him," Rebecca said. "At first she decided to think about it, and later on said yes."

As they started planning their future together, Lacey introduced her new fiancé to her parents and other members of her family.

"We were acting like we were a couple," Hill explained. "I [wanted] to see if we could make it work."

One night he brought home a book of baby names, and they went through it, trying to select one.

"We came up with the name Kayden," he recalled, "and all of a sudden, one day she changed and said, 'I want it to be Garnett.'"

Although Hill didn't like the name Garnett, Lacey insisted.

"She just decided that on her own," Hill said, "and right then I knew that she doesn't want me in his life."

A few days later, Lacey coldly informed Chris Hill that he was not the father of her child, that her old boyfriend Blake was. She said their relationship was over and she never wanted to see Hill again.

"Out of the blue, she acted like I didn't exist," said Hill, "and 'You're not the father.' We didn't even argue. We never got into fights. It was the strangest breakup ever."

Then Lacey started sending him "hurtful" text messages. When he came upstairs to reason with her, she threatened to call the police and get a restraining order.

Hill was devastated by Lacey's painful rejection, feeling she had just used him to get pregnant.

"I think she wanted a child," he said, "but didn't want a father figure in the mix. She kept caring for other mothers' kids up there, and now she just wanted a child all to herself."

Years later, Rebecca Spears would dispute Hill's version of what happened.

"[Chris] became ugly and mean," she claimed, in 2015. "He would scream at [us]. I became afraid he would hurt her. Eventually [Lacey] decided that she did not want to be married to him."

On June 1, 2008, Lacey Spears threw a pool party for Jon-Jon and his little friends Brayden, Katie, and JD. She posted a series of photographs from it on her new LaCey SpEars MySpace page. Dozens of pictures show the infants splashing around in an inflatable pool, with captions like "Splashing," "Having So Much Fun," and "He Loves This Little Pool."

Six weeks later she posted more photographs on MySpace. One showed her kissing JonJon on the lips, with the caption "A Mother's Love Is Unexplainable."

In early October, as Lacey Spears approached her twenty-first birthday, she had a baby shower at the community center in the Cedar Key apartment complex. Her mother and sister attended, and her father, who was working, sent over a green wooden rocking horse he had built for his new grandson. More than twenty people came with presents to congratulate the expectant mother.

"Lacey was super excited to be having a baby," recalled Shawna Lynch, who came with her two sons. "I think that she had wanted a baby of her own for a long time, and she just lit up."

At the entrance to the community center hung a sign, "Baby Shower Here," and a blue ribbon ornament hung on the front door. And as guests entered, they saw a larger poster, reading, "A NEW LITTLE SPEARS IS ON THE WAY, WELCOME TO A SHOWER FOR LACEY TODAY!" Another, on the opposite wall, read, "It's a Boy."

The centerpiece of the shower was a large cake with a little iced baby in a flower. "Welcome Baby Garnett Paul" was written in yellow marzipan above it.

"There were lots of presents," said Shawna. "Clothes, toys, and diapers."

Although Lacey was now telling friends that the baby's father was a policeman named Blake, Shawna knew better, but she never challenged Lacey.

"She denied it was Chris's baby," said Shawna. "But I knew he was the father."

Later, Lacey posted photographs from her baby shower on MySpace, in an album entitled "Baby Shower (for Lacey)." In it were photos of a very pregnant Lacey, with captions: "Look @ That Belly!!!" and "Big Baby Belly."

The final photo in the album was a photo of a smiling Lacey holding her belly, with the comment "Hurry Up Garnett Paul & Get Here."

4

"HE'S ALL MINE"

Garnett-Paul Thompson Spears was born on Wednesday, December 3, at Huntsville Hospital, weighing six pounds, fourteen ounces. He was a healthy baby, and within minutes of him entering the world, a jubilant Lacey was posting photos of him on MySpace.

"Labored only 4 Hours And My Blessing Was Here," she wrote under one, in Garnett's first MySpace photo album. "He's All Mine," she captioned another. A third one said, "Right Before All My Fans Come to See Me & Mommy."

Shawna Lynch and several other friends visited Lacey in the hospital. But when they went to the nursery to see Garnett, there were no babies there called Spears. Later, Lacey told them she had used an alias, in case Chris Hill came to see his new son.

During the first week of Garnett's life, Lacey posted dozens of photos of herself posing with him. "Forever Mine," she wrote by one picture. "Love Him So Much . . . The Best Christmas Present Ever," she captioned another.

On Friday, December 5, Huntsville Hospital doctors discharged Garnett, declaring him a healthy baby with no medical problems. Lacey brought her two-day-old baby back to her apartment, dressing him in a smart four-piece "Going Home Outfit," comprising a camouflage shirt, denim pants, and green shoes. Then she took photographs to post online.

That Sunday, Lacey brought her four-day-old baby into the emergency room at Decatur General Hospital, complaining that he was running a high fever, had jaundice, and was pulling at his ears. Garnett was then examined by Dr. Hope Weeks, who found him to be healthy and sent him home.

When Lacey brought Garnett home, Chris Hill came out and demanded to see his son.

"I confronted her," he recalled. "I said, 'I know that's my son, and I would like to see him.' She said, 'He's not yours, and you need to leave me alone.'"

From then on, Hill had to be content with the occasional glimpse of his son from his window, as Lacey came and went with him.

"I would hear her car door shut," he said, "and look out of the blinds and try and get a look at him. Even if I was outside and she was carrying [him], she wouldn't make eye contact. She just acted like he wasn't mine altogether. I stayed up nights crying because I couldn't see my son."

Upstairs in her apartment, Lacey introduced JonJon to Garnett, posting photographs of them both on MySpace. She posed JonJon holding baby Garnett in his arms, writing, "Big Bro & Little Bro . . . He loves Him So Much."

Over the next few weeks, Lacey posted numerous photographs of JonJon and Garnett, calling them brothers.

In one series of MySpace photographs, she dressed them in identical clothing, photographing them playing in the park on a wooden train. "Brothers and Best Friends," she wrote alongside it.

Then she sat both little boys on her lap and took a selfie she called "Me & My Babies."

On Sunday, December 14, 2008, the *Decatur Daily* carried a brief birth announcement for Garnett-Paul Thompson Spears.

"Born Dec. 3 to Lacey Spears of Decatur," it read. "Grandparents are Terry and Tina Spears of Tanner."

Over the next several weeks, Lacey prepared for the holidays, posting photographs of "My Sweet Babies." She dressed Garnett in a red-and-white suit with "I'm On Santa's Nice List" embroidered in large letters on the front.

On December 25, Lacey photographed her sister, Rebecca, with Garnett and JonJon, opening presents in the living room by a decked-out Christmas tree. One shot in Lacey's new "Garnett's 1st Christmas" MySpace album showed "Baby G" lying on his inflatable bed, in his red-and-white-striped pajamas, surrounded by all his presents.

The day after Christmas, Lacey brought Garnett back to the emergency room, complaining that he was sick again. She posted pictures of him in the hospital, in a Gap T-shirt, with an IV coming out of his arm. "Poor Baby Boy . . . See His IV," she wrote alongside the photo. "My Entire World . . . He Is My Life."

In early January 2009, Lacey Spears started bringing Garnett to Decatur General Hospital or the Southern Rural Health Care clinic almost daily. She complained that he was not eating properly, was vomiting, and was bleeding from both ears. Pediatrician Me'Lissa Young-King treated him at the clinic on numerous occasions, but she never saw him vomit and could not determine the cause of his chronic ear infections.

On January 13, Young-King wrote in a medical record that she suspected Lacey Spears might suffer from Munchausen syndrome by proxy.

"I became concerned that the infant might be a victim of induced illnesses by the guardian or caregiver," Dr. Young-King later told detectives, "a condition known as Munchausen by proxy syndrome [sic]. I became suspicious of this phenomenon."

The doctor also thought it "odd" that Lacey was so well versed in medical terminology and infant illnesses.

"I recall . . . asking the mother, Lacey Spears, if she was involved in the medical field," said the doctor. "She explained to me, at that time, she was either a nursing student or a nurse graduate."

The doctor also witnessed Lacey becoming "overly emotional, distraught, and demanding," and she and her colleagues voiced concern that she presented "some high-risk red flag indications."

Years later, medical records from the Alabama Department of Public Health would reveal just how worried doctors were about Lacey's mental state during the first weeks of Garnett's life.

"It was presumed she suffered from Postpartum Depression and Munchausen Syndrome by Proxy," stated a subsequent New York State child fatality report. "The mother verbalized on 1/14/2009 that she wanted to harm [Garnett] and was referred to Medical Social Services . . . for interpersonal conflict, and dysfunction."

The next day, Lacey was interviewed by Diane Moore, an investigator for the Parental Assistance Agency to Prevent Child Abuse (PACT). Moore saw Lacey in her office, later recalling that Lacey did not "seem concerned" or "pay attention" to her son.

Over the next few months, the social worker arrived at Lacey's Cedar Key apartment numerous times to inspect it, but Lacey was always out. She never returned Moore's calls, and the investigation into possible child abuse never went any further.

Munchausen syndrome by proxy is a mental disorder in which caregivers deliberately harm their children to receive attention and sympathy. First identified nearly forty years ago, it is now known clinically as part of a condition called "factitious disorder imposed on another" and is included in the appendix of the American Psychiatric Association's *Diagnostic and Statistical Manual of Mental Disorders*.

The term "Munchausen syndrome by proxy" was first coined in 1977 by Dr. Roy Meadow, a professor of pediatrics at the University of Leeds, England. In an article in the British medical journal *The Lancet*, Dr. Meadow called it the "hinterland of child abuse."

Over the past few years, the Internet has seen Munchausen syndrome by proxy grow exponentially, as sufferers bask in worldwide attention, posting gory photographs of their sick children in distress. Dr. Marc Feldman, a psychiatrist and forensic consultant in Birmingham, Alabama, believes the Internet is responsible for many new cases of Munchausen syndrome by proxy.

"I sometimes call it illness porn," said Dr. Feldman, the author of the definitive book on the subject, *Playing Sick?*. "It's creepy . . . because of the preoccupation with posting photos with the [feeding] tubes and the child essentially sleeping or unresponsive. Could they not have removed the . . . tubing for the photograph? Well, no. They want the photo to show that."

Dr. Feldman says that medical staff often ignore the possibility that a mother may suffer from Munchausen syndrome by proxy because they don't want to deal with the possible legal ramifications and complications of accusing a caregiver of deliberately harming her child.

"Initial suggestions that [Munchausen syndrome by proxy] is at work may be viewed angrily by many staff," he explained. "No one wants to believe that he or she could be duped so completely. Also, in our litigious society, doctors may worry about the consequences if they make an accusation of [Munchausen] and are proved to be wrong."

Dr. Feldman believes Lacey and Garnett clearly exhibited many of the following warning signs for Munchausen syndrome by proxy:

- signs and symptoms begin only when the mother is alone with her child and are resolved when they are separated;
- other children in the family have suffered similar unexplained diseases;
- the problems consistently fail to respond to appropriate medical treatments;
- the mother is proved to have provided false information or to have fabricated a problem;
- the only diseases that remain as possible diagnoses are exceptionally rare;
- unusual symptoms, signs, or hospital courses that do not make clinical sense;
- caregiver has features of Munchausen syndrome (multiple diagnoses, surgeries, and/or hospitalizations with no compelling diagnosis);
- repeated hospitalizations and vigorous medical evaluations of child without definitive diagnoses;

- a parent who welcomes medical tests of her child, even when painful;
- care at more than one hospital within six months;
- the presumptive diagnosis is based solely on caregiver report;
- experienced physicians state, "I've never seen a case like it before"; and
- the child has been to numerous health-care professionals without a resolution or even sustained improvement.

5

"POOR BABY WAS SICK"

During the third week of January, Lacey Spears brought Garnett back to Huntsville Hospital, complaining that he was projectile vomiting and was not gaining weight. The six-week-old baby was diagnosed with reflux and had a surgical procedure. Presumably, the staff at Huntsville Hospital had not been informed of Decatur's Southern Rural Health Care's concern about Lacey's mental stability. Nevertheless, Huntsville doctors did place Garnett in a room for twenty-four hours without his mother, to see what would happen.

"Lacey was very upset," Autumn Hunt later told police.

On January 22, Lacey posted a series of photos on MySpace of Garnett recovering from his surgery, with a blue pacifier in his mouth.

"@ Hunts Hospital 4 Surgery," she wrote.

Soon after Garnett was discharged, Kristina Boger, who had gone to high school with Lacey, had dinner with Lacey and Garnett at a Chick-fil-A fast-food restaurant on

Beltline Road, Decatur. Although the two were never close in high school, Kristina had visited Lacey in the hospital when Garnett was born, and they had become friends. Boger later told police that, during the meal, Lacey became angry with Garnett because he was "acting out," and had "popped" him in the leg.

Boger also told April Chambers how Lacey had made Garnett cry at the restaurant.

"She said he was eating," said April, "and [Lacey] reached over and gave him a spanking for basically no reason. And I asked her, 'Did you call CPS?' And she said she hadn't, because she didn't think it was her place to."

On February 1, Lacey began screaming at Garnett in a Walmart parking lot. A friend who witnessed this became so concerned about the baby's safety that she reported Lacey to the Alabama Department of Human Resources.

Three days later, Garnett Spears underwent a Nissen fundoplication procedure. Lacey had brought Garnett to Huntsville pediatric gastroenterologist Dr. Randall McClellan, who diagnosed the nine-week-old baby as suffering from failure to thrive and reflux disease.

At Dr. McClellan's request, pediatric surgeon Dr. James Gilbert performed the radical procedure. With Garnett under a general anesthetic, Gilbert made a small surgical incision in Garnett's stomach. He then wrapped the upper curve of the stomach around the esophagus to form a cup, which was then sewed into place. It functioned as a barrier, preventing formula and feedings from coming back up through the esophagus.

From now on, it would be impossible for Garnett to ever vomit again.

Soon after the operation, Lacey brought Garnett back to the Southern Rural Health Care clinic, complaining that he would not take formula. He was seen by Dr. Adrienne Shuler, who observed that Garnett refused to take the bottle of formula that Lacey had brought with her. After trying unsuccessfully to feed Garnett herself with his mother's formula, Dr. Shuler sent Garnett to Decatur General Hospital to have a nasal feeding tube inserted.

After the procedure was done, Lacey posted on her MySpace page several photographs of Garnett with the nasal tube in place.

"He Had To Get A Feeding Tube," she wrote in the photo, showing her unconscious two-month-old baby hooked up to it. "That's How He Ate For Weeks."

On February 11, Lacey brought Garnett to Decatur General Hospital, complaining that he was refusing to take formula. Dr. Shuler would later tell detectives that a nurse had finally succeeded in feeding Garnett from Lacey's bottle of formula, but then he had become "lethargic."

When Dr. Shuler asked Lacey about it, Lacey replied that it was "improper formula."

Blood tests were then done that showed Garnett's sodium level was critically high, at around 180. Then he started having seizures and stopped breathing. He was intubated and airlifted to Children's of Alabama hospital in Birmingham for emergency treatment.

Lacey Spears flew to Children's with her son, now critically ill with hypernatremia—high serum sodium. By the time Garnett arrived at the hospital's pediatric intensive care unit, his sodium level had dropped slightly, to 165.

"He was so severely dehydrated that he was in shock," said Dr. Robert Pass, who treated Garnett.

Doctors were so worried about the nine-week-old child suffering possible brain damage that he was put on a spinal tap. He was also treated with IV fluids to correct his dehydration and bring his sodium back to normal.

Lacey was told that Garnett had been diagnosed with hypernatremia and that the plan was to carefully lower his sodium levels, using replacement fluids of dextrose and half-normal saline.

Rebecca Spears first learned what had happened from her father, who said her small nephew was critically ill.

"And we came over to the hospital," she said. "We didn't know if he was going to be okay or not. It was a very scary night."

Over the next day, Garnett's sodium levels dropped, and he was extubated so he could breathe on his own. And, as her son lay critically ill, his mother chronicled Garnett's brush with death on MySpace, with a series of gory photographs.

"He Was Very Sick And We Didn't Know It," she wrote next to one. "I Don't Feel Good Mommy," she captioned another.

On February 13, Garnett was transferred out of the PICU to the hospital's general floor, where he spent the next eleven days. Two days later, Dr. Sarah Tucker, a gastrointestinal specialist, was assigned to conduct feeding evaluations on Garnett, to find out why he was having so many problems putting on weight. Although Lacey maintained that she was unable to bottle-feed Garnett, Dr. Tucker had no such problem. During the two-day evaluation, the doctor never observed him having any feeding problems.

Baffled, doctors also ran a series of tests to see why Garnett's sodium levels had risen so precipitously, since there was no medical explanation for it.

"We didn't understand," said Dr. Pass, "how he had what he had in the serum sodium when he came in."

Garnett underwent an MRI and a CAT scan, both of which were found to be normal. He was also given an upper gastrointestinal exam, to determine if there was any genetic or metabolic reason for his failure to thrive.

"It was normal," said Dr. Pass. "No genetic or metabolic abnormalities were found."

On February 14, Valentine's Day, Lacey posted photographs of her sister, Rebecca, visiting them in the hospital. Aunt Becca was pictured holding Garnett up next to a heart-shaped HAPPY VALENTINE'S DAY balloon and a bunch of flowers.

After seeing some of Garnett's hospital photographs on MySpace, Autumn Hunt wondered whether Lacey might be doing something to make him sick.

The Children's of Alabama hospital staff were so concerned that Garnett's feeding problems had something to do with his mother that they quarantined him from her. Over the next four days, hospital nurses conducted all his feedings, and the boy ate normally.

"He did not have problems with vomiting or spitting up," observed Dr. Pass. "Nurses' observations conflicted with his mother's reports that he often refused feedings."

On February 23, Dr. Pass asked Lacey how she fed Garnett. Lacey said that she had been feeding him breast milk diluted with Pedialyte (an oral electrolyte to prevent dehydration), with three parts water to one part breast milk. She also gave him half-strength formula with Pedialyte. Lacey claimed that she was doing this on the advice of a physician.

"I did not believe her," said Dr. Pass. "No physician would advise a patient to feed breast milk or formula diluted to this extent, because it would cause electrolyte abnormalities and malnutrition."

The following day, Garnett was discharged from the hospital and was returned to the care of his mother. It was still a mystery how his sodium level had gotten so high, but Dr. Pass had his suspicions.

"We were clearly concerned about Garnett's mother's ability to properly feed and care for him," he wrote in 2015. "It could be as the result of intentional administration of inappropriate . . . episodic administration of extra salt to Garnett. The addition of salt could result in his high serum sodium."

Dr. Pass noted that "very salty feedings" would cause vomiting, but after Garnett's recent Nissen fundoplication, he would not be able to get rid of the poison.

"Feeding large quantities of diluted formula to a baby with a high serum sodium," he wrote, "could result in excess retention of water, brain swelling and even death of some brain cells, which would raise the protein level in CSF—Cerebral Spinal Fluid."

Back in Decatur, Lacey posted more photographs of Garnett's stay in the hospital PICU, hooked up to IVs and various other medical equipment. She photographed him unconscious with his pacifier, writing that he was "Knocked Out & On Pain Meds."

"My Little Man Had To Be Sick Again," posted Lacey on MySpace. "Poor Baby Boy."

A few days after Garnett's discharge from Children's of Alabama, Lacey met Kara Couch for lunch at a Mexican restaurant. Couch knew all about Garnett's recent Nissen fundoplication, so she thought it "odd" when Lacey started putting hot salsa in Garnett's mouth.

6

RED FLAGS

That spring, Lacey repeatedly brought Garnett into the Southern Rural Health Care clinic. Dr. Adrienne Shuler later told police that she felt Lacey was "genuine" but was "overwhelmed" with motherhood.

Garnett suffered persistent chronic ear infections, with blood in both of his ears. Dr. Shuler became so concerned that she notified the Alabama Department of Public Health's parental assistance agency.

The only time Dr. Shuler ever broached the subject of Garnett's father, Lacey gave her an icy stare.

"We do not discuss the father," she informed the doctor.

Southern Rural Health Care nurse practitioner Judy Collier also treated Garnett for feeding issues and ongoing ear infections. She suspected Lacey might be responsible for inflicting the injuries to both Garnett's ears because, despite treatment from numerous ear, nose, and throat doctors, they never cleared up.

Lacey, she later told investigators, loved using medical terminology and claimed she had attended nursing school. Lacey had told her that Garnett's father was named Blake and that his family owned a local day care center.

On March 31, Garnett Spears was examined by Dr. Kinney Copeland of Decatur ENT Associates, after being referred by Dr. Shuler. Dr. Copeland, whose office had previously treated Jonathon Strain for ear infections, observed "bloody drainage" and "perforations" in both of Garnett's ears. He thought the high number of ear infections the child had suffered was "unusual."

On April 6, Dr. Copeland operated on Garnett's ears for large bilateral perforations of the child's eardrums. After the operation, Lacey Spears duly photographed the tubes protruding from Garnett's ears, posting them as part of her new "Garnett's Hospital Stays" album on MySpace.

Five weeks later, Dr. Shuler referred Garnett to Dr. Alice Morgan for a second opinion about Garnett's baffling ear infections. Beforehand, Dr. Shuler sent medical documents and reports about Garnett's health problems to Dr. Morgan's office in Cullman, Alabama. One report stated that his mother might have Munchausen syndrome by proxy.

When Dr. Morgan examined Garnett, she observed bilateral ear infections in both ears as well as a large perforation in his right one. There was also "fresh blood" in his ear canals.

Dr. Morgan thought it a "red flag" and "suspicious," because the referring doctor had also noted fresh blood in Garnett's ear canal a month earlier, and it should have been healed by now.

* | * | *

On June 3, 2009, Garnett Spears turned six months old, and his mother celebrated with a new album on MySpace, entitled "Garnett @ 6 Months Old . . . Priceless Memories."

A few days later, she brought Garnett to Decatur General Hospital for dehydration caused by vomiting. Nurse Ginger Dabbs-Anderson, age thirty-nine, who was on call that day, had first met Lacey three months earlier, when Dabbs-Anderson had helped save Garnett's life before he was airlifted to Children's of Alabama.

"[Lacey] said he was throwing up everything," Dabbs-Anderson told writer Shawn Cohen. "I took him to the nurse's desk, with an IV in his vein and everything, and I fed him."

To see if the little boy could keep formula down, she kept him at her nursing station for two hours, the time it takes for food to start digesting. Garnett did not throw up and was fine.

"So we tried to teach [Lacey] how to hold him when he was eating," she explained. "Hold him upright. Feed him slowly. Stuff like that. But it just didn't seem to sink in . . . and she continued to tell . . . different nurses that he was throwing up."

Lacey, who was now on Medicaid as well as receiving Supplementary Security Income payments for having a disabled child, constantly brought Garnett into the hospital, complaining of gastric problems.

"We were suspicious," said Dabbs-Anderson. "One time I gave her some formula to feed Garnett. Within minutes she was calling me down there, saying he threw up on the bed."

When Ginger rushed to his hospital room, it was obvious that Garnett had not vomited, but his sheets were soaked in water.

"And I [asked] her about it," recalled the nurse, "and she was just kind of quiet. She didn't say yeah or a no or whatever."

There were also the mysterious never-ending ear infections, which could not be explained.

"He had massive ear infections that kids don't get," said Ginger. "It was kind of gross. Pus and blood would leak out of his ears. They had to put towels and stuff under his ears to catch the pus. I don't know what she was doing, but that child was the sickest child I've ever seen."

One time, Lacey turned up at Decatur General Hospital, saying she was "stressed out" and couldn't deal with Garnett.

"She said she didn't know what to do with him," said Ginger. "[He] wouldn't eat and would just cry. So they admitted Garnett to the hospital."

According to Ginger, the Alabama Department of Human Resources, which runs a child protective services unit, was then alerted by hospital staff.

"We just thought they needed to be involved," she said. "Felt more comfortable knowing somebody else was watching. [DHR] got there, basically did a plan of action, tried to talk to her and teach her."

The nurse claims that DHR visited Lacey's Cedar Key apartment several times and monitored her over the next year.

In 2014, however, DHR spokesman Barry Spear said he had no record of any investigation into Lacey Spears.

On June 20, Lacey Spears brought Garnett back to Decatur General Hospital. He was in such serious condition that, once again, doctors decided to fly him to Children's in Birmingham. While emergency preparations were being made to airlift him eighty-five miles south, the hospital alerted DHR.

"Child en route to hospital," stated the call log, "with bleeding from the eyes, nose, mouth, and ears."

On arrival, Garnett was admitted, where he spent the next few days under observation. Four days later, he underwent surgery.

The night before his operation, Lacey posted on MySpace half a dozen photographs of her ailing son lying helplessly in his hospital bed.

"Good Night Little Prince," "He's My Whole World," "He Sleeps With His Mommie Everynight," read her various captions.

The next day Lacey posted more photos of Garnett, before and after surgery.

"He Was Getting Ready 4 Surgery," she captioned a photograph of her seven-month-old sitting in his bed in a hospital gown, hooked up to an IV tube. "Playing Before Surgery," she wrote in another, showing the blond-haired infant with a large stuffed toy duck.

A few hours later, she posted a further set. "Sleeping After His Surgery," she wrote by a photo of Garnett, still under the effects of anesthetic. "That's My Little Prince."

Because neither hospital ever filed a report of suspected child abuse or neglect, DHR never investigated the initial call it received before Garnett was airlifted out of Decatur.

"It's just a courtesy call, so that we have knowledge that the child was arriving," said DHR spokesman Barry Spear. "But it wasn't reported as suspected abuse . . . It was just reported that the child was on his way."

That summer, nurse Ginger Dabbs-Anderson became so concerned about Lacey's fitness as a mother that she deliberately befriended her to keep an eye on Garnett.

"She didn't know how to be a mother," explained Ginger. "She would come to see me at the hospital, telling me that she had no family support and needed a sitter for G. I thought I could teach her to be a better parent, so I became a sitter at first on my off days."

Soon the nurse was socializing with Lacey and Garnett, often having them over to her house.

"I started spending time with them together," she said. "I did want to protect him by teaching her."

When Lacey asked Ginger to babysit Garnett overnight at her home, Ginger agreed. They soon settled into a routine.

"I would meet her at Walmart," recalled Ginger, "and get Garnett and bring him back to my [home] and babysit him."

Whenever Garnett stayed over with Ginger, who lived with her grandmother, he had no problems eating.

"He would eat with us . . . at the dinner table," Ginger said. "I would feed him whatever he could chew. He ate fried potatoes, mashed potatoes . . . whatever we would have. He loved fried okra."

As Lacey grew closer to Ginger, she seemed to lose interest in JonJon and became increasingly unreliable. Autumn Hunt later told police how Lacey would volunteer to babysit JonJon and then not show up. Eventually, Hunt found someone else to look after her son, and his ear infections stopped.

On Independence Day, Lacey Spears brought Garnett to a pool party with her parents. She dressed him in a stars-and-stripes T-shirt, sunglasses, and a hat. It was a sweltering day, and Terry Spears took his grandson for a cooling dip in the pool before he fell asleep in an inflatable plastic serpent.

Soon afterwards, Lacey posted a new MySpace album, "Garnett's 1st July 4th."

"It's Hot Mommie," she wrote by one photo. "Swimming With His Pawpaw," she captioned another.

Three days later, Lacey posted more photographs of Garnett, at home, surrounded by all his toys, now numbering in the hundreds. She boasted that 90 percent of them came from Walmart.

"Garnett Is Already 7 Months Old," Lacey noted in a new MySpace album, with captions reading "My Mommie Is The Best," "He's My Whole World," and "I Love You Mommie."

A few days later, Mallory McWhorter ran into Lacey at a local mall, meeting Garnett for the first time.

"He was really little, and probably about eight months old," Mallory recalled. "He was so cute and cuddly, and I wanted to hold him."

Mallory congratulated her old school friend for having such a beautiful little boy.

"And that's when she told me her spiel," Mallory recalled. "Like he's been in the hospital this many days and this is how sick he is. And I just felt horrible. Wow, this kid's been through a lot, but he was out in a public place."

In August, Lacey brought Garnett to Clearwater, Florida, to meet his great-grandmother, Peggy Florence, and his great-uncle, Bo. During the visit, she took Garnett to Honeymoon Island, posing for photographs on the beach with him wearing her sunglasses.

"Mommie & Baby," she wrote in an album on MySpace entitled "Garnett's First Beach Trip." She also posted pictures of Garnett and his sixty-eight-year-old great-grandmother.

"My Gramma @ Garnett," she wrote by it. "She Loves Him So Much."

She also posted a picture of Uncle Bo, who had just been diagnosed with cancer.

"Oh How We loved The Beach," she wrote. "Going To Live There Again Someday Soon."

7

"MY SWEET ANGEL IS IN THE HOSPITAL FOR THE 23RD TIME"

After returning from Florida, Lacey Spears decided Garnett should have a gastrostomy feeding tube implanted in his stomach. She repeatedly asked Decatur General Hospital doctors to perform the operation, claiming he went for days without eating. But they refused, saying Garnett did not need it.

"I didn't think the feeding tube was necessary," said nurse Ginger Dabbs-Anderson, "because when he was with me he ate [everything] and didn't have a problem with throwing up."

Lacey then started going from hospital to hospital, requesting the procedure. Eventually, Dr. Albert Chong at Children's of Alabama agreed to perform it after diagnosing Garnett with failure to thrive, secondary to inadequate oral intake.

On September 1, Dr. Chong inserted a MIC-KEY feeding tube into the ten-month-old baby's stomach. During the forty-five-minute operation, Dr. Chong placed a small one-and-a-half-inch plastic tube into Garnett's abdomen. At the end of the tube was a balloon to prevent any leakage.

Within minutes of Garnett coming out of the operating room, Lacey posted a post-op photograph on MySpace, captioned "Mommie I Feel Bad And My Belly Hurts."

From now on, Lacey would have visible proof that Garnett was suffering from severe gastrointestinal problems. She would also be able to feed him anything she wanted through the tube going directly into his stomach.

On September 23, Lacey Spears signed up for a Twitter account, under the tagline @Garnett'sMommy. The next day she tweeted, "Please Pray 4 My Little Prince He Has Another Bad Ear Infection :) Poor Baby Boy."

The following Saturday, Lacey invited Dabbs-Anderson over to her apartment, renting the new Will Smith movie *Seven Pounds* and then tweeting about it.

Several days later she took to Facebook, gushing, "I am so Thankful 2 be a mommy!!! My life is 4 my baby boy @ he is my life!!! I love you Garnett Paul!!!"

By now she was telling friends that she wanted another child and had already picked out the name: Granite.

"She wanted to give Garnett a brother," said Kathy Hammack, who worked in day care with Lacey. "She had baby fever."

On Friday, October 16, Lacey Spears turned twenty-two and celebrated by getting a tattoo.

"Happy Happy Happy Happy Birthday To Me!!!" she tweeted. "Is Getting Ready 2 Go Get A Tattoo."

On Halloween, Lacey dressed Garnett up as a turtle, bringing him to a children's party.

"Happy Halloween Everyone!!!" she told her Facebook

friends. "My Little Prince Is Going As A Turtle :) Got Lots Of Fun Plans For Today :)"

On November 9, Lacey asked everyone to pray for Garnett, because she was taking him to the doctor.

"Please Pray Baby G Doesn't Have To Be Put In The Hospital," she wrote on Facebook. ":(Poor Baby Boy Has Spent Much Of His Life In One :("

Two days later, Garnett was back in the hospital, and Lacey tweeted the news in extra-large type.

"My Sweet Angel Is In The Hospital for the 23rd Time :(Please Pray He Gets To Come Home Soon . . . " she wrote.

Two days later, Garnett was back home, and his mother was happily tweeting about shopping for his birthday presents.

"Gotta Work Till 12," she tweeted. "Then Going Shopping For Garnett's Birthday With My Mommy, Ginger & Of Course My Little Prince!!! It Shall Be A Great." [sic]

Later that day, Mallory McWhorter asked Lacey on Facebook how she and Garnett were doing.

"We are great!" Lacey replied. "hard 2 believe he will be 1 in 2 weeks! Seems like yesterday I was bring [sic] home from the hospital . . . he is a true blessing."

"You would have thought she was the best mother," said Mallory in November 2014. "This woman is putting her sweat, blood, and tears . . . to get the best care for her son. She's feeding him the best. She's doing the best for him. She is awesome."

On Thursday, December 3, Garnett Spears turned one year old, and his mother threw him a party.

"Happy 1st Birthday Garnett-Paul!!! Mommy Love You," she tweeted.

From now until Christmas, Lacey would post daily

progress reports on her preparations for Garnett's second Christmas, as well as pictures of their decked-out tree.

"Going Shopping For Garnett-Paul A Big Boy Seat," she tweeted, "& Then Shopping With Ginger For Christmas Stuff."

Nurse Ginger Dabbs-Anderson, who was recovering from a brain surgery, was now spending more and more time with Lacey. She had heard all about Blake and about how Lacey had been molested by a relative. She would later claim not to have believed a word of it.

"[Lacey's] the biggest liar I have ever met," she said.

Chris Hill's only contact with his son was glimpsing him through the blinds when Lacey came and went from the Cedar Key complex. So he relied on updates from Shawna Lynch, who occasionally saw Lacey and Garnett and was friends with Lacey on Facebook.

"Yes, it was very frustrating," Hill remembered. "She had me blocked on Facebook, and I could only see just a couple of photos of my son."

On New Year's Eve, an upbeat Lacey Spears was looking forward to a long, four-day holiday weekend.

"Gonna Have Some Fun with Garnett-Paul & My Sister," she tweeted.

But by January 3, Lacey was posting new concerns about Garnett's health on Facebook.

"Hoping 4 a night without seizures, high fevers & trips 2 the hospital," she wrote.

After a frustrating year of trying to treat Garnett's recurring ear infections, Dr. Hope Weeks had run out of ideas. So she referred Lacey to Dr. Christopher Wooten, an ear, nose, and throat specialist at Vanderbilt University Medical Center in Nashville, Tennessee.

On February 2, 2010, Lacey drove Garnett 115 miles to see Dr. Wooten. Lacey informed him that Garnett had had a chronic ear infection for the past three weeks, as well as bleeding from his nose, ears, and eyes. Attempts to place tubes in his ears, she said, had been unsuccessful.

When he examined Garnett, Dr. Wooten found him perfectly normal. The boy's nasal passage was fine, and Wooten did not observe any bleeding from the eyes or pus from his ears. Dr. Wooten prescribed an antibiotic and a nasal steroid.

Three weeks later, Lacey was back in Wooten's office, complaining that Garnett had severe earaches. While in the waiting room, Lacey took out her smartphone and started posting on Facebook.

"Well we r checked into the hospital," she wrote, "is so thankful 2 all my friends 4 checking on garnett-paul, your sweet words of encouragement and prayers."

While Lacey waited outside, Dr. Wooten examined Garnett in the operating room, finding that his left ear was healed but his right ear had a fresh perforation in it. He described that as "unusual," because he had expected to see both ears completely healed. He thought it suspicious and decided against putting tubes in Garnett's ears.

But Lacey's Facebook postings over the next several days told a different story.

"Garnett is finally back in surgery," she wrote that night. "Please pray 4 Garnett, he is in the PICU due to complications during surgery."

The following afternoon, she posted an update on her son's condition. "Garnett-Paul is being moved from the PICU to the critical care unit :) Yay!!!"

At 2:00 the following morning, Lacey told her Facebook friends that she hoped Garnett would soon go home.

Several days later, Lacey had further bad news for her Facebook friends, who had commiserated with her over his hospital stay.

"Poor Garnett-Paul has a 103 temp!" she informed them. "And now his ears & nose are bleeding :("

Two hours later, after someone apparently voiced suspicions, a furious Lacey lashed out on Facebook.

"Someday all the lies, gossip, & judgments I watch you create will come back around & smack you in the worst way possible."

In early 2010, Rania Cottingham moved into the Cedar Key apartment complex, close to her old high school friend, Lacey Spears.

"I lived diagonally downstairs to her," said Rania, "and I'd run into her and we'd hang out."

Over the next few months, Rania, who was pregnant, spent a lot of time with Lacey and Garnett.

"Garnett would come over," she said. "He was very friendly and outgoing."

One time, Lacey brought Garnett downstairs, and he looked terrible.

"He was sick that day and looked pretty pitiful," recalled Cottingham. "She said he had an ear infection."

Lacey told Rania that Garnett was a failure-to-thrive baby who had to be fed through a feeding tube.

"She would talk about how he would have problems eating," said Rania, "so she had to use whole foods and organic foods and blend things down."

Although Chris Hill lived across the hallway, Rania only realized years later that he was Garnett's father.

"I'd heard through people that his father had died," she said. "I never asked, and she never said anything."

That spring, April Chambers became pregnant, and Lacey Spears immediately reached out to her old high school friend. They reconnected on Facebook, finding a common interest in natural foods.

"We became close," said April.

Lacey often spoke about Garnett's health problems, claiming he had just had open-heart surgery and trouble with his ears.

"She said the doctors couldn't figure out what was wrong," said April, "and they wanted to put tubes in his ears, but she wouldn't let them. There was always something wrong with him."

Lacey and Rebecca Spears would bring Garnett to churches in and around the Decatur area, asking for money and supplies to help care for him. Rebecca took him during the day, and then Lacey took him at night.

"They church-hopped," said Tonya Wallenstein, who runs the Sunday school at Willowbrook Baptist Church in Huntsville, Alabama. "Lacey would go to churches with Garnett, as a single mom in need and asking for donations. They did Tuesday, Wednesday, and Thursday Bible studies and Sunday services. They went to every women's ministry they could hit."

At first Lacey acted like a "timid girl," pretending to be too shy to talk. Slowly, she would open up and share her story about being molested by a family member, and about how Garnett was always ill.

"He was sick all the time," said Wallenstein, "and [Lacey] said he had an appointment at Vanderbilt hospital. We trusted her, so we gave her bus money."

Generous church members opened their wallets to Lacey, helping to pay her rent as well as giving her toys, clothes, and nursery furniture.

"All that was donated," said Wallenstein. "I mean, she got our sympathy."

One time Lacey claimed that she had just lost a child, showing a church official a forged death certificate to get financial help.

"She was taking advantage of several churches," explained Detective Dan Carfi of the Westchester County Police, who would later investigate Lacey's background. "We started to see a pattern of church abuse, and in Alabama, there were churches on every corner."

Years later, Rebecca would say her sister enjoyed going to church.

"They were always there if we needed them," she said. "That's part of what church is about."

Among the half dozen churches Lacey belonged to was the First Bible Church in Decatur, which eventually asked her to leave. Church secretary Erline Baker later told police that Lacey had "issues" and couldn't be left alone in a room.

"[She'd] lie, cheat, and steal anything not tied down," Baker explained.

Rachel Landers first met Lacey at the First Baptist Church, also in Decatur, and soon heard all about Garnett's health woes. Lacey told Landers how Garnett had been born without muscles at the base of his stomach, had undergone open-heart surgery, and had cochlear implants. She also claimed Garnett had contracted Methicillin-resistant *Staphylococcus aureus* (MRSA), a serious staph infection that can cause deafness in children, and could already lip-read.

Recovering from brain surgery, Ginger Dabbs-Anderson spent more and more time with Lacey and Garnett. Several times a week, Garnett would stay over at her house.

"He would eat with us," said Ginger. "He'd eat breakfast, lunch, and dinner at our table. My grandmother [cooks] big country meals—fried chicken, mashed potatoes, and okra. The boy never had any problems eating with me. I never fed him through a feeding tube. He ate food in his mouth."

In Lacey's apartment, Ginger would often see Lacey pureeing fruit and vegetables and then feeding Garnett through his G-tube.

"She always just wanted to give him the feeding tube stuff," said Ginger. "Doing the feeding tube thing."

One night, Garnett was so hungry that Ginger bought him a McDonald's Happy Meal. When Lacey walked in and saw him eating it, she had a fit.

Another time Ginger was over at Lacey's apartment during Garnett's bath time.

"She had him in the tub," Ginger recalled, "and he was whining because she was pouring water over his head."

Suddenly, Lacey flew into a rage, grabbing Garnett's head and holding it under the water.

"And I literally jumped on her to stop her," said Ginger. "Then I got him dressed and took him out of the house."

Later, Ginger confronted Lacey about her abusive behavior.

"I yelled at her," said Ginger. "She said, 'You can't tell me that you have never lost your temper with your children.' I told her . . . I have absolutely never lost my temper with them. It made me feel like she did it before, and more than a couple of times."

On another occasion, Lacey posted a mea culpa on Facebook after losing her temper with Garnett.

"Feeling like a rather horrible mother tonight," she wrote. "Screamed at my child because he screamed at me. Worst of all I gave him a freezing cold bath because I asked him not to play with the spigot. I've cried, held my little boy as he slept, asked for forgiveness. He is this little person who had to fight & fight with all he had to survive. Man did I blow it tonight."

When Kathy Hunt read Lacey's posting, she was horrified, wondering what Lacey might have done to Hunt's grandson, JonJon, during the two years Lacey had looked after him.

"It was the most disturbing thing," Hunt said. "I wouldn't give a dog a freezing bath. My grandson had twenty-one ear infections while she babysat him, so was she putting water in his ears? Was she holding him under water? What was she doing? I don't know."

Hunt said she became so concerned for Garnett's welfare that she reported Lacey to the local child protective services.

"And they didn't do anything," she said. "No, the DHR dropped the ball."

8

CLEARWATER

In July 2010, Lacey Spears took Garnett to Clearwater, Florida, to get away for a while. Uncle Bo was now in a hospice with terminal cancer, and Lacey volunteered to help her grandmother look after him.

"It worked out well for both of them," said Rebecca Spears. "Lacey wasn't really working because Garnett was sick, and my grandmother needed someone to come and take care of her."

Peggy Florence's next-door neighbor, Kimberly Philipson, met Lacey and Garnett the day they arrived.

"Miss Peggy introduced me," she recalled. "I thought Garnett was a girl, with his long hair. Lacey was very, very shy, so I did all the talking, but I thought she was nice."

Over the next few days, Lacey "warmed up," and they became friends as Kimberly drove Lacey and Garnett to and from the hospice in nearby Pinellas Park. In the car, Lacey told Philipson all about Garnett's ongoing medical problems and his G-tube.

"She explained all the stuff about Garnett," said Kimberly. "He was always running around without a shirt on, so I could see the tube. She seemed to be educated in the hospital setting and medical vocabulary."

The cheerful little boy often came over to Kimberly's house to play with her stepdaughters, and he never seemed to have any problems eating.

"Garnett ate regular food all the time," said Philipson. "He would want a popsicle or some ice cream. He would eat crackers. He would eat scrambled eggs. You name it, he ate it just fine."

And it always puzzled her why Garnett needed a G-tube.

"It didn't make sense," Philipson said. "Lacey's saying he couldn't digest food and needs it for nutrition. Well, I'm thinking this child eats everything . . . but I'm not questioning a parent, because it's not my child. "

Kenwood and Rebecca Paulen also lived next door to Peggy Florence on Radcliffe Drive East. They soon got to know Lacey and Garnett, who started coming over to play with the model train set Kenwood had built in his garage for his grandson.

"He called me Mr. Ken," Paulen remembered, "and Lacey did too. Lacey was a great mom. She was always around Garnett, who was always well dressed and well cared for."

Most mornings, Garnett would stand outside their house shouting, "Mr. Ken! Mr. Ken! Come and play with me."

"He was happy and full of life," Kenwood recalled, "and got along with everybody. He liked playing with the trains, and I let him operate them once in a while."

One day, Lacey asked to borrow Kimberly Philipson's laptop computer so she could go on Facebook.

"She was freaking out," said Kimberly, "because her grandmother has no computers in the house. I said, 'You can borrow my laptop, but I don't know what kind of [Wi-Fi] signal you're going to get, because I'm across the street.' From then on, she would sit on Miss Peggy's porch with my laptop, for hours, while Garnett's playing in the driveway."

Over the next few weeks, Lacey began confiding in Kimberly, during the drives to and from the hospice. Lacey always appeared preoccupied with something, but when Kimberly asked why, Lacey refused to answer. As a survivor of sexual molestation herself, Kimberly intuitively wondered if that could be the problem.

"And I said, 'Lacey, did something happen to you as a child?'" said Kimberly. "She had her head against the window of the passenger side, and you could just see the tears."

She then told Lacey about her experiences of being molested as a child, asking if this sounded familiar.

"Oh, my gosh," said Kimberly. "Did I get the lowdown, starting that day, and every day after that. She told me all kinds of stuff about what had happened in Alabama."

Lacey said she had been continually raped by relatives over the years, and one of them was Garnett's father. She said he called her every night for phone sex, knowing her grandmother stayed overnight at the hospice.

"Then Lacey started calling me late at night, telling me what he was doing," said Kimberly. "She would say, 'He won't stop. He has me on the phone all night, telling me what he wants to do to me.' I completely believed her and felt terrible. I told her to change her cell phone number so he couldn't send any more photos of his penis. But Lacey said she couldn't, as she was on a family plan."

Then Lacey announced that the abusive relative was

coming to Florida for a few days and would be staying in her grandmother's house. So Kimberly told her to come over to her house if she needed to get away from him.

"I said, 'You need to have a plan,'" said Philipson. "'Grab Garnett and just run to my house. My side garage door will always be unlocked.'"

A few weeks later, Lacey said she was pregnant by a family member. Kimberly was so shocked that she offered to arrange an abortion, saying she knew a doctor who would do it.

"She hesitated," said Kimberly, "and then she said yes. I said, 'Okay, do you want me to make an appointment for an abortion?' She says yes."

Kimberly then made some calls and arranged for Lacey to have the abortion the following morning. But when Kimberly arrived to drive her to the doctor, Lacey said it was no longer necessary because she had just had a miscarriage.

Soon afterwards, Kimberly Philipson cut her long hair into an extreme crop. Lacey immediately admired Kimberly's new hairstyle, saying she'd love something similar.

"Lacey had long, straight, pretty hair," said Kimberly. "She said, 'I want to cut my hair off for Locks of Love, for Uncle Bo.'"

So Kimberly brought Lacey to her hairdresser, paying for "a real cute haircut." Two weeks later, she was stunned when Lacey went back and had her hair cropped short.

"Her hair was exactly like mine," said Kimberly. "This is very odd."

That night, Lacey posted a photograph of her new look on Facebook.

"Are you gay now?" asked a male friend.

"No, why would you think that," she replied.

"The hair," came his reply.

"Really? I donated my hair to locks of love!!! I can't believe you pass judgment like that!!! Hair is hair no matter how long or short!!!"

"I was jw [just wondering] not judging," he replied.

"Well no I'm not gay," Lacey wrote back, "just too busy to date right now!!! My son is far more important."

In late August, Tina Spears arrived in Clearwater to see her dying brother, Bo. It was the first time Kimberly Philipson had met her, and she was intrigued by Tina's strange relationship with her daughter.

"Tina was lazy and controlling," Kimberly explained. "She would bully Lacey: 'Get up and make me a sandwich!' Do this! Do that!"

One afternoon, at the hospice, Kimberly was playing with Garnett and saw Tina viciously pinch Lacey's arm when she thought no one was looking.

"Lacey was sitting next to her on the love seat," said Philipson, "and I saw Tina reach behind Lacey's arm and pinch the shit out of her, telling her to shut up. Lacey gave her mom a dirty look but kept her mouth shut."

A few days later, Uncle Bo came home to die. As a registered nursing assistant, Kimberly came over to nurse him, but she could feel the growing tension in the house. One afternoon, Kimberly got in an argument with Tina Spears, and Peggy Florence ordered her out of the house. On her way out, Kimberly told her how Lacey had claimed to have been molested by a relative, who might even be Garnett's father.

"And I said, 'Let me speak my piece. This is what you need to know,' " she said. "And Miss Peggy is going crazy. I said, 'Lacey's just had a miscarriage in your house.' Then Miss Peggy goes, 'Kim, you don't know. Lacey has a problem with the truth.' "

* * *

On Wednesday, November 3, 2010, Uncle Bo died of cancer at the age of forty-four, surrounded by his family. The night before, Lacey had spent several hours with her favorite uncle.

Soon after he passed, Lacey posted a tribute to him on her Facebook page.

"My wonderful Uncle Bo went home to be with the Lord and my grandpa 2day . . . I love you Bo & miss you greatly!!! Your spirit is with us always and in my heart you will live forever!!! I will think of you when I catch my next raindrop and know you are shining down on me when I see the sun rise again!!!"

Later that day, Lacey texted Kimberly Philipson that he had died.

"I wasn't allowed to go over," said Kimberly, "because Miss Peggy was still mad at me. All I was doing was trying to protect this woman who says she's sexually molested . . . and then I get my ass reamed out by Miss Peggy and everything goes sour. But I'm thinking, why is it that I'm trying so hard to protect Lacey and everyone else is enabling her to continue this behavior?"

Five days after Uncle Bo's death, Lacey and Garnett flew back to Decatur to pack up their stuff and move to Clearwater permanently. Her grandmother had agreed to allow them to live there in return for Lacey taking care of her.

The night before they flew north to Alabama, Lacey went on Facebook, saying she was contemplating suicide.

"Isn't happy & doesn't have much of a desire to live anymore," she wrote. "I have been knocked down, beat on & let down too many times . . . My heart and soul can take no more pain & sorrow. I look in the eyes of my son and gramma & I know they love me and that my life is for them & them only but I just can't handle anymore . . .

My every move is controlled by 1 person & it has 2 end before its 2 late."

During the two weeks Lacey spent packing up her belongings and moving out of her Cedar Key apartment, she said good-bye to many of her old friends.

"She told me that she wanted a fresh start," said Rania Cottingham, who met Lacey and Garnett for a farewell lunch. "There was too much drama in Decatur, and she was going to stay with her grandma and help her out."

Lacey told Shawna Lynch that she was moving to Florida because its weather was good for Garnett's health.

"I told her good luck," recalled Shawna.

When Chris Hill saw Lacey packing up to leave, he made one final attempt to see his son. Once again, Lacey threatened to call the police, and he backed off.

"She moved to Florida with Garnett," he said. "I couldn't do anything. I didn't have enough money to fight [for his custody]. I barely was able to pay the bills myself."

The night before leaving Decatur, Lacey had a farewell dinner with friends at a Logan's Roadhouse. Then, on Thanksgiving weekend, she and Garnett flew to Clearwater to start a new life.

9

SUN AND BEACHES

Uncle Bo left most of his money to his mother and a small sum to his niece, Lacey Spears. With the insurance money, Peggy Florence immediately bought a brand-new Hyundai Santa Fe, which soon became Lacey's.

She also started remodeling her house, walling in the back porch to make a playroom for Garnett. It was soon filled with piles of toys, including a wooden train set and a drum kit.

On December 3, Garnett turned two, and Lacey threw a small party for her grandmother's friends. The beautiful little boy with shoulder-length blond hair happily devoured several slices of birthday cake.

"Garnett's birthday party was wonderful," Lacey later posted on Facebook. "Gone to pick up Garnett's birthday pictures, will have them posted later!!!"

After the party, Lacey released six balloons in memory of "my wonderful Uncle Bo & my amazing Grandpa Paul."

In the run-up to Christmas, little Garnett Spears became

a fixture on Radcliffe Drive East, driving his green electric John Deere tractor or pulling his toy wagon around the driveway. While Lacey sat on the porch typing on her laptop computer, Garnett drew on the sidewalk with colored chalks, planted pinwheels in the ground, or tried to catch the tiny lizards on the sidewalk.

Kenwood Paulen could not believe the number of toys that were neatly stacked in Garnett's new playroom.

"His room almost seemed like a toy shop," he said. "I mean, they got him everything."

Although Garnett appeared healthy and active to everyone else, Lacey complained on Facebook that he refused to eat and that she was feeding him through his G-tube.

"UGH Garnett just won't eat!" she wrote on December 11. "I struggle to get him to take 1 or 2 bites but I mean that's a struggle! He takes meds that make him hungry but he just [won't] eat. At this rate he is gonna be 40 & still eating through his 'G'!!!"

The Paulens were both impressed by Lacey's doting maternal skills.

"Her whole life revolved around Garnett," Kenwood said. "She wasn't interested in dating. They were like buddy-buddies and not just mommy's little boy. She played with him. She would do everything with him."

On December 22, Terry and Tina Spears arrived in Clearwater for a family Christmas, bringing many gifts for Garnett.

"Can you say SPOILED!!!" wrote Lacey on Facebook.

On Christmas Eve, Lacey wished all her Facebook friends a happy holiday and posted a seasonal message for them.

"Christmas as a child—Magical!! Christmas as an adult—Fun!! Christmas watching your child smile for days on end—Priceless!! Merry Christmas to all."

* * *

In late January, 2011, Lacey Spears bought health insurance for Garnett, who previously had been on Medicaid. Then she started bringing him to doctors and other health providers for a variety of ailments. He was seen by Dr. Peter Orobello, a pediatric ENT specialist; Dr. Michael Wisley, a pediatric gastroenterologist; and primary care physician Dr. Jan Arango.

Then, on January 28, Lacey announced that she would be starting nursing school in June.

"Yay!!!" she wrote. "Can't wait."

In the meantime, she spent her time renovating her grandmother's home using Uncle Bo's insurance money, choosing new furniture and pricey fixtures.

"Going to be making a lot of home repairs & improvements!!!" she wrote on February 7. "Tomorrow morning I am going to have hardwood floors laid in my new home & Tuesday my new furniture will be here!!!"

Most mornings Lacey would drive to Honeymoon Island, where Garnett made sand castles on the beach and waded into the warm water. Then they ate lunch at Frenchy's, which was famous for its grouper sandwiches.

"Baby Garnett had a wonderful time out on the water today!!!" she wrote March 20. "Nothing beats a nice day out on the beach!!!"

Lacey also began attending various attachment-parenting group meetings around Clearwater, soon espousing their philosophy. Named by pediatrician William Sears, attachment parenting teaches that children forge strong emotional bonds with parents during childhood, which last a lifetime.

Over the next few months, Lacey joined many parenting groups, including Mom's Circle and the Consciously Parenting Project, where she became close friends with founder Rebecca Thompson. Thompson describes herself as a holistic family consultant and has written three books.

During meetings, Lacey would share emotional stories about her struggle to bring up a very sick son alone. And she seemed to feed off all the attention and sympathy from the other women.

"Had a wonderful time at Mom's Circle today," Lacey posted on March 30. "So glad I went!!!"

"And I'm so glad you came," replied her new friend Emma Bryant. "It was so nice to see you :)"

Young mother Kerri Alcott first met Lacey and Garnett at a women's group meeting in Clearwater, and they became friends. During the meetings, all the women would breast-feed their young children, with the sole exception of Lacey. This surprised Alcott, because Lacey claimed to use a breast pump every three hours in addition to breast-feeding Garnett.

In April, Lacey began taking Garnett to Dr. Holly Johantgen, a doctor of Oriental medicine with a master's degree in Chinese herbology. Dr. Johantgen specialized in pediatrics and gastrointestinal disorders.

"Taking Garnett to see Doc Holly was the best decision I could have made!!!" Lacey wrote on Facebook. "I am blessed to have found someone that is willing to really help him!!! It will be a long process to heal Garnett but it can be done!!!"

She also met Meka Taulbee, a holistic health and fitness consultant, and they became friends. Taulbee devised a vegan, plant-based meal plan for Garnett. Lacey fed him these meals through his G-tube.

"Ooops, just gave Garnett 8 hours worth of herbs in 20 minutes," she wrote on Facebook. "Guess next time I better double check his flow rate."

For Lacey, this was an epiphany. And from now on she

would proselytize about her new holistic health approach to Garnett's medical problems.

"I'm a co-sleeping, baby wearing, breastfeeding, rear-facing, organic all natural, attached parenting momma!!!" she declared on April 17. "& love it!!!"

A few days later, Lacey announced, "DONE with modern medicine!!! One week of herbs & I have seen all the proof I needed."

When Lacey's old Alabama friend Riley Vaughan read about Lacey's new natural approach to Garnett's many health issues, she was shocked.

"All of a sudden she didn't believe in antibiotics," said Vaughan. "She didn't want to take him to a doctor . . . she believed in holistic medicine. You could tell she wasn't getting him the help he needed, if he really was as sick as she claimed he was."

On April 28, Lacey brought her son to Dr. Theresa Hohl's office with a severe ear infection. Over the next year, the pediatric chiropractic physician would treat Garnett for multiple ear infections and failure-to-thrive problems. Dr. Hohl repeatedly asked to see Garnett's medical records, but his mother never produced any.

On May 4, Lacey Spears drove Garnett to an appointment with Dr. Elisa Lynskey of Saint Petersburg, Florida. Dr. Lynskey placed tubes in both Garnett's ears. She also prescribed eardrops for Garnett, which Lacey refused to use.

Two weeks later, Lacey wrote that Garnett was feeling very sick and that she was looking for a doctor to remove the drainage tubes in his ears.

"He has been sick long enough," she posted on Facebook, "and enough is enough."

Lacey's decision to go vegan and turn her back on Western medicine caused much "friction" in her family. Her grandmother was concerned about the effects on Garnett's health, and told Lacey so.

"It was really difficult for all of us," explained her sister, Rebecca. "And very quickly Lacey changed from going with Western medicine to holistic medicine, and from eating an American diet to eating a very holistic, plain, organic diet. And there was a lot of concern of was it the best thing for Garnett or not. It definitely created some friction."

Peggy Florence had loved baking her great-grandson cookies and cakes, but now Lacey refused to let him eat them.

"That did create some tension," said Rebecca, "changing his diet so drastically. But then everybody settled into a new routine of being able to make it vegan and organic."

On Wednesday, June 1, 2011, the Florida Department of Children and Families began investigating Lacey Spears for inadequate supervision of Garnett after receiving an anonymous call to its hotline. The caller alleged that, although Lacey's young son was "constantly in and out of the hospital," Lacey still took him to "football games and other outings."

At 2:18 P.M. the next day, Child Protective Investigator Arilu Diaz arrived at Peggy Florence's home to investigate. Florence told the social worker that Garnett was at home but that his mother was out. Florence then called her granddaughter, telling her to come home immediately to meet the social worker.

"Garnette [sic] Spears," Diaz later reported, "was observed to be sleeping, he was free of any marks or bruises and he was wearing a turquoise diaper."

While they were waiting for Lacey to arrive, Florence

told Diaz that Lacey and Garnett had been living with her since Thanksgiving.

"She advised that her son passed away," wrote Diaz, "[and] Lacey came down to help her."

Florence said Garnett was often ill and suffered from frequent severe ear infections. He was being treated by several doctors.

"She advised that Lacey is doing a good job with caring for the child," wrote Diaz in his subsequent report. "That she has not observed the child to ever be mistreated by Lacey, nor has she ever put her hands on the child. Garnett has his own room but he mainly sleeps with his mother."

The investigator then asked about Garnett's constant fever. Florence said that this was because of his medical condition, but the doctor was aware and treating it. She said that Garnett had swimming lessons but that if he was sick he did not go in the pool.

When Lacey came home she was interviewed by the investigator, who told her about the abuse allegations being made.

"She denies that she ever hit her son," wrote Diaz.

Diaz then asked about Garnett's medical history. Lacey told him that when Garnett was born he had severe medical problems and needed surgery. He was in and out of the hospital until he was one year old.

She said Garnett was now being treated by a doctor for his ear infections and was seeing a pediatrician.

"She advised that she has also started taking her son to a doctor of oriental medicine," wrote Diaz. "He [is] treated by herbs and antibiotics. She is also looking into alternative methods of treatment."

Lacey claimed to be in regular contact with all of Garnett's doctors, saying he was being well cared for.

"Lacey has a good support system," reported Diaz, "with her parents and siblings coming to visit and maintaining regular contact with her and the child. She denies any critical risks."

A few hours after the Department of Children and Families visit, Lacey announced plans for a new blog on Facebook. It would be called Garnett-Paul's Healing Journey and would enable her friends to chart her son's medical progress on Facebook.

"Or maybe a fan page," she wrote, "where you can check out how he is & what's going on as you please . . . "

"I think you should do it," commented one of her friends. "You have an amazing, inspiring story that can perhaps show a lot of women that despite many obstacles, they can still be the best MOMMY they can be!"

A few weeks later, an official report from the Florida Department of Children and Families stated, "Garnett has lost 50 percent of his hearing and bleeds from his ears, nose and eyes. Mom will slap him for no reason as hard as she can. He begins to cry and she can hug him."

Nevertheless, the report conceded that the anonymous person reporting the alleged abuse had never met Garnett, had not seen Lacey in more than three years, and had heard these details thirdhand.

10

GARNETT'S JOURNEY

At 9:20 A.M. on Friday, June 3, Lacey Spears opened a new Facebook account called Garnett's Journey, to run in tandem with her two other accounts, Lacey Spears 16 and Lacey Spears 33. Each account had different privacy settings, allowing Lacey to control exactly who saw what she was posting. Over the next several years, there would be numerous postings about Garnett's "father," Blake, that her family would never see.

Lacey's new profile for Garnett's Journey read, "Join us on our journey to bring healing to Garnett!!! Embarking on a new way of living to find peace, happiness and health!!! Check in to see how Garnett is doing daily, send him love, healing & peaceful vibe!!!"

That same day, she started a blog called Garnett's Journey. Its first entry was entitled "Mommy Where Is My Daddy?"

"Like any other morning in our house," it began, "I stood at the kitchen sink somewhere between 1 am & 3 am washing dishes. It was something that had to be done, so the time meant nothing."

Garnett was sitting in his "rock chair," watching cartoons on television.

"Yes that's right 1 in the morning & he is awake," she wrote. "He decided when we start our day . . . we enjoy our early mornings."

Lacey wrote that she was washing dishes at the sink, lost in thoughts of doctors' visits, when she felt a little hand tugging her shorts.

"Mommy where is my MY DADDY?" asked Garnett. This was not the first time he had asked, wrote Lacey, saying she had given much thought about what to tell him.

"Do I give him details?" she asked. "Do I tell him the truth or do I 'butter it up' for him?"

As a parent, Lacey wrote, she wanted to protect Garnett from anything that could hurt him, but she had finally found a way to explain where his daddy was. So she dried her hands and kneeled down to his level to answer his question.

"I looked at my son in the face," she wrote, "and said, 'your daddy is in you, He is in your ears, eyes, nose, arms, legs, heart & soul. Your daddy is half of you & mommy is the other half.' "

Garnett had "glared" at her, she wrote, speaking just one word, with a "sweet, blissful voice."

"Awesome," he said, before running off.

Lacey asked how someone so young could find that awesome, but felt "pleased & at peace" on hearing that.

"I know the day will come," she wrote, "when Garnett will ask again where is daddy but for today he thinks its awesome. No matter where Garnett's father is he will always be in him & he will always be apart of him!!!"

After posting a brief summary of her blog on her new

Garnett's Journey Facebook page, she received half a dozen admiring comments.

"You are awesome, beautiful response," wrote Kerri Alcott.

"Perfect response," wrote another friend. "You are a great momma :)"

Later that day, Lacey Spears brought Garnett to Dr. Theresa Hohl's office, where he was treated for a G-tube infection and another ear infection.

"Garnett & his ears, need I say more," wrote Lacey on her Garnett's Journey Facebook page.

The following day, June 6, Lacey wrote that her son could "really use some happy healing thoughts tonight . . . he's having a rough go at it!!!"

Two days later, Lacey posted an update after returning from Dr. Johantgen's office.

"Garnett had a visit with Doc Holly," she wrote, "& let's just say his ears are not doing well. Currently waiting on some herbs to be overnighted, hoping they will help him & fast."

On June 8, Lacey wrote that Garnett's condition had worsened.

"G's ears are infected again :(" she wrote. "At the moment he is asleep & for now we are taking it hour by hour . . ."

"Poor baby!!! Hugs to you both!!!" commented Danielle Jolly, who had recently met Lacey at a mother's group. "Your [sic] such an amazing mommy!!"

By June 10, according to his mother, Garnett's condition had deteriorated still further.

"Please think of Garnett today," she posted at 9:40 A.M. "He is having one rough day & has really taken a turn for the not so good . . . "

April Chambers had been closely following Garnett's

latest health scare from her home in Decatur, Alabama, and was very concerned about his 103-degree fever. So when Lacey posted photographs of Garnett playing on the beach a few hours later, April reported Lacey to the Florida Department of Children and Families.

"Somebody needed to call them," April explained in 2015. "The posts on Facebook were enough to worry me. Like, Garnett would have a fever of 103 and she wouldn't take him to the doctor. But the next day she would take him to the beach. That was concerning."

By June 14, Garnett's condition had improved.

"Garnett has had two wonderful days!!!" Lacey wrote. "I haven't seen him this happy in sometime :) So I would have to say that his raw herbs from Doc Holly have helped."

Four days later, Florida Child Protective Investigator Arilu Diaz interviewed Tina Spears by phone as part of his ongoing investigation. Tina told the investigator that she was aware that Lacey regularly brought her grandson to doctors. She said Lacey had "fought" to have tubes put in Garnett's ears to fight his ear infections.

"She has no concerns with the way the child is cared for," Diaz later reported, "nor has she ever seen her daughter shake or intentionally make the child cry just to comfort him. Garnett is disciplined by consequences."

Over the next few days, Diaz would interview a number of Lacey's friends and medical professionals, including her new nutritionist, Meka Taulbee.

"Lacey was very concerned," said her sister, Rebecca, "because she didn't understand why the child protective services had been called on her to begin with."

On June 27, Lacey Spears updated her Garnett's Journey Facebook friends on his condition.

"Today I put on a brave face but I am far from brave," she wrote. "My heart hurts & tears run as I watch my son hurt . . . His healing journey is by far a challenge we must continue to concur [sic] so that one day he may hold the joy of good health."

"We love you," wrote Kerri Alcott. "You are a brave mama and Garnett is a brave boy."

That July 4, Lacey posted that Garnett was enjoying his first Independence Day outside of the hospital.

"Garnett has a visit with Doc Holly this morning," she wrote, "& then we are off to enjoy a wonderful weekend :)"

Two days later, the Florida Department of Children and Families received another anonymous call, reporting Lacey for not seeking any medical attention for her sick son.

"There are concerns that the mother is looking to get into holistic medicine," read the investigator's subsequent report. "CPI [Child Protective Investigator] advised reporter that the allegations are being addressed."

Lacey Spears was then summoned to the Child Protective Investigation unit's Clearwater office to answer the allegations against her.

At 2:45 P.M. on July 13, Lacey met with investigator Cindy Kuhack. Lacey explained that Garnett had been diagnosed with reflux, failure-to-thrive issues, and ear infections in Alabama. Later, Kuhack recalled the meeting, saying Garnett was a "small child," and she did not observe any "issues with the ears." She said Garnett appeared to be interactive and had "good speech."

At the end of the meeting, Kuhack instructed Lacey to put Garnett on "a proper diet" and to make an appointment with a pediatric doctor.

"One can only be so strong," Lacey posted on Facebook after the meeting.

On July 16, the investigation was officially closed, clearing Lacey of any medical neglect or abuse. The Department of Children and Families found that no further intervention would be necessary, although it expressed concern about Lacey's lack of follow-through with some of Garnett's medication and about his strict holistic vegan diet.

"His mother reports that she became discouraged with western medicine," the report stated. "Giving children, especially young ones, herbal remedies, is concerning as these are not regulated and the effects are not known especially in young children. He and his mother eat a vegan diet, but this has only been initiated since April of this year. He is breast fed. Children of mother [sic] who are vegan are at risk for vitamin B deficiency."

Nevertheless, the investigation concluded that Lacey appeared to have a good support network and that there were no signs of medical neglect or abuse.

"Her [grandmother] advised that she has no concerns with the way the child is cared for. In addition, [she] has advised that the mother is very appropriate with the child."

The abuse report concluded by saying Lacey had been told to keep Garnett's medical appointments as well as all recommendations by his doctors.

The investigation into Lacey Spears was then officially closed.

That night, she was jubilant.

"Out of despair, disappointment and pain comes determination, strength, focus, self love and drive," she wrote on Facebook. "Taking a much needed break . . . Spending the night snuggled up with G :)"

Several weeks later, in August, the Child Protective Investigation unit received yet another complaint, which claimed that Lacey was not following up with doctors' recommendations and that Garnett was losing weight. Once again, an investigation was initiated.

"Mom's lack of follow-up may have contributed to the weight loss," read the findings. "Mom was made aware of the importance of the follow-up, but she hasn't followed several recommendations."

The agency classified Garnett as being of "intermediate risk," because Garnett was so young and because of his extensive medical history, but then closed the case with no recommendations for any further action.

Over the next few months, Lacey started relying more and more on Dr. Holly Johantgen and nutritionist Meka Taulbee. Lacey told Meka that she was hard up, so they came to an arrangement by which Lacey cleaned Meka's house in exchange for nutrition services.

Later, Meka told detectives that Lacey would call her late into the night, often disrupting her sleep. During one late-night conversation, Lacey told the nutritionist that she had been raped by a relative and had had an abortion.

"Lacey was always looking for attention," Meka later explained.

That summer, Lacey portrayed herself on Facebook as a tirelessly inspirational mother. After spending the night playing with Garnett, whose health appeared much improved, she would go for long runs on the beach.

"2am and G is table surfing, watching a yoga video and jabbering about coffee," she posted on September 1. "That is my boy, full of life, love & ENERGY."

A few hours later came an update.

"Started my morning with a 6 mile run . . . even got to see the sunrise over the ocean."

A few days later, after she posted about an "8 mile run

in the rain before 6am," several friends asked if she took Garnett along in his stroller.

"Hey ladies I do not run with Garnett!!!" she replied. "I sneak out before he gets up in the mornings! I doubt I could run a mile with G in a stroller."

"Oh . . . okay . . . I know you were a superhero," commented one of her friends, "but come on now!!! LOL!!"

Besides attending various mothers' support groups around Clearwater, Lacey also joined several Facebook groups, including one for mothers who have lost children.

She struck up an online friendship with Pam Hamilton, who lived in Mesa, Arizona, and had recently lost a child. Lacey portrayed herself as a nurse, claiming to have lost two children at birth—a boy and a girl. The two women would regularly text each other or speak on the phone, but they never met in person. Over several months, Lacey told Hamilton about being sexually abused and that Garnett had spent two straight years in the hospital.

Laura Jarosch, who runs the Love of Learning Families group for homeschoolers, received a Facebook friend request from Lacey after Meka Taulbee suggested they meet.

"Meka knew her pretty well," said Laura. "She was giving nutritional advice to Lacey, to help Garnett because he was sick. I remember her saying that Lacey needed friends, [so] I accepted her friend request."

When Laura first met Garnett at a group function, she thought he was a girl.

"He was so pretty," she recalled. "He had this beautiful blond hair and a little pacifier in his mouth. Lacey was just sitting with him, smiling. She was very quiet and seemed really shy."

Lacey also befriended Jessica Wilson, a young professional mother she met at an attachment-parenting group in Clearwater. In August 2011, Wilson hired Lacey as a nanny for her young son and daughter. Later, Wilson would tell police how Lacey claimed she suffered from a brain tumor and Crohn's disease. Then, after Lacey learned that Wilson had celiac disease, Lacey claimed to have developed it, too.

Now settled in Clearwater, Lacey decided she wanted another baby, constantly bringing up the subject at mothers' group meetings. Eventually one of her new friends offered her husband for sex and to give Garnett a sibling. Lacey accepted and began sleeping with the friend's husband. According to detectives who later investigated Lacey's life in Florida, things turned bad when Lacey's friend became jealous. The friend finally joined her husband and Lacey in bed for a threesome, but their friendship broke up soon after that.

Later, Lacey alluded to the incident on Facebook.

"Garnett informed me tonight that Santa Claus was going to bring him a baby sister," she wrote on August 29. "Where the heck does he come up with this stuff."

Ultimately, Lacey did not become pregnant, but it would not be the last time she would try.

In mid-November, Lacey put up a Christmas tree in preparation for the arrival of her mother and sister, who were visiting for the holidays. She and Garnett were now on a strictly organic diet, which Lacey preached about on Facebook.

"My child WILL NOT eat chemicals, wood particles, processed foods, dairy, meat or gluten!!!" she wrote on November 20. "If you have an issue with this please remember he is MY CHILD!!!"

Lacey also continually posted about breast-feeding Garnett, although no one had ever seen her do so.

"Today I am thankful for the breastfeeding relationship I have with my son for nearly 3 years," she wrote on November 28. "We are 5 days short of 3 years [and] looking forward to nursing many more babies down the road."

That winter, as many mothers prepared to get their children winter flu shots, Lacey announced that Garnett would not be getting one.

"I STRONGLY DISLIKE DOCTORS," she wrote on Facebook. "They are a MAJOR waste of time & energy!!! Why the hell do I want to give me [sic] child a flu shot? WELL I DON'T We do not vaccinate & we sure as heck do not believe in flu shots!!!"

At the end of November, Lacey Spears hired professional photographer Melissa Ramos to photograph her and Garnett on the beach, to mark his third birthday.

"This is what I am looking for," she told Ramos on Facebook. "Garnett & I walking holding hands, I want the picture to be taken from the back down on the beach."

But when Ramos told her how much it would cost, Lacey balked.

"I think she wanted them for free," said Ramos. "She was financially strapped at the time . . . so it didn't end up happening."

On December 3, Lacey threw a birthday party for Garnett, serving only vegan, gluten-free, and sugar-free dishes. She invited "a few of our dearest and closest friends" to the party, telling her Facebook friends that she and Garnett would celebrate by themselves afterwards.

"Taking the Birthday Boy out for dinner & to walk on the beach :)" she wrote. "The best part is we are going ALONE!!!"

On Christmas Day, Lacey wished all of her Facebook

followers a happy holiday, writing about the perfect day she and Garnett had shared.

"Spent most of Christmas Day out on the beach [with] Garnett :)" she wrote. "What an amazing past few days we have had!!! Merry Christmas Everyone!!!"

On New Year's Eve, an upbeat Lacey reflected on her first full year in Clearwater.

"What a year," she wrote. "Made some incredible friends, journeyed to new places, said goodbye to one amazing person, watched my son's health slowly but surely be restored. Bring in 2012, the good, the bad & the amazing we shall concur [sic]!!!"

In early January, Garnett Spears's ear infections started again. Lacey was now treating his ears with breast milk, but reported on Facebook that it had been unsuccessful. When she brought Garnett to his pediatrician, Dr. Jan Arango, the doctor observed bilateral ear infections, a very rare occurrence.

Several weeks later, Lacey furiously lashed out on Facebook after being called a "hippie" for buying organic goods in a Publix store. Her outburst sparked a lively discussion among her online friends.

"Was called a hippie . . . for the simple fact everything I was buying was organic," she wrote. "Wonder what they would think of me if they knew I still breastfed, co-sleep, give my son a bottle and cloth diaper."

Meka Taulbee advised taking it as a compliment.

"Show them that bright smile," she wrote, "and say thanks."

April Chambers said she was proud to be a hippie at heart.

"I just laugh and ignore them," she told Lacey, "because I know that I'm doing what is best for me and my child."

Rania Cottingham viewed her old high school friend as an ideal mother because of her new age lifestyle.

"Garnett was gorgeous and still had a pacifier when he was four," she said. "And they co-slept and everything . . . Just the way she talked about everything natural, she seemed like the perfect parent."

At the end of January, Lacey got Garnett a dachshund-mix puppy she named Odie. Garnett called him "Owie," and for the next eight months they would be inseparable.

"We got a new friend Odie," posted Lacey. "From the moment Garnett laid eyes on [him] he was in love."

Kimberly Philipson would often hear Odie loudly barking, when Lacey locked him in the garage for hours at a time in sweltering temperatures.

"You could just hear the dog screaming and crying in the garage," she said. "I'm like, 'Lacey, you can't leave a dog in the damn garage.'"

On February 9, Lacey took Garnett and Odie to Orlando for a four-day visit. On their return, Garnett had a bad toothache, so Lacey brought him to Dr. Susan Blankenship in North Palm Harbor, Florida. The dentist, who had already fitted Garnett with two crowns because of tooth decay, warned Lacey that he had bad oral hygiene. Blankenship recommended a fluoride treatment, but Lacey refused, saying she did not believe in it.

On March 6, Lacey wrote that Garnett had been in "intense mouth pain" for several days and was unable to eat or sleep.

"He just starts screaming and holding his face!!!" she posted on Facebook. "His teeth look wonderful, no thrush in his mouth."

The next morning, after half a dozen sympathetic Facebook comments, Lacey announced Garnett was now suffering from a spinal disorder.

"G's C1 disk is severely compressed," she wrote, "either

from a fall or growth!!! He also has some fluid built up around his C1 disk!!! He was adjusted tonight along with a cranial adjustment!!! He goes back Friday for another adjustment!!! Hoping this helps."

Several days later, as Garnett struggled with an ear infection, Lacey posted an online article by Jake Fratkin, a doctor of Oriental medicine, titled "Pediatric Ear Infections And Chinese Medicine."

"If your child has an ear infection," Lacey wrote, "DO NOT PUT THEM ON ANTIBIOTICS!!! They are not needed & are more harmful then helpful!!!"

On Saturday, March 10, Lacey and Garnett flew back to Decatur for an eight-day visit. Before leaving, Lacey went on Facebook, posting, "Now Garnett has a fever!!! What next????"

Soon after arriving in Decatur, Lacey brought Garnett over to Rania Cottingham's apartment.

"Garnett was sick that day, and he looked pitiful," Rania recalled. "We were sitting in the living room, and she said he had an ear infection and a cold. He was just kind of wrapped up and wouldn't move or talk."

On March 15, Lacey and Garnett attended a birthday party for Shawna Lynch's son, McKelly, in Shawna's garden. By now Garnett had improved somewhat and was playing with the other children there, with a pacifier in his mouth.

"Lacey came to [my grandson's] party," recalled Jeannine Lynch. "She was a little heavier than the last time I had seen her."

Lacey, who was wearing a pink T-shirt, appeared to be in a bad mood all afternoon. A photograph taken that day shows her sitting with her arms crossed, staring down at the floor, grimacing. Later, Jeannine was really disturbed by that photograph.

"Any time you look at children playing and having a good time," she explained, "it makes joy in your heart. But the picture depicts such a sadness in her gaze."

Two days later, Lacey announced that she was taking a break from Facebook for a while.

"Been a mentally, physically & emotionally draining week!!!" she wrote. "If you need me call or text!!! HOPING to be back home in Florida Monday!!!"

On Monday, March 19, Lacey was back in her grandmother's house in Clearwater, Florida, and back on Facebook.

"Went to put G in the shower only to realize HE HAS 2 FULL BLOWN EAR INFECTIONS!!!!" she posted. "Really??? Really!!!"

Four days later, at 6:07 A.M., before leaving to take Garnett to a holistic pediatrician for treatment for his ears, she took to Facebook.

"8 mile run & yoga with Garnett, all before 6 am!!!" she wrote. "Now to tackle a trip to the pediatrician without antibiotics, an antibiotic shot or a trip to the hospital! May the force be with me!!!"

"Just one question," asked one of her Facebook friends. "I know you don't believe in antibiotics, so if he has an infection what would they give him? I'm just curious."

11

"YOU ARE AN INCREDIBLY STRONG WOMAN AND MOMMA"

On March 31, 2012, Lacey Spears killed off Garnett's purported father, Blake. Posting on her new Garnett's Journey Facebook page, which did not include any family members, she announced that the dashing young police officer had died in a tragic car crash, in the line of duty. From now on, Lacey would portray herself as a young widow bringing up a fatherless child.

"Nearly 9 months ago Garnett's father & my life long best friend was tragically killed," she wrote. "Tonight while driving home Garnett woke out of a deep sleep & simply said, 'mommy . . . daddy loves you.'"

Lacey wrote that she held her son "a little tighter tonight," and that memories of Blake will live on, even if he is not still here physically.

"We were supposed to grow old together," she wrote, "yet I said goodbye to you during the prime of our life's!!!!"

"Breathe deep mamma," commented Meka Taulbee. "Dance with the memories and love love love."

Another friend told Lacey that she was an inspiration.

"You are an incredibly strong woman and Momma," she commented. "Garnett is extremely lucky to have you as his mommy! <3 [heart]."

A week later, Lacey celebrated Easter with Garnett. On her Lacey Spears 16 Facebook page she was upbeat.

"Simply beautiful day!!!" she wrote. "Played on the beach, dyed eggs, went to the park, hunted eggs and lastly watching a home video! Best part of the day was spending it alone with Garnett!!!"

But her more private Garnett's Journey page painted a far different picture.

"Bittersweet Easter weekend!" she wrote. "1st without Daddy Blake, family or friends. Garnett struggled to find out why daddy wasn't here & well I struggled with his absence equally."

When her old friend Ginger Dabbs-Anderson read these posts back in Alabama, she was amazed, because Lacey had never even mentioned Blake to her.

"I found it online, on Facebook," she recalled. "I went, 'What bull crap! Blake, your soul mate, died in a car wreck.' I never saw her with anybody named Blake . . . It was a wholly made-up, fabricated situation. I met Garnett's daddy. He lives in Decatur."

Although Mallory McWhorter, who had known Lacey since kindergarten, had never heard of Blake, she assumed Lacey must have been too upset to talk about him.

"After she posted this up on Facebook," recalled Mallory, "I said, 'I'm so sorry that happened. I'll pray for you, and hopefully you'll find someone that can fill that role for Garnett. A father figure.'"

April Chambers was also surprised by the Blake posting, but she gave Lacey the benefit of the doubt.

"I don't know what happened or who he was," she

wrote on Lacey's timeline, "but the two of you created such an amazing little person <3"

On Mother's Day, Lacey posted a photograph of Blake on her Garnett's Journey Facebook page. It showed a ruggedly handsome, dark-haired young man in a T-shirt and jeans, slumped against a brick wall, looking brooding and pensive.

"My best friend. Garnett's daddy," she wrote underneath. "Our strength, my unfailing love and support!"

"Beautiful," gushed Meka Taulbee.

"My heart goes out to you Miss Lacey," wrote another friend.

Back in Decatur, April Chambers saw Blake's photograph and was suspicious. She then did a Google search, discovering that it was a stock photograph on a photo agency's Web site.

"She kept posting the exact same photo of him," said April, "but it would be different crops and edits. I don't know if she thought we were all stupid enough to fall for it, but I wasn't."

Five days later, Lacey began posting anguished messages about Blake to new friends she had recently met on a survivors' Web site.

"I just want him back!" she wrote one Facebook friend. "Today I feel insane, numb, angry, out of control."

"I'm sorry," she replied.

"I feel like I'm drowning in pain," Lacey continued, "pain that no one understands!"

"It's unimaginable. It's hard to understand how we survive it," her friend wrote. "I know that nothing makes it better right now, but know that someone understands what you're going through."

That same week, Lacey met a sympathetic Texas

grandmother in another survivors' Facebook group. When she asked Lacey for her life story, she was only too happy to oblige. It would be just one of several different far-fetched versions of her life story she would send to various Facebook friends over the next few months.

> May not be able to write it all out tonight but I'll start . . . On Dec. 28, 2007 my partner and I gave birth to a beautiful baby boy (Grayson Grayer) who never made it earth side . . . A few short weeks later I became pregnant with Garnett . . . His brother and him were born less then a year apart . . . The hurt, unknown fears of being pregnant again so soon separated their father and I! I raised G alone until he was nearly 1! G was 6.14 at birth and by the time he was 9 weeks old he was 3.4 pounds, he was unable to hold down food . . . He had emergency stomach surgery to save his life (his organs had began to shut down) however the hospital who did his surgery did it WRONG, gave him the wrong amounts of fluid and his sodium levels began to rise, he started having seizures, stopped breathing, was med flighted to Tennessee were [sic] he spent the next 14 weeks on life support . . . I never once was able to hold him for 14 long weeks, babies/children need touch, connection!

> Once G was off life support we were moved to the floor where we stayed for another 2 months. During these months I battled to feed G . . . If he ate I had to use a syringe to feed him. In September 2009 Garnett got a "G" tube and that is how he eats 90% of the time now! After getting his eating/reflux under control we began to battle MRSA . . .

He was and still bleeds from his ears, eyes and nose. Finally in September 2010 when G was nearly 2 I was told he needed to have his intestines cut out from all the medicines he had been on . . . Wasn't working for me, G was 21 months old and 16 pounds . . . So his father and I decided I would leave with him and come to Florida. I fought everyday to keep him alive until April of last year when I had the opportunity to meet a DOM [doctor of Oriental medicine] who YES SAVED HIS LIFE! G went on a special diet and began to take herbs instead of mainstream medicine, within 2 weeks there were signs of improvement! He doesn't eat gluten, dairy, meat, sugar of any form, soy, any processed foods, vinegar, all his food is organic. He still battles infections, takes time for your battle to heal . . . Just in the last few weeks he began a cancer prevention diet (or really it is a diet that has been known to cure any form of cancer) no he doesn't have cancer but the diet heals the body like no other medicine can! People with final stages of brain cancer, women with breast cancer have been cured within weeks . . . So that was our life until September. September 3rd I lost my daughter (Journey) at 23 weeks . . . 33 days later my best friend and son's father was killed in an auto accident . . . My life stopped on that October night, I struggle to place one foot in front of the other . . . I often feel robbed of Garnett's 1st 2.5 years of life and now I feel robbed of this part of his life . . . That's our journey, today we add more to it!

G has been in the hospital 33 times thus far, med flighted 2 times and had 12 surgeries for various things to do with the MRSA, his stomach and ears!

After reading this, the grandmother was moved.

"All I can say is WOW and God bless you!!" she wrote. "I have found through my parents, my husband and my own illnesses that you have to be your own advocate. You have done and are doing an amazing job for Garnett. You should be so proud of yourself."

The last week of May, Lacey Spears told her holistic family consultant, Rebecca Thompson, that she was suicidal. She claimed to be "terrified" and "paralyzed," complaining her life had no purpose.

"Am I insane?" she posted on Thompson's Facebook timeline on May 22. "Is there something wrong with me? Why is this happening?"

"No, you're not insane," Thompson reassured her. "This is part of your process and it is understandable given what's happened in your life. Breathe slowly, like you're blowing out a candle. And then slowly back in."

"I can't breathe," Lacey replied, "and my son is screaming for his father!!!!! He has been dead 7.5 months already!!!!!! He is never coming home, why can't he just stop asking???? I can't do this, I don't want to do this."

"Cry together about it," advised Thompson. "He needs you to see that this is really hard for you both."

A few days later, Garnett was back in the hospital with a blockage in his G-tube. His mother told her Facebook friends that she was in "utter disbelief" and "struggled" to understand why he suffered so much.

"My sweet little boy . . . has had to fight for his life since day one," she wrote. "I'm looking forward to the day he no longer needs raw herbs around the clock for weeks on end . . . To the day he is infection free, pain free . . . We have been on this journey of healing 13 months, looking back I'm amazed at how far he has come, we still have a long road ahead."

Soon afterwards, she boasted of donating 3,600 ounces of her breast milk to a local mother, and delivering it in person.

"As I approached her door," Lacey wrote on Facebook, "I saw a mother standing there with tears streaming down her face & a little boy in arms! In my eyes I was just getting rid of milk that I no longer had room for . . . In her eyes I was giving life to her child. I was not just donating milk I was also a little piece of inspiration for that mother and son!"

Her posting generated a flood of comments.

"Sweet soul you have!" wrote one friend. "Just brought tears to my eyes," said another. "You are goodness :)" gushed a third.

On May 30, Garnett was rushed to the dentist after a "flying" accident in the kitchen had "left his two front teeth mangled." Dr. Susan Blankenship examined him and found that one front tooth crown was pushed up into the gum and the other was infected. The following day she removed his two front baby teeth.

On Facebook, Lacey reported that Garnett was suffering a far more serious medical condition.

"Update On Garnett," she posted. "Found out this morning he has Osteomyelitis in his upper jaw. To clarify he has a major bone infection. Please send healing, strength, love and guidance to him and I. This is absolutely not were [sic] we need to be right now. I'll post more details later this afternoon."

The next day, Lacey wrote that she would have to give Garnett antibiotics to clear up the osteomyelitis. She hoped it did not travel to his brain.

"I have very deep reservations over the use of antibiotics," she said. "Watching these run into him has broken my soul! G has fought since day one for his life and 3.5 years later he is still fighting!"

12

"BLAKE, I WILL LOVE YOU ALWAYS"

On June 2, Lacey Spears asked Rebecca Thompson if the rest of her life was going to be "a slow form of torture."

"I see no end in sight," she wrote. "I miss Blake and our home seems empty without him."

The holistic consultant assured her that things would eventually improve, saying she was sorry that Lacey's life was so hard.

On June 6, Lacey marked the eight-month anniversary of Blake's death with a tribute on her Garnett's Journey Facebook page.

8 months ago today an [innocent] life was taken by a careless driver who ran a red light. 8 months ago a fiancé, father, son, best friend, soulmate and the person I spent 21 years of my life knowing was killed. I have no idea where his journey has taken him or what his journey looks like . . . I do know that I miss him, his connection, his love, the sound of his voice, the security he brought to our lifes [sic]. He

has a son that will grow up without his physical presence and I have no idea how I will survive without my best friend and soulmate. Life without him is a nightmare that never ends, a form of torture and today is certainly no different. There's no beauty, no happiness, no joy. Life is raw, unbearable and utterly pointless.

Later that day, Lacey told Rebecca Thompson she wanted to die and be reunited with Blake. She wrote of being unable to function, saying she could not even breathe.

"How do I live without him?" Lacey asked. "Rebecca, I haven't functioned today. I've done nothing! What's wrong with me? This kind of pain is debilitating! How will I survive tonight, the moment he was killed?"

Thompson suggested writing Blake a letter, or pounding out some Play-Doh as a catharsis.

"I hear that you don't want to be here without him," she wrote. "I can only imagine what that must feel like for you. I'm listening Lacey. And I'm sorry this is so hard for you right now."

"I WANNA BE DONE!!!!" Lacey replied. "DONE WITH EVERYONE AND EVERYTHING!!!!"

Just hours later, Lacey was back on Facebook, marveling at the amount of breast milk she produced.

"Was away from G for three hours and pumped 30 oz of milk when I returned home!!!!! Did I mention he nursed right before I left!!! Brings me to the grand total of 120 oz pumped and countless nursing sessions today alone."

Back in Alabama, Riley Vaughan was suspicious.

"Have you nursed for three years now?" she asked. "I thought you bottle fed for a while."

Soon afterwards, Vaughan unfriended Lacey on Facebook and stopped communicating with her.

"All her lies were kind of building on top of each other," she later explained. "That's why I stopped Facebooking her. I was just done with her after that, after realizing that most of the stuff she was saying just wasn't true."

Taking Rebecca Thompson's advice, Lacey did write a letter to Blake, posting it on her Garnett's Journey page on Facebook.

"Life without you is bizarre and unnatural," she told him. "I miss the scent of your pillowcases, the way you would wrap your arms around me at every opportunity just to hold me close. The sound of your laughter that filled the walls of our home. I miss [you] Blake and I [will] love you always."

On June 14, 2012, Lacey announced that Garnett had "2 full blown ear infections . . . [with] blood and pus draining from both."

A concerned friend asked what treatment he was receiving, noting the danger of permanent ear damage and loss of hearing. Lacey replied she would be taking him to her doctor of Oriental medicine if he didn't improve soon.

"Typically I clean his ears out with breast milk and herbs," she explained. "Do around-the-clock herb drips, push as much fluid as he will tolerate and just wait it out."

"With blood and pus I would be [taking] him to the ENT," advised the friend.

"Been there, done that!" came Lacey's swift response. "That doesn't help only makes the situation worse."

On Saturday, June 16, Lacey declared that she and Garnett would celebrate Father's Day at Crystal Beach Park in Palm Harbor, Florida. The next day she posted a closely cropped version of the stock photograph that she claimed was Blake.

"Happy Father's Day Blake!" she wrote beneath it. "Thank you for the honor of knowing you, loving you and being the mother to your children! I miss you dearly, long to hear your voice just once more. Today may have been the hardest day since your death. Happy Father's Day to the most courageous father, son, best friend and soulmate one could ever imagine!"

On January 19, at 1:22 P.M., Lacey told Rebecca Thompson that she feared she had cancer, was "falling apart at the seams," and had hit "rock bottom."

"What if I'm dying?" she asked. "Why isn't Blake here? What is wrong with me? Why am I incredibly angry. Why doesn't some of the pain go away? Why can't I tackle one thing before being handed another?"

A few minutes later, after getting no response, Lacey sent Thompson another post.

"What if I don't have cancer?" she wrote. "It's only a possibility. What if I'm making myself sick for no reason."

A few minutes later, Thompson answered, telling Lacey to take it "one step at a time" and to find a "bit of calm space."

"You're grieving," she wrote, "and you're continuing to be handed more. I'd be angry too."

Lacey replied that she was unfit to be Garnett's mother and he deserved better.

"I don't want to be a mother to G anymore," she told her holistic mentor. "I suck as his mother! I cry, scream, put him in time out, don't play with him. Can't understand what he needs most of the time. I'm over it! I'm over life! I need a hug. One person to try and understand."

When Thompson promised to help in any way she

could, Lacey wrote that there was something important she could do. Then Lacey asked if she could tell Dr. Holly Johantgen how she had been raped throughout high school and forced to have an abortion.

"Rebecca," she wrote, "you know just about every dark place of who I am. Hoping you still . . . see the real me and that your thoughts and views haven't changed."

"I think you are even more endearing the more you share," replied Thompson.

Lacey said that she had only told Dr. Holly that she had been raped, but nothing more.

"Tell her what happen[ed]," Lacey wrote. "I was raped, 5 LONG years, pregnant at 17!!!!!!!! I was a junior in high school!!!!!! Had an abortion AGAINST my will, what else was I to do? BEFORE YOU SAY A WORD I NEED YOU TO TELL HER I DO NOT WANT THIS SPOKE TO ANOTHER SOUL EVER!"

Thompson promised to tell Dr. Johantgen and to warn her not to tell anyone.

"Oh, Lacey," wrote Thompson. "I'm SO sorry."

That summer, Lacey argued with Peggy Florence over how Garnett should be fed. Lacey complained to friends that her grandmother was "too controlling" and wouldn't let her parent the way she wanted to.

Kenwood Paulen would later claim that Peggy Florence had told him that Lacey was jealous of the attention Peggy gave to Garnett and felt intimidated.

Some members of the various women's groups that Lacey belonged to were also having misgivings about her. They saw glaring inconsistencies in her tearful and increasingly elaborate stories about her ordeal of raising a sick son whose father had tragically died.

Emma Bryant first met Lacey at a breast-feeding mother's group in Clearwater, and they became friends.

Over a period of time, she noticed discrepancies in Lacey's stories. She later told police that Lacey had said she was having a miscarriage, but she did not seem pregnant. Lacey also claimed to have had a brain tumor. Bryant told detectives that there also was gossip that Lacey had had sex with a friend's husband in an unsuccessful attempt to get pregnant. She said that Lacey appropriated sicknesses and treatments from other people and then claimed them as her own. She described Lacey as "a compulsive liar."

Jessica Wilson also was becoming disillusioned with Lacey, who had been her children's nanny for a year. She eventually fired Lacey after coming home to discover that her daughter had somehow gotten Icy Hot back-pain ointment in her eye, for which Lacey had no explanation.

Her daughter, who always refused to take a bottle from Lacey, had also begun getting gastric and ear infections after Lacey began caring for her. These all cleared up as soon as Lacey left.

Wilson would later tell detectives that she had caught Lacey stealing some of her clothing. After Wilson confronted Lacey about it, the clothing was returned.

On June 28, Lacey defended her new holistic, herbal lifestyle on Facebook. In a manifesto, she defiantly told her critics that, from now on, Garnett would not be receiving any Western medicine.

I'm not one to often speak my mind, I can when needed! No my child does not eat off plastic, have his food cooked in a microwave, play with plastic toys that light up and talk . . . No he does not watch tv, drink purple kool-aid, eat ice cream or consume sugar of any form . . . He isn't vaccinated, doesn't follow western medicine . . . No I won't take his pacifier until HE IS READY TO LET IT GO!!! He doesn't get put in time out, won't spank him, don't scream at him, will not force him to do something he isn't ready to do . . . He isn't abused, mistreated, is not missing out on life!!!! I could sit and explain my reasons behind each of the listed but does it really matter??? NO! What matters is he is MY son, I birth [sic] him, I'm raising him. At the end of the day he is loved, nurtured, thriving, happy and always put 1st!!!

On July 4, Lacey wrote of falling into a deep depression. She complained that all her friends had abandoned them after Blake died, leaving her and Garnett alone.

"I HATE life!" she wrote. "I hated life yesterday, I hate life today, I'll surly [sic] hate life tomorrow. I encounter smiling faces daily, smiling faces!?! What's wrong with people? There is absolutely nothing to smile over."

The bleak posting brought more than a dozen sympathetic comments, offering "big juicy hugs," love, and prayers.

"We're all here for you," wrote one friend. "Hang in there. (((hugs)))"

Soon after moving to Clearwater, Lacey Spears learned about the local Suncoast Waldorf School, in Palm Harbor, from her friend Rebecca Thompson. Then, in early July 2012, Lacey was hired by Jak and Nicole Plihal to take care of their three young children at their home in Palm Harbor. Nicole was well acquainted with Waldorf schools in Maryland, Pennsylvania, and Clearwater, and she told Lacey about them.

Established in 1919 by the Austrian philosopher and founder of anthroposophy Rudolf Steiner, Waldorf education integrates holistic values with the academic development of pupils. There are now more than one thousand independent Waldorf schools all over the world, and 150 in North America, from pre-kindergarten through twelfth grade.

"It was just something I mentioned to [Lacey]," Nicole Plihal told writer Shawn Cohen. "That if I was a single mom with a child, this is the place I might end up. And she decided to look into it. She did her own research."

After researching the Waldorf education system online, Lacey decided it would be the perfect lifestyle for her and Garnett. She particularly liked the Green Meadow Waldorf School in Chestnut Ridge, New York, which was on the grounds of the Rudolf Steiner–inspired Fellowship Community. Lacey learned that, in return for working for the Fellowship Community, she would get free room and board, plus an education for Garnett at the private Green Meadow.

"How many people are going to help her support her child?" asked Nicole Plihal. "Being a single mom is scary all on your own."

On July 30, 2012, Lacey filled out an official application form to join the Fellowship Community. The application was riddled with lies about Garnett's health and her past employment history.

She wrote that she had heard about the community from several friends, naming Rebecca Thompson. Asked why she wanted to join, Lacey wrote, "Looking for a very simple, organic lifestyle for both my son and self."

She was then asked to describe her own and Garnett's state of health, because a medical exam would be required.

"No current medical needs," she wrote. "Overall healthy."

Lacey wrote that she wanted to stay "long-term" and listed all her jobs, including working as a nanny for Jessica Wilson. But when she was asked her reason for leaving, Lacey wrote, "Mother wanted to stay home."

She was then told to list any skills she could bring to the Fellowship Community.

"Nursing skills," she wrote, "hospital experience, worked with children for many years, took care of my 70-year-old Gramma."

Lacey was then asked if any of her interests could be developed further in the community.

"Working with children," she wrote. "Helping the elderly."

She gave her doctor of Oriental medicine, Dr. Holly Johantgen, and her employer, Nicole Plihal, as references.

Finally, she was asked to write a brief biographical sketch, including any previous work in anthroposophy or other spiritual movements.

"Interests or experience in working with older people or handicapped," she wrote. "Home schooling. Unschooling. My 3-year-old son. Believe in helping others. My son's life is based around Waldorf."

After submitting her application, Lacey was interviewed over the phone by several members of the Fellowship's executive circle, who run it. As Lacey's reference, Nicole Plihal was also contacted by the Fellowship, to see whether Lacey would be a good fit.

That summer, executive circle member Matt Uppenbrink and his wife, Elizabeth, who had started their Waldorf careers doing marketing and music, respectively, for the Suncoast Waldorf School, happened to be on the Gulf Coast, visiting family. During their visit, Rebecca Thompson introduced them to Lacey and Garnett, and they were most impressed.

"They got in a conversation with Lacey about the Fellowship and invited her [to join]," said Christine O'Brien, who lived at the Fellowship at the time. "And that's how she came."

But it would be another three months before Lacey and

Garnett finally arrived in Chestnut Ridge to join the Fellowship Community.

On August 6, Lacey marked the ten-month anniversary of Blake's passing with another eulogy. Now she was claiming they had been high school sweethearts.

> 10 months ago I heard my best friend, sons father and soul mates voice for the last time, never would have thought in a matter of hours he would travel onward. We had an amazing relationship, one that had been evolving for 21 years. See we met each other when he was 3 and I was 2. For many years we were best friends, inseparable. We would finish each others sentences, most times we didn't need words to express what the other needed, we just knew. I couldn't look into his deep dark brown eyes without smiling, when he would wrap his arms around me I knew we would always prevail through anything. After high school there was college, 2 children, countless hospital stays with our son, a move to Florida, another child and life was full circle. As crazy as life was we were in love, deeply in love. I looked forward to the weeks he was here, yearned for him while he was away working and hoped we would soon be together again, as one, as a family. I miss him everyday, his voice, his laughter, his scent, mostly the security he brought by his touch. I don't know how I've managed without him or how our son and I will begin to rebuild our lives [sic] without him. 10 months without him seems much longer.

In late August, Garnett's beloved pet dachshund, Odie, was found dead under a neighbor's window. Lacey told some people the puppy drowned in a bathtub, others that it had eaten a poisonous frog.

"That didn't make any sense," said Kimberly Philipson. "I've had dogs my whole life that are always in the backyard. Never saw a poisonous frog."

Soon after burying Odie, Lacey vented on Facebook.

"I swear I have experienced enough death in my life!!!!" she wrote. "I lost a child almost a year ago, my best friend and soulmate 10 months ago and today my son lost his best friend, his puppy, Odie. . . . What the hell did I do to ever deserve a life like this????"

When someone suggested trying to explain to Garnett that death was a natural part of life, Lacey lashed out.

"What the hell are you thinking????" she wrote. "He is 3 years old, he knows all too much about death. If you can't remember his father was killed!!!!! I seriously wonder what the hell people are thinking."

On September 7, Lacey Spears received Garnett's new Kangaroo pump for his G-tube and posted a picture of him playing with it.

"Meet September," she wrote, "Garnett's tubie friend! He arrived in the mail this morning! After promptly naming him he went right to work giving him his daily herbs :)"

Two days later, Lacey informed her Garnett's Journey friends that Garnett had hit "another rough patch." He had not eaten for days, and despite being given "countless herbs and home remedies," nothing seemed to be helping.

The following morning, Lacey posted that Garnett was suffering from a serious blood disorder called hereditary spherocytosis. She said he needed an immediate blood transfusion, but she promised to get a second, third, and fourth opinion before allowing him to undergo surgery.

"He will eventually need his spleen removed," she wrote. "Just another part of his amazing journey. Hasn't he been through enough?"

At 10:24 P.M. on September 11, Lacey posted that Garnett was now undergoing tests in the hospital.

"The sounds of a night in the hospital are all to [sic] knowing," she wrote. "The humming of G's joey pump as it nourishes his body, the steady beep of his O2 monitor, the clicking of his IV and the ticking of the clock hung on the wall. I've spent many nights here, I'll spend many more here."

"Poor G can't catch a break," commented Ginger Dabbs-Anderson. "Love y'all and miss y'all."

The next day, Lacey wrote that Garnett definitely had a red blood cell disorder, with only 75 percent of his liver working.

"I think I need to go for a run," she wrote. "A long run!"

By Tuesday, September 18, Garnett was out of the hospital and apparently much improved. Lacey told her Facebook friends that she had just returned from a seven-mile run in heavy rain.

"Did I mention I had my toddler in tow," she wrote. "Exactly what we both needed to start the day."

That afternoon, she posted the second and final Garnett's Journey blog. It consisted of a month-by-month photographic essay of her and Garnett's life since Blake's passing.

"We've done OUR unthinkable," she proclaimed. "We have together survived nearly 365 days, a complete year without Blake, my soulmate and Garnett's daddy. The past year has been the hardest year of my life, I don't imagine the next will be any easy [sic] but worth living through."

She described the fourteen-hour drive back to Alabama in March for "Daddy Blake's" memorial service, posting pictures of Garnett in the backseat of her Hyundai Santa Fe.

"July 1st would have been Daddy Blake's 26th Birthday," she wrote. "Garnett spent many hours playing with water beads."

August was an "ugly month," she wrote, after Odie the puppy had journeyed onward. This was accompanied by a photograph of a grinning Garnett playing with his pet dog.

"Here's to another year," wrote Lacey. "Many memories. Lots of laughs. Most of all hoping we both find peace, balance, happiness and light."

13

"I HATE MYSELF"

In the weeks before her move to New York, Lacey Spears's behavior became more and more erratic. She canceled numerous doctors' appointments, telling none of her Facebook friends about her and Garnett's life-changing decision to move north. She also began berating herself on Facebook for not being a perfect mother.

"Thank you Garnett for pulling your G Tube out," she wrote on September 22, "and laughing as stomach contents sprayed all over the living room!!!"

A week later, she described how she and Garnett had gotten into a shouting match after he refused to brush his teeth.

"I admit I'm far from the perfect parent," she wrote. "Tonight I was reminded of this. As my child was SCREAMING at me because he didn't want to brush his teeth, I screamed back 'You accomplish anything by screaming at me!' As I screamed at him it begin [sic] to dawn on me I wasn't helping him understand how to better communicate what he needed. I sure didn't win the parent of the night award."

Her post elicited a stream of supportive comments from her online friends, including one saying, "You're a great Mom Lacey Spears."

She replied that she was "the worst mother ever" because she had "failed majorly" with Garnett.

"Not only will I never forgive myself," she posted, "my child will more than likely never forgive me . . . When he informed me he hated me, I completely agree, I hate myself."

Lacey's Blake postings were becoming more and more fanciful. On September 29, she thanked his parents for being so supportive.

"I have the sweetest in laws," she informed her Garnett's Journey friends. "Weekly they send us a care package with random items. Today before they left my mother in law left a weeks worth of meals prepared, apple pie, cinnamon and pumpkin candles (just happens to be my favorite scents). I'm thankful for my sweet in laws."

"That is soooo sweet!!!" commented Mallory McWhorter.

On October 2, Lacey raged against a mother she had just encountered in a park.

"[She] informed me I was a LAZY MOM because my son still had a pacifier, wore diapers and nursed," she wrote. "Really? She has not the first idea of what he's been through. Then to top it off after she noticed he had a G tube she snatched her son up and left. Lady my son doesn't have a disease nor am I lazy."

A dozen Facebook friends rallied to her support, including her nutritionist Meka Taulbee.

"Ignorance can be cruel," Taulbee wrote. "She's

lucky I wasn't there. She probably would have gotten an earful."

"I love you Meka (: Thank you!" Lacey replied.

On Saturday, October 6, Lacey marked the first anniversary of Blake's death by pledging to post one new fact about him every day for the next year, which she would then print up and save for Garnett.

"One year ago today my soulmate and son's father was involved in an automobile accident that claimed his life," she wrote. "I was in no way prepared for this experience. I lost a part of myself that horrible night and I'll never get it back. He had a beautiful country accent, heart warming smile, joyous laugh and an amazing soul. We miss him every morning and every night. So if in the passing days you see a police car as your [sic] drive, walking up on a dragonfly or perhaps you see an owl one night think of us, our journey, most of all Blake."

From now on, Lacey would tell Garnett that his dead father had come back as an owl to watch over them.

On October 16, Lacey turned twenty-five and received more than thirty happy birthday greetings on Facebook, including many from her old school friends in Decatur.

"Dislocating my shoulder AGAIN is exactly how I did not plan to start my day," she posted on her Lacey Spears 16 Facebook account. Her heartbreak about not having Blake to celebrate with her she saved for the Garnett's Journey page.

"One year ago today I celebrated my 24th birthday," she wrote on it, "one of many I would celebrate without my soulmate. Today I celebrated my 25th birthday. Birthdays just aren't the same. Most days I wish tomorrow would never come, tonight being one of those days. I never dreamed life would turn out as it has. I know there's a lesson to be learned . . . Tomorrow's another day, another chance. Through everything I still have my son, he's the only reason I have to live and for him I'll do anything to insure he has a for filling [sic] life."

The next day, Lacey announced that Garnett's blood levels had suddenly dropped and he needed a blood transfusion. She asked for "positive healing vibes."

Her dramatic post elicited more than a dozen responses promising prayers for Garnett, including one from Nurse Ginger Dabbs-Anderson.

"I hope everything goes well with G," she wrote. "Text or call me if I can help."

"Thanks everyone," wrote Lacey. "He's wonderful (: Took for a blood transfusion, changed his herbs around to help fight off the infection and increased his G tube feeds."

That fall, the Pinellas County Sheriff's child abuse unit began investigating Lacey Spears after receiving several anonymous complaints about her parenting. An investigator called Lacey on numerous occasions, requesting an interview with her and Garnett. Several appointments were made, but Lacey always canceled them at the last minute.

Then Lacey and Garnett flew to New York, leaving the investigation on hold.

14

THE FELLOWSHIP COMMUNITY

On Sunday, November 4, 2012, Lacey and Garnett arrived in Chestnut Ridge, New York, to live at the Fellowship Community. They should have gone six days earlier, but their flight was canceled due to Hurricane Sandy.

Lacey's sudden announcement that she and Garnett were leaving Florida took everybody by surprise.

"Garnett and I are packing up and moving to New York," she posted on Facebook. "I decided to move a week ago. Short notice. Excited, terrified and ready to see how our journey pans out."

Shawna Lynch remembers Lacey telling her that they were moving for a better life.

"I just said, 'Good luck. I hope everything goes well for you,'" she recalled. "I would still see them from time to time on Facebook."

Mallory McWhorter saw it as yet another example of Lacey's selflessness.

"I thought she was an awesome mom," explained Mallory. "This woman is putting her sweat, blood, and tears and moving all over the country to get the best care for her son. She's doing all she can for this child."

Lacey's neighbors in Clearwater also were caught by surprise by her abrupt departure.

"All that we were told," said Kenwood Paulen, "was that she thought it would be a better life for Garnett. He would get some good schooling, and of course it was a good job offer for her."

When Kimberly Philipson saw Lacey loading her car up with twelve boxes to ship to New York, she asked what was going on. Lacey said she was leaving Florida because she was fed up with her grandmother's constant criticism.

"She says her grandma won't let her parent the way that she wanted to," said Kimberly. "Miss Peggy was apparently very aware of what was going on, because she would be like, 'Lacey, stop it! Let him eat that! Let him do that.'"

In the days before she left, Lacey sent a series of instant messages to Rebecca Thompson, complaining about her grandmother.

"My gramma said I'm worthless!!!" she wrote. "I'm hollow, worthless, unloved, unlovable, a waste of space, a *uck up! That's who I am. I want to die."

Her good-hearted mentor tried to bolster her spirits, saying that many people loved and cared about her and that the $800 in donations she had received from Facebook friends to help pay her moving expenses proved it.

"They believe in you," wrote Thompson, "and they don't even know you. They believe in you because I believe in you."

"You do?" asked Lacey.

"Yes I do," she replied.

At around 10:00 P.M. on Sunday, November 4, 2012, Lacey and Garnett landed at John F. Kennedy airport, going straight to the Fellowship Community at Hungry Hollow Road, Chestnut Ridge. They moved into Matt Uppenbrink's house until a permanent apartment could be found for them.

Perched on a hilltop in Rockland County, just thirty miles north of New York City, the Fellowship, which is spread out over eighty acres, looks like a relic of the past. The entrance on Hungry Hollow Road leads up a path to Hilltop House, which is the hub of the community and is surrounded by various outbuildings. There is a thirty-three-acre farm with a garden, where herbs are grown for the seventy residents, or "coworkers," as they are known. Horse-drawn carts till the farm's soil, utilizing a form of holistic organic farming known as biodynamic agriculture, which was first developed by Rudolf Steiner. Solar panels on the barn roof generate some of the Fellowship's energy, but its main power and water supplies had been knocked out by Hurricane Sandy and were only restored the day before Lacey and Garnett arrived.

After unpacking and putting Garnett to bed, Lacey went on Facebook to announce their safe arrival.

"[It's] during the night," she wrote. "I'm still unsure of what the area looks like. Lots of trees, beautiful fallen leaves and quietness. May venture out once G is awake and begin to check the area out and meet a few people."

On Monday morning, Lacey and Garnett ate breakfast by a roaring fire in the Hilltop House dining room.

"I came up and introduced myself," recalled Oona Younger. "That was her very first day there."

Oona, who worked as a day planner on the scheduling committee, showed Lacey the ropes. Lacey would be starting off as a coworker, mainly working in Hilltop House, doing many different tasks, including cooking, cleaning, and nursing the elderly.

That night, Lacey informed her Facebook friends that she had made a big mistake in coming.

"I hated today," she wrote, "and would love nothing more than to get on a plane and go home!!!!"

The Fellowship Community warmly welcomed Lacey and Garnett, doing its best to make them feel at home. Lacey, now wearing a diamond engagement ring, would tearfully explain how Garnett's father, Blake, had died in a traffic accident, leaving her to bring Garnett up alone. She described Garnett as a failure-to-thrive child who had been in and out of hospitals his entire life. Her tragic stories touched the hearts of many in the community, who opened up their arms to her and Garnett.

But, strangely, the little boy did not appear to be ill. He was full of energy and always running around introducing himself to everybody he encountered.

"He had such a spark," recalled Matt Uppenbrink. "He was very outgoing and would greet everyone when he came in the door by saying, 'Hi, everyone.'"

Despite Lacey's initial reservations, she and Garnett soon settled into the community.

"It's really family orientated," said Nellie Grossenbacher, whose four children attend the Green Meadow Waldorf School affiliated with the Fellowship. "And they embraced this single mother. They welcome people. Somebody has a baby, everybody's making a meal."

Coworker Valerie Plauché began working with Lacey, and they soon became close.

"I saw Lacey and Garnett just about seven days a week," recalled Plauché, age fifty-one, who lived at the Fellowship with her twelve-year-old daughter. "We talked . . . and I saw quite a bit of her. We were friendly."

Valerie became especially close to Garnett, who loved playing on a tree swing outside Hilltop House.

"Garnett was a really special child," said Plauché, "and I used to hang out a lot with him at work. He'd say, 'Can we go swing?,' I was like, 'Yes,' so we'd go and I'd push him on the swing. We were very good friends, actually."

Every morning, Garnett arrived at Plauché's top-floor apartment in Bow Top House, wanting to play.

"He was really cute," she said. "In the beginning, he used to come up without telling me. So I said, 'Well, if you have to, let me know if you're coming up.' So pretty much every day [after that], he would come in the morning and yell at the bottom of the stairs, 'Valerie! Valerie! Can I come up?'"

Two days after arriving, Lacey brought Garnett to see Dr. Gerald Karnow, who runs a family practice at the Fellowship. He specializes in anthroposophic medicine, in line with the community's Rudolf Steiner–inspired beliefs.

"It was a quick visit," he recalled, "with the complaint of an ear infection."

Dr. Karnow referred Garnett to Dr. Kenneth Zatz, a pediatrician in nearby South Nyack. But it would be another four months before Lacey made an appointment with him.

On November 8, Lacey updated her Facebook friends on how things were going in New York.

"We've been here in NY for 4 days nearly," she wrote, "and time is flying by! Mixed emotions over this HUGE move. With time things seem to be settling down a little and calming into something of a routine . . . only time will tell."

Lacey wrote that it had snowed the previous night, and Garnett, who had never seen snow before, made snowballs. He had also been to the greenhouse and the farm, where he gathered chicken eggs.

"We have certainly been busy, crazy busy!!!" she wrote.

Two days later, Lacey wrote that she loved her "wonderful" job and was looking at a couple of houses to live in.

"We are living with a friend and [their] family at the moment," she explained. "Garnett . . . does enjoy all the friendly faces he encounters daily. He's made a couple of friends and is slowly, very slowly adjusting to life here."

On November 25, Lacey and Garnett moved into a ground-floor apartment in North House, on the perimeter of the Fellowship. They had their own bedroom and bathroom and shared a living room and kitchen with Christine O'Brien, who was out of town, visiting family.

"Moving into our beautiful farm house today," Lacey announced on Facebook. "Looking forward to putting up our Christmas tree."

A week later, Garnett turned four, and his mother celebrated on Facebook by listing every hospital where he had spent his previous birthdays. She also posted this:

The moment Garnett was placed upon my chest the person I was prior melted away and a new one began to transform. 4 years have come and gone. Garnett and I have both evolved into 2 very different people since that afternoon and yet we are one, connected and forever tied at the heart and soul. He fought to survive, lived in the hospital for weeks, months, years and proved all wrong. He's survived the unthinkable and is today thriving, happy, healthy, joyful and a delight to all who encounter him. Don't remember who I was before him and couldn't imagine life without him. Have been told children pick there [sic] parents for a reason, maybe, just maybe Garnett picked me to be his mother to show that we can all live, survive and thrive through the unthinkable events life deals us. HAPPY 4th BIRTHDAY, to my little man who is will [sic] forever be my baby boy, heart and unending love.

A few days later, Christine O'Brien returned to the Fellowship and met her new housemates, Lacey and Garnett. Soon after, she discovered that somebody had gone into her bedroom, taking clothes, furnishings, and toiletries. She suspected it was Lacey after seeing Lacey wearing some of her clothes and spotting her comforter and other personal items in Lacey's bedroom.

When O'Brien confronted Lacey about it, she just walked away without saying a word. O'Brien then reported the theft to the leaders of the Fellowship.

"They told me to let it go," she recalled. "That it was time for me to move on."

She also filed a theft report with the Ramapo Police Department, but they have no record of it.

Not wanting to make waves at the Fellowship, Christine let it go. She decided to try to get along with her new neighbors, since they shared a living room and a kitchen.

One night, after dinner, Lacey told O'Brien about Garnett's chronic health problems and his father's tragic death.

"We were just getting to know each other," recalled O'Brien. "She said that Garnett's father had died in the line of duty as a police officer. And then she went into the whole owl thing . . . that she had told Garnett that his father had turned into an owl and was always watching him. That's why she had owls everywhere."

Soon afterwards, Christine came home early one morning, after milking the cows, and noticed that Lacey's bedroom door was open.

"I glanced in," she remembered, "and I saw Lacey leaning over Garnett. There was a tube sticking out of him, and she was doing something to it. I was flabbergasted."

Not wanting to get involved, O'Brien went into her bathroom and showered before coming out into the kitchen.

"Garnett was outside with his head down and was kicking the dirt," she said. "And it was very unlike him to be so down. And I said, 'Garnett, what's the matter?,' and he said, 'I don't feel good. My ear really hurts.' And I said, 'I'm sorry, sweetheart. You'll feel better later.' He kept on kicking the dirt and then he said, 'Have a good day, Christine.'"

Later that morning, she asked Lacey about the tube protruding from Garnett's stomach, saying she should know if he had any medical issues because they lived together. Lacey explained that, because of his troubles eating normal food, Garnett was often fed through his G-tube. Christine replied that she had never noticed him struggling to eat, but she mentioned that, earlier, he had been complaining about his ears hurting.

"She told me not to worry about it," said O'Brien, "and then she just walked away."

During her first weeks at the Fellowship, Lacey gravitated toward Oona Younger and her husband, Howard Friedman, who took her and Garnett under their wings. Before long, Oona, the middle-aged coworker with a grown-up son, viewed Lacey as the daughter she had never had.

Oona often would spend her days off with Lacey and Garnett, driving them into Paramus, New Jersey, and going to Barnes and Noble and Starbucks. She even bought Garnett his own car seat because she drove him around so often.

She could never understand why Garnett's feeding tube was necessary when she had seen him eat all kinds of food, including spicy Chinese dishes.

"Garnett used to eat a lot of chicken," Oona said, "sometimes hamburgers. There wasn't anything that he would refuse to eat."

Christine O'Brien often ate meals with Lacey and Garnett in their shared kitchen, where he would eat everything that was put in front of him. When she asked why Garnett still needed his G-tube, Lacey said he couldn't swallow normally.

"And I said, 'No, he doesn't [need the tube]. He's always eating animal crackers, donuts, and all that crap.'"

Living on the same floor in North House, Christine often saw Lacey lose her temper with Garnett, sometimes getting physical with him.

"When she didn't think anybody was looking," said Christine, "she would yell at him and yank him by his arm—so hard that I thought she was going to pull it out of its socket. Then, if he started crying, she would pick him up and soothe him. It would be like, 'Oh look what a great mommy I am.'"

One night, in their communal kitchen, Garnett was sitting alone at the table, picking at his dinner. Suddenly Lacey started screaming at him to eat. Christine told her that maybe he would eat if they went and sat at the dinner table with him.

"She just gave me this clipped look," said Christine, "and walked away."

During their time together, Christine bonded with Garnett, who was always friendly. He always asked how her sick father was doing whenever she went to visit him.

"He would come up to me and say, 'Hi Christine. Did you see your father today?' she remembered. " 'How's he doing, and what about his wife? Was the dog outside? You look really good today. I hope you have a great day. I can't wait to see you later.' That's how he spoke. Articulate. Smiling ear to ear."

But, according to Christine, his mother was the polar opposite, frequently moody and prone to fits of anger.

"The only personality that existed was when the anger came out," she explained. "It happened at least daily, and it didn't take much. All you had to do was ask a question or move something . . . and you could actually see it. The eyebrows would go down and her mouth would open up a little bit . . . and she would just give you this look."

15

By mid-December, Lacey was seriously considering moving back to Florida, telling her Garnett's Journey friends that New York was not good for Garnett.

"Stay in New York or go home to Florida?" she questioned. "Been here in New York almost 2 months and my heart desires home, Florida. Maybe going home is best."

Before Christmas, Lacey made several trips into Manhattan to buy gifts. She also sent Christmas cards to all her friends in Alabama.

"Christmas shopping for my tiny love is complete," she wrote on December 18. "Thanks to my dear friends for the help, you guys are awesome. Even managed to grocery shop without any meltdowns!!!"

On December 23, Lacey posted a sonogram photo of an embryo on her Garnett's Journey page. She wrote that it was Grayson Grayer, who would have been Garnett's elder brother, had he survived.

"Grayson Grayer was born sleeping at 38 weeks," she

wrote. "Happy Birthday Grayson, may you and your daddy enjoy the day together."

"Oh Lacey, I'm so sorry," commented a friend. "I had no idea. You are one incredible strong woman and a wonderful mom."

On Christmas Day, Christine O'Brien gave Garnett a wooden owl with feathers, which she had bought in a local crafts store.

"I just hung it on his door, and he woke up to find it in the morning," she said. "He was like, 'Look, there's Daddy.'"

A few hours later, Lacey posted on her Garnett's Journey Facebook page, "Garnett: Momma, I wish daddy was here with us on Christmas . . . Me too Garnett, Me too. We love and miss you Daddy Blake!"

With a sick son to bring up, Lacey Spears was given far less work than the other coworkers. It led to much resentment. She often would bring Garnett with her when she cleaned rooms or worked in the greenhouse. And she was allowed to take off between 1:30 P.M. and 5:00 P.M. to take care of her son.

"She had a particularly light schedule," said Oona Younger, who helped coordinate the daily tasks. "She did some caregiving of elders [and] fed them. She would do some cleaning tasks [or] bringing things from the outer buildings into the kitchen that we would cook that day."

Christine O'Brien worked up to seventy hours a week, and she complained to the executive circle about how easy Lacey had it. She was told not to interfere.

Soon afterwards, Christine again complained about Lacey screaming at Garnett every night as she was giving him a bath.

"Her bathroom wall bounces up against my bedroom,"

Christine explained. "I hear screaming as she's fighting with the kid while he's taking a bath. And he's saying, 'Mommy, that doesn't feel good.' And she's telling him to shut up and then there's splashing."

O'Brien claims she told Fellowship executives that she feared for Garnett's safety.

"They called me a troublemaker," she remembered. "They said, 'Oh, she's just a nice, good mom.' And I'm like, 'I really don't think so.'"

A few weeks later, Christine O'Brien left the Fellowship because she could no longer live with Lacey Spears.

By early January 2013, Lacey Spears had decided to stay at the Fellowship and was already preparing for the next fall, when Garnett would join the Green Meadow's kindergarten.

"Can't wait to learn how to knit & looking forward to joining in on pottery once Garnett is in school," she wrote on Facebook. "So many new opportunities opening up now that my baby will be in the Waldorf school."

Apparently, Lacey now loved living in the Fellowship Community.

"Life is truly beautiful these days," she wrote on January 20. "Waited a long while to be able to say that . . . Enjoying every moment."

The following day, Lacey wrote that their move had brought "such healing" into her and Garnett's lives.

"Experiencing this unreal love of life," she told her Facebook followers. "One that has been lacking for some-time."

She now fully embraced the Waldorf ideas of bringing up children naturally, in line with the teachings of Rudolf Steiner.

"Who ever said children needed colored, plastic, battery operated toys must never have met a Waldorf child," she wrote. "Garnett's been happily playing for awhile. We own no plastic & few toys that are not natural colors. Let children be children & develop their [imagination]."

At the end of January, Oona Younger and her husband, Howard, entertained Lacey and Garnett at their home.

"Thank you for coming over," Younger posted on Lacey's Facebook timeline the next morning. "You and Garnett bring so much light to my life that my heart feels as though it will burst."

In the first week of February, Chestnut Ridge had two feet of snow, and Lacey shot several dozen photographs of Garnett sledding.

"G's ready," she told Rania Cottingham, who had voiced concern about him being out in the snow.

"She'd post that Garnett was sick," said Rania, "and 'I'm taking him to the hospital.' And the next day she'd post pictures of Garnett playing in the snow. That got my attention."

Just after midnight on Wednesday, February 13, an emotional Chris Hill desperately reached out to Lacey, asking how she and Garnett were doing. Shawna Lynch had been feeding him photographs of his four-year-old son, and he now wanted to establish contact.

"Garnett is a cutie," he wrote on Lacey's timeline. "You 2 seem to be doing okay, and I'm glad :) i'm sure that I don't have to say this, but make sure you teach him right . . . which I know you will. Didn't mean to worry you if I did, just wanted to say hi, and im glad you, and lil man are doing alright :) . . . ok . . . tty!"

Ten minutes later, after getting no response, Hill sent her another message.

"Oh, and you don't have to worry about me doing

anything stupid . . . you 2 just crossed my mind is all. I looked you up a year ago, and never said anything too [sic] you. I wanted to, but I knew you wouldn't talk to me, but its ok :/ . . . night."

When there was no reply, a frustrated Hill sent her a third and final message.

"And you don't have to block me," he told Lacey. "I know how you are, I'm not going to bother you."

Two days later, Lacey Spears informed her Facebook friends that she was now thinking about adopting a baby with Down syndrome.

"We all need a family & someone to love us," she explained.

Soon afterwards, Lacey told Oona Younger that she was going to a bar to pick up a man for sex so she could get pregnant. Oona then suggested that her husband, Howard Friedman, father her child. Later, Howard would tell police about Oona's offer while denying he had ever had any sexual relations with Lacey.

But there were persistent rumors within the Fellowship that Howard had "developed a personal relationship" with Lacey, who reportedly had been seen sitting on his lap in public. Friedman would later say the rumors were false.

On March 22, Lacey Spears finally took Garnett to pediatrician Kenneth Zatz, more than four months after being referred by Dr. Karnow. For the next nine months, Dr. Zatz would become Garnett's primary pediatrician.

"He appeared a healthy child [and] very playful," remembered Dr. Zatz, "running around the office."

When Dr. Zatz asked for his prior medical history, Lacey said Garnett had aspirated at birth and had been transferred to the intensive care unit. By the time he was two months old, she told the pediatrician, Garnett's weight had dropped to less than four pounds, almost three pounds below his birth weight. She said Garnett had undergone abdominal surgery at nine weeks for a Nissen fundoplication, developing seizures soon afterwards.

"At that point," said Dr. Zatz, "she told me that he was placed on life support—a ventilator—for six weeks. And at nine months of age he basically had come to eight pounds of weight, which is the size of a newborn, and he had another surgery to place a gastrostomy tube.

"She had also mentioned he had had a history of increased sodium and Methicillin-resistant *Staphylococcus aureus* (MRSA), requiring eight sets of ear tubes for chronically recurring ear infections."

After learning of Garnett's extensive medical history, Dr. Zatz conducted a physical examination of him.

"He was pretty typical height and weight," the doctor recalled. "He seemed like a healthy child with a gastrostomy tube and chronic ear problems."

The doctor also took a blood sample, which came back completely normal.

At the end of the exam, Dr. Zatz told Lacey that he was referring Garnett to several ear, nose, and throat specialists as well as a dentist—Garnett had bad teeth because his mother disapproved of fluoride.

"He certainly had what appeared to be a very complicated medical history," said the doctor. "I made referrals for him . . . and he also needed a gastroenterologist to evaluate the necessity of a feeding tube."

Two weeks later, Lacey drove Garnett to Middletown, New York, for an appointment with pediatric gastroenterologist Ivan Darenkov.

"One hour drive to the GI doctor this morning," she posted on Facebook. "Must squeeze in a trip to the health food store too."

Before the examination, Lacey outlined her son's

extensive medical history for the Russian-born pediatric specialist. She informed him that Garnett had been
diagnosed with celiac disease and Crohn's disease.

Dr. Darenkov told Lacey that he wanted Garnett to
have a feeding evaluation, to see how many nutrients he
was taking by mouth and through his G-tube. He urged
Lacey to get Garnett a feeding evaluation on this and on
several follow-up visits.

"Every visit, I would have a talk about how Garnett
definitely needs [this evaluation]," he said. "I did this on
numerous times, and she never followed up."

16

TULIP HOUSE

At the beginning of April, Lacey and Garnett moved into a small one-bedroom basement apartment in Tulip House, a two-story building in the woods. The apartment consisted of a kitchen, a living room, and a bedroom off to the side.

"Decided to decorate my new home in owls!!!" she told her Facebook friends, noting that she could use more space. "Can't wait to be moved and settled."

There was no television, and Lacey would proudly tell people that Garnett had never watched TV.

On moving day, Lacey wrote a cryptic posting on Facebook.

"Two worst emotions . . . Sad & lonely!!!" she told her followers. "Blah."

Oona Younger immediately offered support.

"I love you and Garnett so much," she wrote, "and am totally here for you if you need me."

That April, Lacey became friends with Juani Tantillo, who regularly visited her elderly, terminally ill mother at the Fellowship. On April 17, Lacey texted Juani that Garnett was having ear and throat surgery. A few hours later, Lacey went on Facebook, blaming fluoride for causing cancer in children.

"Enough of our children are fighting & dying from cancer," she opined. "Let's wake up & realize this is one of the reasons why!!!! NO FLUORIDE!!!"

The next day Lacey was back, pledging never to allow Garnett to have his tonsils out.

"Will be taking a holistic approach!!!" she announced. "Mommas read up before having your child's tonsils removed, life long health problems occur!!!!"

Later, Juani Tantillo would remember her gut reaction when she first met Lacey Spears.

"Something just wasn't right," said Tantillo. "She told us all about the feeding tubes and food, and yet the kid was happy as can be."

At the end of April 2013, Stuart "Shaiya" Baer, age fifty-seven, and his wife, Charisse, moved into the first-floor apartment in Tulip House. Charisse soon became friendly with Lacey while Shaiya was still packing up their old home. When Shaiya came three weeks later, he met Lacey and Garnett.

Charisse, age forty, later told detectives that Lacey often talked about wanting to have another child, once asking if Shaiya would be the father.

The Baers were both "shocked" by her proposal, and their friendship with Lacey became "strained." After that, she never brought it up again.

That spring, Lacey made the first of several claims about being sexually harassed by men at the Fellowship. Ramapo police were called in after she reported that a man had twice exposed himself to her. The man vehemently denied her allegation and was told to avoid Lacey. No further action was taken.

Christine O'Brien, who was still in close touch with friends at the Fellowship, questioned why the executive circle always sided with Lacey.

"Why is everybody believing this woman?" she asked. "It always just came down to, 'Oh, she's a single mom, and she's doing such a good job.'"

A few months later, Lacey accused Brazilian-born volunteer Ricardo Alv of sexual harassment. He and his wife were then asked to leave the community without being given the opportunity to defend themselves.

"[Lacey's] behavior caused me and my wife trouble," said Alv, who moved back to Brazil with his wife soon afterwards, "so we were obliged to leave the Fellowship."

Alv described Lacey as "a liar" and "out of balance," refusing to discuss the incident further.

"The problem is much more deeper [in the Fellowship]," he said in October 2014. "We don't want to talk about it."

That summer, as Garnett Spears prepared to start kindergarten, a former Green Meadow Waldorf School pupil, Kate Christensen, published her autobiography, *Blue Plate Special: An Autobiography of My Appetites*. In it she claimed to have been sexually abused by her math teacher, John Alexander, for a year during the late seventies. She alleged that the abuse was widespread at Green Meadow, extending to other teachers and involving eleven other girls. Christensen claimed that she had told her mother, who reported it to the school authorities, who took no action.

In the wake of her accusations, the Green Meadow Waldorf School launched an independent investigation. It resulted in a damning report that concluded that the school had failed to take action after becoming aware of the allegations.

In a letter to all members of the Green Meadow school community, including Lacey Spears, the school officially apologized to the victims. And it pledged to make the school "the safest, most hospitable learning environment it can possibly be."

In early May, Lacey brought Garnett back to pediatric gastroenterologist Dr. Ivan Darenkov, who once again said Garnett needed a feeding evaluation. Dr. Darenkov then wrote out prescriptions allowing Lacey to obtain an IV pole with a Kangaroo pump enteral feeding device, a MIC-KEY button and connector tube set, and feeding bags and syringes.

A week later, Lacey announced on Facebook that Garnett would soon undergo another round of surgery.

"My anxiety, stress, fear and worry," she wrote, "are already through the roof!!! It's only Tuesday, wonder how I'll be Sunday night?!?"

Several days later came an update.

"Worst feeling is knowing your child is in pain & discomfort," she wrote, "& not being able to take it away :("

On June 4, Dr. Darenkov performed a gastrointestinal endoscopy on Garnett at the Orange Regional Medical Center in Middletown, New York. The procedure confirmed that Garnett did not have celiac disease, and after telling Lacey the good news, the doctor again urged her to get Garnett a feeding evaluation.

On Monday, July 1, Lacey and Garnett flew to Florida for the start of a three-week vacation. Suddenly, Lacey seemed obsessed with the idea of traveling the world with Garnett.

"Call me crazy," she wrote on Facebook. "Considering moving out of the country in a few years. Africa or Australia. I'm young and I don't want to miss an opportunity to experience life to its fullest!!!"

After a twelve-hour delay at Kennedy airport, they touched down in Tampa at 1:15 A.M., going straight to Lacey's grandmother's house, where they were staying.

Over the next few days, Lacey and Garnett "enjoyed some beach time," looked up old friends, and ate lunches at Frenchy's.

On Saturday, July 6, they flew to Decatur, and while waiting for the plane, Lacey pledged she was "Going Raw!!!" on her return to New York.

"Yes, that's right," she told her social media followers. "Once we return from our adventures, Garnett & I will be going from grain free, vegans to grain free, raw vegans. Excited to see what this adventure brings for both Garnett & I!!!"

Two days later, Lacey arrived at April Chambers's house with Garnett. It was the first time April had seen them since she had left Decatur. And while Garnett was playing with April's daughter, Priscilla, April admitted that she had called the Florida Department of Children and Families on Lacey.

"I felt guilty," April explained. "[The agency] had determined that Garnett was fine and there was nothing to worry about. I apologized to her and she was extremely, and oddly, accepting and forgiving. She said her parents had also called CPS on her at one point, and then someone when she was in Florida had called as well."

Lacey did not seem angry, saying she was glad people cared enough about Garnett to do that for him.

"We actually became closer," said April, "after I apologized to her."

During the course of the afternoon, Garnett was very hungry and wanted to eat some potato chips that were on the table. Lacey kept telling him no, because they were not "raw vegan."

"And finally I was like, 'Please, Lacey, he can eat them,'" recalled April. "'It's not going to bother me.' And he ate almost the entire family-size bag."

That night, April thanked Lacey on her Facebook timeline.

"I'm so glad we got to talk and see one another," she wrote. "We should definitely hang out whenever you guys are out here again! Keep doing what you are doing because you have such a sweet boy. You are doing an amazing job and I actually look to you for inspiration."

Lacey also saw Mallory McWhorter, who had just given birth to a premature baby boy named Blackstone.

"She was telling me her deal," recalled McWhorter, "about how her son was in the hospital for so many days."

Then Lacey told Mallory how lucky Mallory was to have a husband, because Lacey had to bring up Garnett alone.

"She was like, 'Garnett's dad passed away,'" said Mallory. "And I said, 'I wasn't aware of that. I'm so sorry.' And then she went into this spiel, like 'His name is Blake. He's a police officer and Garnett doesn't get to grow up with his dad.'"

On their last night in Decatur, Lacey planned a big reunion dinner at Logan's Roadhouse, but no one turned up.

Later, Lacey posted scores of photographs on Facebook, in an album entitled "Our Summer 2013 Adventure."

"After 21 days away," wrote Lacey, "lots of fun, little sleep, many adventures, tons of giggles, yummy food & memories to last a lifetime. Garnett the Great & I will be flying home to NY tomorrow night."

* * *

Back in New York, Lacey Spears announced that she and Garnett would be "going raw" for the entire month of August, and then "hopefully forever." She even started a new Facebook page and a blog to chart their progress.

"Our first day of raw vegan adventures was a success!" she reported on August 2. "Now to finish up my new FB page & blog so all can follow our adventures."

Someone then asked why Garnett could not eat peanut butter and jelly sandwiches. Lacey responded:

He's never had peanut butter. Has very little to no nutritional value, even the organic stuff. That being said I have always made a nut butter for him, cashew, almond, sunflower seed. Peanuts also harbor mold, enough to turn anyone off. I also soak & dehydrate my nuts. G's had many stomach/intestinal problems so by soaking the digestive process has already started making it easier on G and your body can gain nutrients from the nuts. Nuts that haven't been soaked & dehydrated give little nutrients off, body can't break them down. Jelly. Well, jelly is sugar. We don't do sugar. He's never had jelly, doesn't have a taste for jelly so why give it to him now. Store bought or processed jellies have nothing to gain from by eating. Yes we do honey. Often he asks for cashew butter with honey on homemade bread (bread made from almonds). We also don't eat grains. Sometimes I wish I didn't know the horrible impact food has on your body, the environment & the future generations. We only eat organic, I make 90% of our food, even milk. I'm a raw grainless vegan & G's a grainless vegan. When he's older & can truly understand the importance of food I'll let him decide what he wants to eat. I don't deny him food, we meet on a middle ground."

The next day, Lacey went shopping to buy Garnett school clothes, as he would soon start kindergarten.

"My baby is growing up & to [sic] fast for this momma," she wrote on Facebook. "Nevertheless he's off to kindergarten in the fall, half day kindergarten & I'm going to be lost without him."

On August 17, Carol Grieder, who would be Garnett's kindergarten teacher, visited Tulip House to meet her new pupil and his mother.

"Surprisingly," wrote Lacey on Facebook, "Garnett is super excited to meet her!"

The two-hour meeting mostly involved Lacey telling the teacher about her son's strict dietary needs.

"[She] related to us which foods he wasn't able to eat," said Grieder, age fifty-three. "He seemed to have a problem with glutens, so apparently he was not allowed to have anything that was wheat and which contained gluten. But then there were also lists of other foods."

It was agreed that Lacey would bring Garnett containers of his specially prepared lunches on certain days of the week.

Later that night, Lacey reported back to her Facebook friends on the meeting.

"We sat and talked for nearly 2 hours," she wrote. "What a beautiful soul she has. Feeling very settled & confident with my decision to send him to school. Garnett's Waldorf education is going to be amazing, much different then [sic] the public school education I received."

In mid-August, Lacey met Nancy Leopold, who had just returned from a leave of absence. Leopold, a registered nurse who had been at the Fellowship more than thirty years, would now oversee elderly care at Hilltop House and was in charge of supervising Lacey.

"She would be caring for an older person," said Leopold, "and I would be sort of checking in on how things were going. If she had a question, she would ask, or I would show her something."

Leopold first met Garnett when he turned up at one of the offices on the outskirts of the Fellowship. The little boy immediately introduced himself before asking her name.

"We're always aware of where are the children," said Leopold, "because we are all feeling responsible for them. He was in the office, so I said, 'Well, where's your mom?'"

Garnett replied that she was working in Hilltop House, so Leopold telephoned Lacey to tell her Garnett was with her.

"I told Lacey I would send him over to her," she said, "and he very happily went on his way."

Over the next few weeks, Leopold frequently saw Garnett coming and going.

"[He was] very friendly, very active," she said. "Always looking around, and he would always say hello to you when he saw you."

On August 19, Lacey Spears started a new Facebook account, which she called HippyHappyMomma. One of the first pictures she posted was of Garnett asleep with his pacifier, his shirt pulled up, exposing his MIC-KEY tube port.

"A simple page dedicated to my son, Garnett the Great's first year of Waldorf Kindergarten," she wrote in its Facebook profile, "& all the many adventures that come along with him, his journey through life & the next year of our lives!"

The next day, Lacey was "gathering clothes" Garnett needed for school.

"Since he'll be in a Waldorf school," she wrote, "they require certain clothing items, snow pants, rain pants, snow boots, rain boots, wool under clothes, etc."

On August 31, Lacey took Garnett to a local store, spending two hours trying on different backpacks. Finally, she wrote, her son picked the one he wanted after trying every backpack in the store at least three times.

"When I asked why this one he sweetly replied, 'Well. Momma I need to look grown up. I'll be a daddy one day.'"

After reading this, Fellowship Community leader Matt Uppenbrink's wife, Elizabeth, urged Lacey to start writing down Garnett's comments.

"This is amazing book material :)" she commented. "I cannot get over how hilarious Garnett is!"

On September 3, a week before Garnett's first day at school, Lacey worried about being separated from him. She wrote of being "consumed in panic" that her son was "about to stretch his little wings and venture out into the world."

"He'll only be away 4 hours," she told her HippyHappyMomma friends. "4 hours is an extremely long time for both him & I. See, Garnett & I have always been together since his birth. I can count on both hands the number of times I've left him."

Lacey then called Carol Grieder, saying she did not want Garnett to start school yet.

"His mother was reluctant to have him go," said Grieder. "She wasn't sure if he would be able to separate—or she would be able to separate. But then she changed her mind and really wanted him to go."

17

STARTING SCHOOL

On Friday, September 13, Garnett Spears officially started at the Green Meadow Waldorf School, although he wouldn't go full time for several more weeks.

"He started gradually," explained Carol Grieder. "Just basically in the playground. Then he started two days a week and moved gradually up to four days a week."

From the beginning, Garnett loved school, getting along well with his dozen schoolmates and enthusiastically participating in all the activities.

"He was great," said his teacher. "He was sharp, attentive, and very happy to be in school . . . and there were no problems at all."

Although the plan was to slowly ease him from two to five days a week, according to Lacey, he wanted to go every day.

"2nd day of school was another huge success!!!" she wrote on Facebook. "This transition thing isn't working for him, he's ready to be in school 5 days not 2."

Each morning, Garnett would stand at the gate, greeting his classmates as they arrived.

"He knew all of their names," said Grieder, "and he would greet all the adults as well. So he was a real big part of the class . . . everyone really enjoyed him."

One afternoon after school, Nellie Grossenbacher's five-year-old twin boys, who were in Garnett's class, were outside playing in a sandbox. Lacey walked over with Garnett, who joined them.

"All the kids were playing together in the sandbox," said Nellie, "so at some point Lacey and I just introduced ourselves. We developed a friendship quite quickly."

The next day, Nellie saw Garnett say something to Lacey about his father.

"No, your papa's dead," Lacey told him. "Remember, he died in a car accident and is not alive anymore."

"And I immediately felt bad for her," said Nellie. "There was a single mother, and clearly the child's father's not alive."

Then Lacey tearfully told Nellie the tragic story of her fiancé, Blake.

"She told me that Garnett was very sick," recalled Nellie, "and she and Blake had decided to move to Florida, so he could seek help through a different doctor, the Chinese herbalist that she had used. While they were in Florida, Blake had gotten into a car accident and died."

Nellie was shocked to hear this and befriended Lacey.

"I saw a single mother that needed a friend," she later explained, "and I was available, and our children played so beautifully together."

When Nellie started visiting Lacey at Tulip House, she noticed that there were no pictures of Blake anywhere.

"So I asked her why she doesn't have any pictures of him in her house," said Nellie. "And so her answer was,

'It's just too painful. I can't have any pictures of him out, but I have one in my bedroom.'"

When Nellie remarked that Garnett should have some photographs of his father, to remember him by, Lacey just walked away.

"Well, I'm not a single mother with a dead fiancé," said Nellie. "So I just chalked it up to maybe she's grieving, and it's hard for her [losing] the man she loved."

As their friendship progressed, Nellie was impressed with how Lacey was bringing up her son.

"She was a doting mother," explained Nellie. "She was a single mom that took really good care of her kid and was concerned about his well-being."

Lacey told her all about Garnett's failure to thrive problems, and that she was still breast-feeding him. But when she proudly said that Garnett, now just a couple of months away from his fifth birthday, still used a pacifier, Nellie asked why.

"She said that the sucking helped relieve the pressure in his ears," recalled Nellie. "Which again, I can't question, because here's a child that supposedly had numerous ear surgeries."

But Nellie was surprised when Lacey said Garnett had a cochlear implant because she knew that the surgically implanted medical devices, which transmit sound signals to the brain, are plainly visible, but there was nothing in his ear.

"I have no problem asking questions," said Nellie, "so I asked her why I couldn't see anything."

Right off the bat, Lacey replied that Garnett's cochlear implants employed a new technology and were placed inside his ear.

"I looked it up on the Internet," said Nellie, "and couldn't find anything regarding brand-new technology for cochlear implants. But I never said anything. Lacey always seemed to have a fine, understandable excuse for every story she told."

Contrary to Lacey's claims that Garnett was a weak, sickly child, Nellie observed a little boy with boundless energy.

"He was so happy and cheerful," she recalled, "and just a regular kid. We have a huge jungle gym in our backyard, and he would be all over that. He just wanted to be in everything that was going on."

Whenever Garnett was over at her house, he would eat anything that was put in front of him, without any problems.

"He ate whatever I fed my children," said Nellie, "which would be anywhere from peanut butter and jelly to lentil stews, pizza, or whatever snacks I would put out. So he had a broad palate."

One time, Nellie asked Lacey about Garnett's G-tube and why he needed it, since he'd always eaten normally in front of her.

"She told me that she used it for supplemental feeding," said Nellie, "because some days he was temperamental and wouldn't eat, so she would feed him through it at night."

That fall, Garnett settled into a daily routine and seemed to thrive. Lacey would drop him off at school and then pick him up at night, Tuesdays through Fridays. Because of Garnett's strict gluten-free diet, she always sent along a hot container with his specially prepared lunch in it.

"So we would open that," said his teacher, Carol Grieder, "and he would eat it instead of whatever the class was eating on that day."

Although his mother claimed that Garnett would often refuse to eat, Grieder saw the exact opposite.

"He always ate well," she said. "He had seconds and,

oftentimes, thirds. And in the beginning I had to ask Lacey to send more . . . because he was eating so much. He was actually one of the children who really ate best."

Garnett also loved playing games at the school and was very competitive.

"His energy level was great," said his teacher. "We had some morning activities that we generally did—drawing or painting or baking bread. He was a real big part of the class."

She later told police that, while playing with his schoolmates, Garnett would often cry out, "Daddy died! Daddy died!"

Although his teachers at Green Meadow were delighted with how easily Garnett had assimilated into the nursery, his mother seemed to think the opposite. On September 29, she wrote that she was planning to tweak his vegan diet by removing all grains from it.

"Since he's been eating them," she wrote on Facebook, "his behavior & temper has [sic] been out of control . . . Poor guy is really struggling. Not to mention school, lots of activities, late night at hilltop and a lingering cold."

Nellie Grossenbacher remembers Lacey continually discussing Garnett's various illnesses.

"It was always about his health," she said, "and how she was just always trying to find solutions to help him be healthier. [She said he was] very sick and constantly needed attention."

On October 9, Lacey informed her Facebook followers that she had finally stopped breast-feeding Garnett.

"Yes, you heard right," she wrote. "I nursed my son until he was 55 months old!!! And I was grateful for our full term nursing relationship."

Soon afterwards, Nellie went grocery shopping with

Lacey, who bought Garnett six and a half gallons of almond milk.

"And I was like, 'Shit! I have four kids and I'm getting two,'" said Nellie. "'What do you need six for?' And she's like, 'Oh, he'll drink one throughout the entire night.'"

On Wednesday, October 16, Lacey Spears turned twenty-six years old, receiving almost fifty congratulatory messages on her Facebook timeline.

"Happy Birthday Lacey!" wrote Oona Younger. "I love you so much and hope your day is really special!" Matt and Elizabeth Uppenbrink sent their best wishes, as did other old friends from Decatur and Clearwater.

"Happy Birthday Precious Sister of Mine!" wrote Rebecca, who was visiting Lacey and Garnett at the Fellowship. "I hope you have a wonderful day! Love and miss you and G doodles and bunches."

Two weeks later, Lacey celebrated the first anniversary of her arrival at the Fellowship Community with a photograph of her and Garnett, in a new Facebook album she entitled "30 Days of Thankfulness!!!"

"Today I'm thankful for . . . New York! It's been a busy year, full of many changes, hard times, joyous times. Most of all one year of healing, healing that was a long time overdue. So here's to another year here in New York!"

On November 22, Lacey brought Garnett back to Dr. Ivan Darenkov's office for a routine appointment. The pediatric gastroenterologist examined the little boy and was told by his mother that he was now taking more food by mouth.

"Once again, the necessity of the G-tube was raised," recalled Dr. Darenkov. "I said we absolutely need to do the nutritional evaluation," recalled Dr. Darenkov.

The doctor referred Garnett to a local hospital for the evaluation, but his mother never followed up.

That Thanksgiving, Rebecca Spears spent eight days at the Fellowship, staying in Lacey's cramped one-bedroom apartment at Tulip House. Rebecca was delighted at how well her sister and nephew had adapted to life there.

"They really embraced the lifestyle that she believed in," said Rebecca. "The whole thing of eating healthy and living [holistically] that she was looking for to make him better. It was a very interesting place."

In the run-up to Garnett's fifth birthday, Lacey shared her joys of motherhood on Facebook.

"Garnett-Paul Thompson Spears Due: December 15, 2008," she wrote. "Born: December 3, 2008. Weight: 6lbs 14 ozs. Repost if your [sic] a proud parent."

She also posted a new photo album on Facebook, called "Garnett the Great's Final Week as a 4 Year Old!"

"Even though he's going to be 5 in 2 days," she wrote, "he'll still be my baby boy."

And on December 3—his birthday—she celebrated by posting fourteen "Random Facts" about her pregnancy with Garnett.

1: I took 40 pregnancy tests, was in complete denial!!!
2: I had PUPPS & clawed nearly all the skin off my legs & arms.
3: I was admitted to the hospital numerous times for dehydration.
4: I work from 5am until 3pm, when I got off work I went straight home and slept from 3 until 7 everyday day without fail.
5: I slept on my stomach every night. G would move to one side of my belly.

6: Fire places, coffee, BBQ restaurants made me instantly vomit.

7: I lost 25lbs during my pregnancy.

8: I went from being a sweet, caring, loving person to someone people hated to interact with. To say the least I wasn't pleasant person.

9: I was 3 cm dilated from 30 weeks until I delivered.

10: I knew I was having a baby boy.

11: I never looked pregnant until 8 months & over night I grew a HUGE belly!

12: Garnett never kicked for anyone but Angela Holyfield!

13: I had a completely natural labor & delivery with very minor pain.

14: After delivery I was terrified to hold Garnett.

On Thursday, December 19, Lacey and Garnett celebrated an early Christmas with Oona Younger and several other Fellowship friends, drinking raw vegan eggnog. For weeks, Lacey had been ordering extravagant Christmas presents for Garnett as she prepared to spend the holidays in Florida.

"Santa is making his special delivery tonight," she posted on Facebook. "Haven't began [sic] to pack, still have to conquer work shifts & everything that comes along with raising a special needs child."

"She had a beautiful custom-made wooden airport made for him," remembered Nellie Grossenbacher. "It was gorgeous, and had the words *Garnett's Airport* on it."

Two days later, Lacey and Garnett flew to Clearwater, Florida, for a family holiday at Peggy Florence's house. Lacey helped decorate the Christmas tree, which was full of purple owls for Garnett.

"Signing off for awhile," Lacey told her Facebook followers on December 23. "Family, friends, beautiful weather, Christmas & Garnett the Great."

On Friday, December 27, Nellie Grossenbacher and Carol Grieder both received alarming e-mails from Lacey, saying that Garnett was seriously ill in the pediatric intensive care unit.

"She told me that he wound up in the PICU in Florida," said Nellie, "because he was having seizures and vomiting."

Garnett's teacher received a similar e-mail.

"She said he had a fever of 104," said Grieder, "and he was very sick and not eating."

Lacey also wrote that Garnett had to "have his port accessed for fluids" and was being treated with "different Chinese herbs and remedies." Grieder, who has also been a registered nurse for thirty years, was "surprised," because she knew that although Garnett had a G-tube, he did not have a port (an intravenous access device) on his chest.

Several days later, Grieder received another e-mail updating her on Garnett's condition.

"[Lacey] said that he was hospitalized in the PICU," said Grieder, "and was vomiting and had an intestinal virus. She also said he had been diagnosed with Crohn's and a milk allergy, and his fever had spiked to 105."

Nellie Grossenbacher also received another e-mail from Clearwater.

"He was in PICU for three or four days for a stomach infection and diarrhea," said Nellie. "She was stressed out."

Later, Lacey would deny taking Garnett to any hospitals during their Florida stay. And no one who had spent the holidays with Garnett remembered him being hospitalized.

"He was okay," said Rebecca Spears. "His ears and stomach were bothering him, but overall he was pretty good. We went to the beach . . . and saw the Christmas lights at night. We did all the fun things that you wanted to do. . . . And we went to Frenchy's—that was our place to always go eat."

On December 29, Lacey and Garnett flew back to New York, and on New Year's Eve, Lacey expressed concern about a virulent new strain of flu that was going around.

"Hoping to ward off this super stomach bug," she wrote on Facebook. "G's getting his normal nightly feed & another feed with apple cider vinegar, vitamin C & a few Chinese herbs. Stay away from my baby stomach bug!!! I don't want G in the hospital, must be proactive."

PART TWO

18

"THE SMALLEST CHANGE IN HIS SODIUM LEVEL CAUSES HIM TO HAVE SEIZURES"

On Tuesday, January 7, 2014, Garnett Spears returned to the Green Meadow Waldorf School and seemed fine. After receiving his mother's disturbing e-mails from Florida, Carol Grieder was much relieved.

"He was the usual Garnett," she said. "He was very happy to be back. Very happy to play. Happy to do what everyone was doing, and eating well."

But Lacey kept him home from school on Friday, saying he had a fever and stomach flu.

It was now, investigators believe, that Lacey Spears began laying the groundwork for what she was planning to do to her son, who was getting too old for her to control. They theorize that she feared that the chatty, adventurous little boy, who was now known as the Fellowship's "Little Mayor," would start talking about what she had been doing to him since he was born.

Just after 8:00 A.M., Lacey went on Facebook, writing that Garnett was "really struggling," and that her attempts to kick her coffee addiction were not helping.

"I've been up since 2 AM," she wrote. "My son lost his mind in the middle of supper & then screamed for another 40 minutes."

Several hours later, she brought Garnett to Dr. Gerald Karnow's office, complaining that her son was having problems in school and was unable to focus or concentrate.

"That he had night terrors," said Dr. Karnow, "was hysteric and he had to be with his mom all the time. That his sleep was very poor [and] he was struggling with food and had to be mostly tube-fed."

Lacey also told the community physician that Garnett disliked school and was "playing with things of death."

The elderly doctor did a brief examination, feeling Garnett's belly and listening to his chest, but could not find anything wrong.

"He was good," said Dr. Karnow, who prescribed Garnett three homeopathic remedies.

The next morning, Lacey posted a photograph of Garnett sitting at a candlelit table, his favorite owl cup by his breakfast plate. Soon afterwards, she e-mailed his teacher, informing her that Garnett was sick and had seen Dr. Karnow.

"I got an e-mail saying that he had a fever . . . of 104," said Carol Grieder, "and he had a stomach virus."

Lacey also told others that Garnett had suffered a relapse.

"She told me he was sick and had a virus," said Nellie Grossenbacher. "He had diarrhea and fever."

On Sunday morning, Lacey photographed Garnett happily eating Chinese food and playing. He looked perfectly well. Then, at 3:45 P.M., she posted more photographs of Garnett happily painting a picture on the kitchen table, wearing a black-and-white polka-dot bandana.

"Garnett is sick with the flu," she wrote underneath it, "but feeling well enough to try out his new homemade paint."

Just after 6:00 P.M., Lacey updated his teacher, Carol Grieder, on Garnett's condition.

"Garnett is still hanging in there," she wrote in an e-mail. "Still keeping 102–104 fever, he's getting enough fluids, hydrated, very sick to the stomach and going to the doctor tomorrow. Just to have his sodium levels checked, the smallest change in his sodium levels causes him to have seizures."

At around midnight, Lacey Spears made three Google searches on her iPhone 4, looking for her old boyfriend, Blake Robinson of Moulton, Alabama. Immediately afterwards, she searched for the exact number of days between October 6, 2011—the day she claimed Blake had perished in a car crash—and now.

Then, on Monday morning at 6:16 A.M., she typed in the words "normal sodium level for a child," followed by another search, in an online medical encyclopedia, for the ratio of sodium to blood.

A few hours later, Lacey brought Garnett to Dr. Kenneth Zatz's office, complaining that Garnett had been running a fever for the previous five days, with a 105-degree temperature.

"I took his temperature," recalled Dr. Zatz. "It was 98.6, which is normal."

The pediatrician did a thorough physical examination of Garnett, telling his mother that there was nothing wrong.

"There were no signs of infection," said the doctor. "He appeared well. Healthy."

Dr. Zatz told Lacey that Garnett might have had a

virus that had now passed and told her to immediately bring Garnett back if his symptoms recurred.

At 8:17 Monday night, Lacey Spears conducted further Google searches about the effects of elevated sodium in children. Over a thirty-seven-minute period, she made eight separate searches, including "dangers of high sodium levels in a child" and "what happens to someone if they have high sodium levels in the blood."

She also searched for the word *hypernatremia,* a sometimes fatal condition caused by an excess of sodium in the blood.

At 11:37 P.M. on Tuesday, Lacey and Garnett arrived at the Good Samaritan Hospital emergency room. It was busy, so they were told to wait in a hallway until a doctor was available. While they were waiting, Lacey took several photographs of Garnett.

Soon afterwards, Nurse Samantha Herman came over and asked what was wrong with Garnett. Lacey said he had suffered two seizures, including one just now in the waiting room. She said he also had a bad headache, retching, and "explosive" diarrhea, mentioning that he had been diagnosed with failure to thrive and celiac disease.

The nurse then helped Garnett undress and put on a hospital gown, sitting him down on a stretcher. A few minutes later, Dr. Angela Ellerman walked over and asked Lacey what was going on.

"She told me that she believed he had experienced two episodes of seizure activity," said Dr. Ellerman. "One prior to coming into the hospital and . . . a second episode while in the waiting room. She said that Garnett was retching [and] he grabbed his head and then his eyes rolled back. He became unresponsive and shook for about ten seconds. Then afterwards he was confused and screaming for about a minute."

Lacey then recounted Garnett's medical history, saying he had been hospitalized multiple times, including once for high sodium when he was a very young infant.

"She reported that he had had seizures in the past," said the doctor, "due to hypernatremia, which means a very high sodium level."

Dr. Ellerman then did a full examination of the little boy, and everything appeared normal except for a feeding tube in his abdomen. Then she asked Garnett what was wrong with him.

"He appeared a little bit shy," the doctor recalled, "but was friendly answering questions, which is normal for a five-year-old in the emergency department."

Then, to test for coordination, strength, and any neurological problems, she asked Garnett to stand up and walk over to her.

"He didn't want to get out of his stretcher," she said. "He kept on telling me no."

Dr. Ellerman then asked Lacey to walk down the hallway and call her son over, thinking he would feel more comfortable going to her instead of a stranger. Lacey then did so.

"He didn't want to go," said Dr. Ellerman. "He still wouldn't get up and go."

She told Lacey that because seizures were very concerning, she would be doing a CAT scan, chest X-ray, and blood work. When the results came back later, everything appeared normal except for Garnett's sodium level, which was slightly elevated.

"It was 147," said Dr. Ellerman, "with the upper limit of normal being 145. The chloride was also elevated. These aren't levels that we would need to treat or would imply seizures."

The doctor told Lacey that although she could not rule out seizures, everything appeared normal, and no treatment was required. But, just to be safe, she offered to have Garnett transferred to the Westchester Medical Center, so he could be seen by a pediatric neurologist in its PICU.

"She declined," said Dr. Ellerman. "She said that she would prefer that he come home, and she'll take him to a pediatrician in the morning."

At 4:07 A.M., Garnett was officially discharged from Good Samaritan. His mother was given copies of the CAT scan and other test results and was told to come back if he had any further seizures.

Back at the Fellowship Community, Lacey started texting about Garnett's condition. She complained that Good Samaritan Hospital was not taking Garnett's seizures seriously.

"Garnett had two more seizures today :(" she wrote to one friend. "Won't know more until tomorrow. Please pray for my baby."

"We'll be saying lots of [sic] and lots of prayers," replied the friend. "R u at the hospital?"

"No," replied Lacey. "Went back home. I'm terrified."

"Hang in there," said the friend. "Try and stay calm."

All through Wednesday, Lacey texted back and forth about Garnett's worsening condition. At 8:35 P.M., Pam Hamilton, an Arizona nurse who had met Lacey on a Facebook women's group but never in person, asked how he was doing.

"Do you have any idea what's going on???" she texted.

"We still have no answers," replied Lacey, "except his sodium levels are 189!!!!!"

As a trained nurse, Hamilton knew how life-threatening

such a high sodium level was and could not believe Garnett was not in the hospital.

A few minutes later, Lacey texted another friend.

"Nina, we are home," she wrote. "G's had 5 seizures since 9 pm last night. My [sic] so worried!!!"

At 7:00 Thursday morning, Lacey updated her friend on Garnett's condition.

"Oh Nina," she wrote. "G had his 6th seizure during the night. I'm just a complete wreck. Poor G keeps screwing [sic] out in pain."

"Breathe," replied Nina several minutes later. "And imagine the both of you surrounded by Light. Breathe."

Half an hour later, Lacey texted another friend that she was taking Garnett for urgent medical treatment.

"G & I [are] going to Nyack 1st to his pediatrician," she wrote.

When she arrived at Dr. Zatz's office, she told him they had gone to Good Samaritan emergency room on Tuesday night.

"She brought him there after he had five apparent seizures," said Dr. Zatz. "She told me that they had worked him up and had done a CAT scan and a chest X-ray. Everything seemed normal at the time, so he was sent home."

The pediatrician then examined Garnett and also could find nothing wrong with him.

"He appeared well," said the doctor. "His temperature was 97.6, and he had a normal exam. But that was an alarming story, so we arranged a referral to see a pediatric neurologist to see if it's possible."

At 10:18 P.M. on Thursday, Lacey texted another friend at the Fellowship Community, who had asked about Garnett's condition.

"He keeps screaming in pain," she wrote. "Says his

head & stomach hurts. Was walking through the living room & fell on his knees in pain. I'm not sure I can handle much more."

"Maybe u should take him to the hospital," replied the friend.

"I don't know," Lacey answered.

Late that night, Oona Younger called Lacey to check up on Garnett.

"She said that he was having seizures," Younger recalled, "and she took him to the Good Samaritan Hospital three times . . . and the pediatric health clinic."

19

"HE'S ADMITTED!"

At 1:20 P.M. on Friday, Carol Grieder arrived at Tulip House on her lunch break to check up on Garnett. She had been receiving updates from Lacey all week and was concerned about her pupil. After parking outside, she walked up to Lacey's front door and called out to her. Lacey told her to come in, because the door was open.

Grieder walked into the living room and saw Lacey on the couch, holding Garnett in her arms. The little boy was in obvious distress, not even recognizing his nursery school teacher.

In the middle of the room stood an IV pole with a Kangaroo pump. Attached to it was a feeding bag full of milk-colored liquid. To the pediatric nurse's trained eye, it looked like it had just been used, or soon would be.

"He was lying there," said Grieder, "holding his head, [which] was arched back, and sucking a pacifier. He was whimpering . . . and he seemed like a child who was having a headache."

When she asked what was wrong, Lacey calmly replied

that Garnett had been "happy and joking" earlier in the morning, and then this had happened. Grieder knew that he was not having a seizure, but his symptoms did not make any sense.

She was also surprised by how "passive" Lacey seemed to be. Grieder told Lacey that Garnett needed to go to the emergency room immediately and asked if she had a ride. Lacey said she would call someone to get a car.

Then Grieder left, telling Lacey she would stop off at the Fellowship's medical office, to have Dr. Karnow come and look at Garnett.

After his teacher had gone, Lacey hooked Garnett up to the feeding machine, turned on the Kangaroo pump, and sent the whitish liquid straight into the little boy's stomach. Then, at 2:01 P.M., she made the frantic call to Oona Younger, screaming that Garnett was having seizures and needed a car immediately to take him to Nyack Hospital.

After dropping Oona Younger off at Hilltop House, Lacey parked the car and took Garnett inside. She saw her friend Valerie Plauché and explained that Garnett was very sick and they were on their way to the Nyack Hospital emergency room.

Plauché would later tell detectives that Garnett asked her to come and get him later that day. She thought Garnett was just setting up a playdate, but later she would question whether it was a desperate cry for help.

On the way to Nyack Hospital, Lacey stopped the car by the roadside, got out, and took a photograph of Garnett sitting in his car seat in the back. She posted it on Facebook at 2:23 P.M.

One minute later, she started texting friends about Garnett, during the ten-mile drive to the hospital.

"Pray for G," she wrote to one. "Hospital now!!!!"

"Loads of prayers [and] drive safely," came the reply. "He's a warrior. He's going to be ok."

At 3:00 P.M., Lacey and Garnett arrived at Nyack Hospital's pediatric emergency room and were directed to the waiting room. After they sat down, Lacey pulled out her iPhone and texted her friend Nina.

"Seizure," she wrote, "lasted 5 minutes."

"What are they saying??" asked Nina.

"What if he dies???? I'm so scared! He's starting to come around! Just shaking!"

"Ask the healing angels and spirit doctors to help him and u," Nina replied.

A couple of minutes later, Nurse Janelle Kimler came into the waiting room and saw Garnett sitting next to his mother. His hands were trembling. The triage nurse then walked them back into the eight-bed pediatric emergency room, where Garnett was put on a stretcher.

After checking his charts and listing any allergies or medications, Nurse Kimler did a visual examination of the little boy. She weighed him and took his blood pressure and temperature, which were all normal.

"He sat on the stretcher," she recalled. "He had a shaking in his hands [and was] a little nervous. He didn't speak to me."

When the nurse asked why they were there, Lacey said her son had suffered three seizures, with convulsions and eyes rolling into the back of his head. She said she had taken him to Good Samaritan Hospital on Tuesday night for seizures, where he had had a CAT scan, X-rays, and blood work.

"She was just basically explaining to me," said Nurse Kimler, "that there were three episodes which led her to come to the emergency room that day."

Then Lacey calmly recounted Garnett's medical

history, surprising the triage nurse with her familiarity with medical terminology.

"She told me that he had an allergy to dairy," said the nurse. "It caused him to vomit. He had multiple surgeries . . . and had had an esophageal stretching, tonsils and adenoids removed. Multiple ear surgeries, a Nissen fundoplication, and a G-tube placement."

Lacey also told her that Garnett had celiac disease and Crohn's disease and was on "homeopathic medications" and multiple probiotics. She said he had not been vaccinated due to her strict Mormon religious beliefs.

Then Nurse Kimler left to brief Dr. Kevin McSherry, the pediatric emergency room doctor on duty that day.

At around 3:15 P.M., Dr. McSherry arrived to examine Garnett and decide on his treatment.

"He was lying on a stretcher, next to his mother," recalled the doctor. "He was quiet [but] alert and awake."

Then he spoke to Lacey, who seemed only too eager to recite his medical history once again.

"She was ready to talk," recalled Dr. McSherry, "and answer any questions that I had."

Lacey said she had brought her son to the emergency room for ongoing seizures.

"He was having what she was calling a seizure activity," said Dr. McSherry, "describing it as hand-shaking, eyes rolling back, and he was retching. She actually provided me with a pretty extensive [medical] history . . . that he had been diagnosed early on in infancy with celiac disease and Crohn's disease."

After telling the doctor about her son's Nissen fundoplication and G-tube, she mentioned that, as a baby, he had been hospitalized in an Alabama PICU for a high sodium level.

"She told me that level was around two hundred," said Dr. McSherry. "I thought that was extraordinarily high, and basically not compatible with life. So I did not believe that."

While his mother was talking, Dr. McSherry observed Garnett trying to vomit, which was impossible because of his Nissen fundoplication operation.

"About three or four times during the interview with his mom," said the doctor, "he would arch his back and make a sort of gagging sound . . . that he was going to vomit."

Dr. McSherry then did a head-to-toe examination of the little boy, who appeared "fairly normal" except for his G-tube.

"I did not find any evidence of any seizure activity," said the doctor. "He was awake and alert, and despite having had those episodes of retching and arching his back, he did not lose consciousness."

Nevertheless, Dr. McSherry decided to admit Garnett to Nyack Hospital for observation, calling his pediatrician, Dr. Kenneth Zatz, and Nyack Hospital's pediatric neurologist, Dr. Ariel Sherbany, for their input. It was then decided to perform a video electroencephalogram (EEG) to determine whether he was having seizures.

At around 4:00 P.M., Dr. McSherry briefed Nyack Hospital's attending pediatric physician, Dr. Sarika Sunku, who would be officially admitting Garnett Spears. He warned Dr. Sunku that he did not believe the boy was having seizures and that he suspected his mother might be suffering from Munchausen syndrome by proxy.

After Dr. McSherry's call, Dr. Sunku went to the emergency room to meet her new patient, Garnett Spears. He was sitting on a stretcher next to his mother and seemed much improved.

"He was not in any distress," remembered Dr. Sunku. "He was happy to answer questions."

Dr. Sunku began by asking Lacey Spears what had brought them to the emergency room.

"She told me . . . he was complaining of abdominal pain that morning. And when she was coming to the emergency room in the car he had a large bowel movement, and then he had an episode which looked like a seizure."

Lacey said that five days earlier Garnett had suffered three "episodes of seizures" and she had taken him to Good Samaritan Hospital.

"She described shaking movements of the arms and legs," said Dr. Sunku, "with rolling of the eyes."

When asked about Garnett's previous medical history, Lacey claimed that a gastrointestinal specialist had recently diagnosed him with Crohn's and celiac diseases.

Noticing his G-tube, Dr. Sunku asked whether Garnett could eat any solid food. Lacey said he mostly ate vegetables and fruits.

"She kept him on a special diet," said Dr. Sunku. "So I questioned why he had a G-tube still in him, and she said occasionally she would feed him pureed vegetables through it."

Lacey also mentioned how, as a baby, Garnett had had a very high sodium level of two hundred, accompanied by seizures.

"Two hundred was way too high," said Dr. Sunku. "It probably would have caused considerable brain damage . . . or taken his life."

At around 4:00 P.M., Dr. McSherry told Lacey Spears that Garnett was being admitted to Nyack Hospital for observation.

"I explained to her that we needed to find out if he really had seizures," said Dr. McSherry, "and . . . a video EEG would be the best way to do that."

He told her that a number of electrodes would be secured to Garnett's scalp to continuously record his brain waves. There also would be a video camera positioned directly on him, so doctors could see what was happening to him alongside his brain wave patterns. If he had a seizure and it correlated to abnormal brain wave patterns, it would be a strong indication of seizure disorder.

"She seemed very passive about it," said Dr. McSherry. "There was no anxiety about admitting him to the hospital. No fear."

The doctor then placed Garnett on an IV and ordered a complete blood count and an electrolyte panel, measuring sodium and chloride. Lacey and Garnett were kept in the emergency room until a bed could be prepared for him on the second floor pediatric ward.

At 4:16 P.M., Lacey texted a friend, "He's being admitted."

"Thank goodness," came the reply.

Then, ten minutes later, Lacey posted the news on Facebook.

"Healing vibes," she wrote. "Garnett's being admitted!"

Her posting elicited twenty-two responses offering prayers, including one from Nellie Grossenbacher, asking what was going on.

At 4:45 P.M., Garnett's blood was drawn. As they waited for the result, Lacey photographed Garnett in a hospital gown with an IV tube in his arm. She posted it online, writing that although he "had a seizure," he had improved enough to "run laps around the pediatric unit."

When the blood serum results came back, they showed Garnett's sodium level was 138 and his chloride was 105, both normal. When Dr. McSherry informed Lacey about the good news, she had no response.

* * *

Ten minutes later, Garnett Spears was brought upstairs to the general pediatrics floor and placed in room 242, right across from a nursing station. The second floor had twenty-two rooms for children as well as some adult patients.

Garnett's room was medium size, with a bed against the back wall and a cot. Directly opposite the entrance was a bathroom. He was delighted to discover that there was a television in his room and a playroom full of toys opposite. As Garnett settled into the hospital bed, his mother texted friends and checked Facebook.

At around 7:00 P.M., Lacey called Oona Younger to ask for a favor.

"She asked if me or my husband could come and stay with Garnett," said Younger, "so that she could come home and get some more things to bring to the hospital . . . because she believed she was going to be staying there for the weekend. I wasn't able to go [because] I was still working, so at that point, my husband went."

A few minutes later, Howard Friedman arrived at the hospital, and Lacey left to go home. Garnett seemed "in good spirits," and Friedman stayed with him until Lacey returned about an hour later.

At around 8:00 P.M., just before finishing her shift, Dr. Sunku came to see how her new patient was settling in.

"He was comfortable and happy," she remembered. "He was very excited because there was a television in the room, and he kept saying he wanted to watch it."

For the next few hours, while they were waiting for a technician to set up the video EEG machine, Lacey was on her iPhone while Garnett happily watched cartoons on the television.

At 10:18 P.M., Lacey updated all her concerned Facebook friends, who had offered prayers and sympathy.

"Thanks everyone," she wrote. "Still no news. Looks like we will be here for a few days."

Over the next couple of minutes, Lacey searched Google forty-four times for "children's eeg," as well as looking up the Nyack Hospital gift shop.

At 11:00 P.M., Lacey asked one of her Facebook friends who lived nearby to bring in some food.

"Hospital food just isn't something I want G to eat," she wrote. "No gluten, dairy or meat. So fruit, veggies, grain, nuts/seeds."

At 12:27 A.M., an EEG technologist finally arrived to set up the video EEG machine. The machine, with its desktop computer and twenty-inch color monitor, was wheeled in and placed in front of Garnett's bed. A camera atop a pole was aimed straight at Garnett.

A series of electrodes were then attached to Garnett's scalp, using a quick-drying cream. Wires from the electrodes were fed into a small box, which amplified the electrical brain signals, and then the box was connected to the machine.

It took an hour to set up and test the EEG machine. After being satisfied that it was working properly, the technician left. Unfortunately, although it had both video and audio capabilities, the technician had not properly connected the sound cable to the back of the computer, so there would be no audio.

20

"HE SEEMED LIKE A NORMAL FIVE-YEAR-OLD"

At 7:00 Saturday morning, Nurse Nora Bompensiero began her twelve-hour shift on the Nyack Hospital pediatric floor. She was assigned as Garnett Spears's primary nurse and was briefed that he had been admitted the previous afternoon for suspected seizures.

Then she went to room 242 and introduced herself.

"Garnett was there with his mother," she recalled. "I said, 'I'm Nora and I'll be nursing him.'"

Despite the large white head bandage and the electrodes tethering him to the video EEG machine, Garnett was in good spirits.

"He seemed like a normal five-year-old boy," said the pretty twenty-three-year-old nurse. "He was awake. He was chatty. He appeared healthy."

After cleaning Garnett's feeding tube, she left the room to continue her rounds, saying she would be back later.

Soon afterwards, a pediatric care associate, Jessica Shields, arrived to take Garnett's vital signs. The little boy politely asked her name and what she was doing, saying that he wanted to "be a daddy" when he grew up.

At 8:10 A.M., Lacey carefully posed Garnett by the EEG machine and took a photograph, posting it on Facebook.

"Here's a short update!" she wrote. "G hasn't had a seizure since 1:30 Friday afternoon. He's completely back to himself. Still no word on his labs. Currently having a 24 hour EEG. Being cooped up in a tiny room, mainly to a bed is already starting to bother him. Visitors are welcome."

An hour later, clinical dietician Sylvia Hawkins arrived to assess Garnett's dietary needs. Lacey stated that her son was "vegan, gluten-free, and had a milk allergy." She said he had celiac and Crohn's diseases, and was fed EleCare formula through his feeding tube at night.

Then, Dr. Neelima Thakur, a specialist in neurology and epilepsy, arrived to check on Garnett. She had already viewed the previous night's EEG video and had seen no signs of any seizure activity. After giving Garnett a brief neurological exam, she told Lacey that, so far, everything looked good.

"I said I'm going to continue the study," said Dr. Thakur, "and get more information."

Just before noon, Garnett's pediatrician, Dr. Kenneth Zatz, arrived to see how his young patient was doing. After Lacey's urgent message the previous afternoon, the doctor wanted to check up on him.

"He was great," remembered Dr. Zatz. "He was sitting in his hospital bed. They were reattaching electrodes for his EEG that was being performed, and he seemed very happy."

After Dr. Zatz left, Lacey called Nellie Grossenbacher, asking her to come and play with Garnett and to bring some "real food."

"She was very specific," said Nellie. " 'You need to come and play with Garnett. I'm tired. I just need a break. Bring some food.' "

So Nellie came right over with leftover rice and beans, fruit salad, and cookies. She walked in to find Garnett bursting with energy.

"Garnett was just running and jumping all over the room," she said, "like any rambunctious five-year-old."

While Lacey took a break, Nellie played with Garnett, who was painting in his coloring book. At one point, she used Lacey's iPhone to take a photograph of the smiling little boy sitting in his hospital bed with electrodes on his head.

After about two hours, Grossenbacher left, delighted that Garnett was doing so well.

"I left there thinking they'll be out of the hospital tomorrow," she recalled.

On Saturday afternoon, pediatric neurologist Dr. Ariel Sherbany came to room 242 to examine Garnett. Immediately, Lacey informed him that she had nursing experience.

"When she said that," said Dr. Sherbany, "it obviously raised my concern. If she thought it was a seizure, then it was. So I needed to work up the child's studies to make sure we're not missing anything."

Once again, Lacey said that her son had been diagnosed with Crohn's and celiac diseases, but Dr. Sherbany was amazed when she claimed Garnett had had a sodium level of two hundred as a baby.

"I recall telling her," said the doctor, " 'Are you sure it was two hundred, because sodium of two hundred is not compatible with life.' "

He then carried out a full neurological examination of Garnett, and everything seemed normal.

"I noted that the child was awake, alert, fluent," said the doctor. "He seemed fine."

But, although Garnett was cooperative, when the doctor asked him to walk across the room, he refused.

"He kind of resisted and didn't want to do it," said the doctor, "and his mother wanted to force him. I just backed off, as I didn't want to get into a situation where the mother's fighting with a child."

At around 7:00 P.M., Nurse Nora Bompensiero stopped off at room 242 before ending her shift.

"[Garnett] was playing with his toys," she said, "and he was asking me questions about what the IV fluid is."

As he would be having overnight feeds of nutritional milk products through his G-tube, she began to prepare it for the night nurse. But, as she was setting up the Kangaroo pump, the feeding bag, and the formula, she realized the hospital didn't have the right size connector tube for his MIC-KEY button port.

"So I asked his mother," said Nurse Nora, "and she had one. She gave it to me."

Soon after the nurse left the room, Oona Younger and Howard Friedman arrived. Oona read Garnett a story while Lacey went off with Howard.

"He looked great," Oona remembered. "He looked like his normal self. I spent time alone with him while Lacey and my husband took a walk in the hospital."

21

CODE WHITE

At 7:30 A.M. on Sunday, Nurse Nora Bompensiero checked in with the outgoing pediatric floor night nurse, Milda Anthony, before starting her shift. Nurse Anthony reported that Garnett had had an "uneventful night" and was doing well. Then they both went in to see the young patient, who was lying in bed, clutching his stuffed teddy bear.

Just before 8:30 A.M., Nurse Nora returned to room 242, disconnected Garnett's overnight feeding tube, and closed up his MIC-KEY port. Then she used a syringe to flush clean the connector tube before handing it back to his mother. She examined Garnett while he happily chatted away to her. He seemed quite normal.

After she left, Lacey took another photograph of her son lying on his hospital bed and posted it to Facebook.

At around 9:00 A.M., Dr. Sarika Sunku, who had just come back on duty, checked in on Garnett. He was on the toilet, so she said she would come back later.

"[Lacey] told me he had a mild headache, which lasted

a few minutes," said Dr. Sunku, "and that was it, and he was doing well."

Then, at 9:08 A.M., Lacey began searching Google for information about iodized salt. Her various searches included "What is iodized salt?," "Why buy iodized salt?," and "Morton Iodized Salt: What's in it?" She then made a series of searches on the central nervous system, benign and malignant brain tumors, and abnormal brain activity.

When Dr. Sunku returned to examine Garnett at 9:30 A.M., he was sitting on his bed with his breakfast in front of him, watching television.

"He was picking on his food," said Dr. Sunku. "He was not eating."

She checked his lungs, heart, and abdomen and found everything normal. Dr. Sunku then told Lacey that, so far, all the EEG recordings had been normal, and if the MRI scheduled for the following morning did not show any abnormalities, he could go home.

"So that's good news," said Dr. Sunku. "He would go home and he doesn't have seizures and won't have seizures."

Upon hearing that Garnett would soon be home with a clean bill of health, Lacey displayed little reaction.

"She was just calm," Dr. Sunku remembered. "She didn't really say anything."

At 10:25 A.M., the video EEG camera captured Lacey bringing Garnett into the bathroom. He looked happy, even grabbing a cookie on the way in. Seconds earlier, the little boy had been gleefully kicking around on the bed and waving his hands while his mother sat with her arms folded, staring into space.

After taking him into the bathroom, Lacey came out and walked out of camera range, toward her bag on the other side of the bed. Thirty-seven seconds later, she reappeared, clutching Garnett's connector tube in one hand and a large cup in the other.

For the next three minutes, Lacey and Garnett were in the bathroom, out of camera shot. Prosecutors believe that, once inside, Lacey attached the connector tube to Garnett's MIC-KEY button port. She then filled a syringe with a liquid containing a high concentration of salt. Finally, she jammed the syringe into the connector tube, sending the poison straight into Garnett's stomach.

When Lacey brought Garnett back out and lifted him onto the bed, he looked lethargic and scared. He kept rubbing his nose, an allergic reaction to the salt he'd just ingested. The little boy looked almost paralyzed with fear, as if he knew what was going to happen.

Then, Lacey went back into the bathroom, emerging fifty seconds later with the connector tube and cup in her hands. There was a strange, blank look on her face as she got onto the bed and leaned over her son, checking that his MIC-KEY button was closed.

For the next several minutes, Lacey waited for the salt to take effect, watching her son almost clinically. She picked up the red nurse call button, moving it up onto the bed in readiness.

Suddenly, Garnett keeled over in bed and began trying to retch. He arched his back as he desperately tried to purge the poisons from his body. But it was impossible because of the Nissen fundoplication procedure.

Finally, at 10:35 A.M., his mother pressed the emergency call button. Within seconds, Nurse Nora rushed into the room and was horrified by what she saw.

"Garnett [was] gagging," she later testified. "He had all the motions behind throwing up, but not the actual vomit coming out. He was dry heaving."

For the next fifteen minutes, the little boy rolled around

on the bed in agony, clutching his head in pain, while Lacey stroked his back to comfort him.

"He was screaming . . . and extremely agitated," said Nurse Nora. "The video EEG fell off because he was so upset."

The nurse paged Dr. Sunku, who rushed in.

"Garnett was holding his stomach and retching," she said, "[but he couldn't vomit] because of the Nissen fundoplication. He was in a lot of pain. He was turning and tossing . . . and he was asking for water, which I felt was strange. Because if you have so much nausea, you won't be able to drink anything."

The doctor ordered Zofran, an antinausea medication, and Motrin, for his severe headache, both of which were given through his IV. She then left, knowing that the only way Garnett could purge whatever was in his system was through a bowel movement.

At 11:30 A.M., Garnett started having explosive diarrhea, which went through his heavy diaper and into his clothing. Dr. Sunku returned to find Nurse Nora changing the child's soiled sheets.

"He had a couple of really large bowel movements," said the doctor, "and then, because of the worry that he would get dehydrated, we ordered a half-amount of saline."

At around midday, Garnett's whole body began trembling.

"The child was having shaking of his arms and legs," said Dr. Sunku. "He was shivering."

She then ordered a dextrose finger stick test to check his glucose level.

"It was 240," said the doctor. "It was high."

After getting the result, Dr. Sunku ordered a complete metabolic profile for Garnett. It would measure his sodium,

chloride, and potassium levels and show how his liver
and kidneys were functioning.

At 1:20 P.M., Garnett's blood was drawn, and while she
was waiting for the results, Lacey posted a new photograph of her suffering son on Facebook.

"Please please send G some love!" she wrote. "Went
from fine to really sick in minutes!"

At 2:30 P.M., the lab results came back, showing Garnett's sodium level was normal, at 144, although his
chloride was slightly elevated, at 114.

By this time, Garnett's condition had markedly improved.

"He wasn't complaining of a headache anymore," said
Nurse Nora. "He wasn't dry heaving, and his shivering
was decreasing."

Soon after the lab results came back, Lacey called
Nurse Nora into the room.

"She was asking about the results of the lab work," the
nurse later testified. "If the sodium . . . was normal."

The nurse told her it was within the normal range before leaving to attend to her other patients. Throughout
the afternoon, Nurse Nora regularly checked up on Garnett.

"He looked better," she said. "He was drinking a lot
of water. His mother was filling up the pitcher, and he was
drinking a lot."

At 4:19 P.M., the video EEG camera caught Lacey haul-
ing Garnett back into the bathroom with a cup and a connector tube in her hands. He looked alert, wearing a
hospital gown, with his head and left arm in bandages.

When they reappeared several minutes later, Garnett
had his head down and looked dazed. As he lay motionless on the bed, Lacey changed his diaper, pulling him

up roughly by the wrists to clean him up. Then, prosecutors believe, she got on the bed and waited for the massive dose of salt she had just pumped into him to take effect.

At 4:30 P.M., Lacey pressed the red nurse call button, and Nurse Nora rushed in.

"He appeared to be dry heaving again," said the nurse, "and again had all the motions of throwing up without actually doing it."

Dr. Sunku was then paged, and she prescribed anti-nausea medication through his IV. Then, as Nurse Nora was administering the drug, she leaned over Garnett and saw his MIC-KEY button was wide open, as if he'd just had a gastrostomy feeding.

"I notice that the G-tube port was open," she said. "So I just said, 'Mom, the G-tube is open.'" And she said 'Okay,' and we closed it up."

Then Lacey asked if there were any further lab results, and the nurse said she would ask Dr. Sunku.

Over the next hour, Garnett's condition deteriorated rapidly as he was given more doses of Zofran and Motrin. Then he began complaining of a very severe headache, his eyes started tearing, and he was rolling around the bed.

While her son was writhing in agony, Lacey texted a friend.

"He's having another episode!!!" she wrote.

Just before 5:30 P.M., Lacey Spears began screaming hysterically. Nurse Nora rushed into room 242 and found Garnett Spears having a full-blown seizure.

"She was screaming, 'Look at him! Look at him!,'" remembered the nurse. "He was totally incontinent. The bed was soaked through. He appeared to be twitching. His eyes were moving around in his head."

Nurse Nora then called an emergency Code White, summoning additional help into the room.

Dr. Sunku, who had heard Lacey's piercing screams from her office down the hall, was already on her way. She rushed in to see Lacey on the bed screaming and Garnett having a seizure. His arms and legs were shaking uncontrollably, and his eyes were rolling back in his head.

The doctor immediately checked his airway, breathing, and circulation before ordering Ativan, a strong antiseizure medication.

"The first dose didn't do anything," said Dr. Sunku, "and we gave him a second dose that . . . stopped the seizure-like activity for a few minutes."

Then Garnett started seizing again. He was given two additional doses of Ativan at 5:40 P.M. and 6:10 P.M., and the seizures subsided for a few minutes before starting up again.

Dr. Sunku then ordered the powerful antiseizure medication fosphenytoin.

"After the loading dose, he stopped for some time," said Dr. Sunku, "and then he needed another dose of fosphenytoin to stop the seizures."

Suddenly, Garnett's oxygen levels started falling, and he began having trouble breathing. Things became so dangerous that Dr. Sunku ordered Garnett to be intubated and put on life support. She also began making arrangements to transport him to Westchester Medical Center, which had its own pediatric intensive care unit and was better equipped to deal with this life-or-death situation.

"It became a critical situation at this point," she later explained. "If he was breathing on his own, and the seizures were under control with the medications that we gave him, we could have managed him over here. But he was not able to breathe on his own, and we couldn't stop the seizures."

While the doctor and nurses were desperately trying to stop her son's seizures, Lacey was texting friends.

"G's not well! Not well!!" she wrote.

"Praying like crazy!!!" came the response, several minutes later.

Just after 6:00 P.M., Dr. Neelima Thakur remotely checked Garnett's brain waves to see if he was having seizures. When she accessed the video EEG on her computer, she observed something far worse.

"I saw a significant amount of slowing in the wave forms," Dr. Thakur later testified. "There was no ongoing seizure activity; however, the brain had a very severe dysfunction."

When Nellie Grossenbacher arrived at room 242 to visit Garnett, he was flailing all over the bed.

"He was having a seizure," she said. "It was scary. The hospital staff were all around him and [Lacey] was standing at the end of the bed and she looked scared."

Nellie put her arm around Lacey to comfort her as the medical staff sedated Garnett so he could be intubated. Then, to Nellie's amazement, Lacey suddenly announced she had to call her grandmother and walked out of the room.

"She was more concerned with calling her grandmother," said Nellie, "than being right next to her child."

At this point, Nellie asked a nurse if she could comfort Garnett.

"Lacey wasn't going to do it," said Nellie, "and I just stood next to him and stroked his head and said, 'It's going to be okay.' "

* * *

At around 6:50 P.M., as the rapid response team was intubating Garnett, his mother returned to the room with a request.

"She asked us to check the labs," said Nurse Nora, "and said the last time this happened his sodium was high."

A few minutes later, blood was drawn from Garnett for another full metabolic profile.

At 7:13 P.M., the hospital laboratory called Nurse Nora with the stunning results. Garnett's sodium level had leaped from 144 to 182 in less than four and a half hours, and his chloride had risen from 114 to 160.

Alarmed at the results, the nurse immediately called Dr. Sunku. When Lacey asked whether the results had come in yet, Nurse Nora told her to speak to Dr. Sunku.

When the doctor heard the results, she was stunned, knowing of no medical explanation to account for such a steep rise in sodium. Dr. Sunku then told Lacey, warning her of the dangers to Garnett.

Lacey calmly replied that she had been expecting this after Garnett's previous experience of high sodium as a baby.

"She just had a smile on her face," Dr. Sunku would later testify.

As soon as the high sodium results came in, Nyack Hospital nurse Beatrice Augustine telephoned Dr. Carey Goltzman, director of the PICU at Maria Fareri Children's Hospital at Westchester Medical Center. Over the previous several hours, she had been arranging with him and his staff to airlift Garnett over the river to the PICU.

When Dr. Goltzman, who has more than thirty years of pediatric experience, heard Garnett's sodium level was

182, he was "flabbergasted." He was certain there had to be a mistake.

"It's impossible," he screamed down the phone. "You need to repeat it. That last sodium they gave you was 144, so how could it go to 182? It's an aberrant value. It needs to be repeated."

Then Dr. Sunku came on the line and agreed to repeat the blood work immediately.

"I mean, this is a really abnormal blood gas," Dr. Goltzman told her. "This kid is much sicker, Dr. Sunku, than you've been telling me."

At 7:30 P.M., the electrolyte tests were repeated. The results came in thirty-six minutes later, and Garnett's sodium levels had dropped slightly, to 178, and his chloride to 155, but these levels were still perilously high.

Lacey was then told that her son was in such critical condition that he would be airlifted to the Westchester Medical Center.

"Is he dying?" asked Lacey.

Nurse Nora told her she could go with her son in the helicopter, thinking she would naturally want to be with him at a time like this. Lacey refused, saying that a friend would drive her over instead.

"She flat-out said she did not want to get in that helicopter," said Nellie Grossenbacher. "And they said, 'What? Your kid's going in a helicopter, why wouldn't you go?' And she said, 'I'm scared. I don't want to get in the helicopter.' That was very strange."

Finally, Lacey reluctantly agreed to fly over with Garnett, after Carol Grieder persuaded her that it was the right thing to do.

The helicopter was delayed by a heavy snowstorm. As her son lay unconscious, on life support, in his hospital room,

Lacey was outside in the hallway, making phone calls and texting.

At one point, her father, Terry Spears, called, saying he and her mother were leaving Kentucky immediately to drive the nine hundred miles to New York.

Nyack Hospital nursing supervisor Frank Druse observed Lacey while she was waiting for the helicopter to arrive, and he was surprised at her lack of emotion.

"The mother did not appear to be in shock," he said, "or demonstrate extreme concern for the situation. [She] had friends at the bedside who showed more concern for the situation than [she did]."

At 9:05 P.M., the Westchester Medical Center flight crew finally arrived. Several medics collected Garnett from his room, carrying him on a stretcher to the waiting helicopter. Lacey picked up her bags and followed her unconscious son out of the hospital and into the helicopter.

At 9:28 P.M., as she waited for the helicopter to take off, Lacey took out her iPhone and typed a message to her Facebook friends.

"Pray for Garnett!!!" she wrote. "He's on life support & being life flighted!!!!"

22

At around 10:00 P.M., the helicopter landed at the West-chester Medical Center, in Valhalla, New York, and a heavily sedated Garnett Spears was carried on a stretcher through the snow and into the pediatric intensive care unit.

"He was very grave," said Oona, who had arrived a few minutes earlier. "He was on a stretcher and . . . bun-dled up."

She asked Lacey how she was coping.

"She smiled," remembered Oona.

A few minutes later, after the nurses settled Garnett into a bed in room 2108, Dr. Carey Goltzman came in to examine him.

"He was intubated and mechanically ventilated," said the PICU director. "He had IVs in both hands. He was anatomically stable."

Dr. Goltzman first drew blood for a new set of met-abolic tests. When the results came back, Garnett's so-dium remained unchanged, at 178, but his chloride was slightly lower, at 147. Both figures were still dangerously high.

When Dr. Goltzman started examining Garnett, he saw the G-tube and became immediately suspicious. Until then, the doctor could not fathom how it was medically possible for the child's sodium level to jump from 144 to 182 in such a short time. Now the answer was staring him in the face.

"I thought immediately," he recalled, "*Could this youngster have been given an exogenous dose of sodium chloride that could account for both his sodium and chloride level going through the roof?*"

Then Dr. Goltzman called Lacey and her two friends into his office, to get more information about Garnett. Lacey seemed composed as she calmly recounted his medical history and the events leading up to this. Then the doctor asked what had happened that day.

"[She said] Garnett was initially doing well in the morning, but later on he was retching," said Dr. Goltzman. "He had [acute] headaches . . . towards the very early afternoon."

Then Lacey said Garnett had been so thirsty that he had drunk at least one hundred ounces of water.

"And I asked her to repeat that," said the doctor. "And she said, 'Yes, one hundred ounces of water.' I said, '[That's] like about six and a half bottles of bottled water that we would get in the supermarket.'"

Lacey insisted he had drunk that much water, even after Dr. Goltzman told her it would be a lot of water for anyone to drink, let alone a five-year-old child.

"I said it's hard for me to believe," he later testified, "because if Garnett drank this much water, why is his sodium precipitously elevated to 182? He would have peed off most of the water, and his sodium . . . should have gone down."

Then Lacey recounted her son's basic medical history, and the doctor was surprised by her extensive knowledge of medical terminology. She also told him that her son had suffered one prior episode of hypernatremia, again surprising the doctor by her use of the correct medical term for excess sodium.

When Dr. Goltzman asked when Garnett had last been fed through his G-tube, Lacey said it had been more than a week prior to his admission to Nyack Hospital.

Oona Younger, who was in the doctor's office along with Nellie Grossenbacher, was astonished. She had seen Lacey feeding Garnett through his G-tube just two days earlier. She also noticed that Lacey neglected to mention many of Garnett's other medical issues, which she had so often spoken about with Oona.

"He asked Lacey some questions and she wasn't really exactly answering," said Oona. "I was very surprised."

Finally, Oona could keep silent no longer. She tried to correct Lacey, who turned around and gave her a cold, withering stare. Oona was so shocked that she walked out of the office and sat in the waiting room.

Like Oona Younger, Nellie Grossenbacher was concerned that Lacey had been strangely selective about Garnett's medical history. When the meeting finished, she took Lacey into an empty hospital room and told her it was vital to tell Dr. Goltzman everything, to help Garnett.

Suddenly Lacey angrily lashed out at the doctor, saying he was accusing her of hurting Garnett, when she had not.

"She picked up right away that he was accusing her of doing something," said Nellie. "I mean, I didn't. She said to me, 'He's accusing me of hurting my child. I didn't hurt my kid.'"

Then Nellie suggested writing down a complete

timeline of Garnett's medical history, to help in Garnett's treatment.

"I tried to get it all out of her," said Nellie, "but it was, 'I don't remember everything. There are so many hospitals. There are so many doctors.'"

Nellie told her it was essential to have a binder of Garnett's medical history available, for doctors to check. Lacey replied that there had been so many hospital visits over the years that she had lost track.

"I said, 'Okay, we'll figure this out,'" said Nellie. "'Don't worry about it.'"

After examining Garnett Spears and talking to his mother, Dr. Carey Goltzman diagnosed him as suffering from hypernatremia, or elevated sodium in the blood. It is a rare condition caused by either severe dehydration or a lack of free water in the body. And it is a potentially lethal condition because it can cause shifts of water in the intracranial cavity where the brain sits. In extreme cases, hypernatremia can result in cerebral edema, or swelling of the brain, causing the brain stem to herniate, and brain death.

The doctor then calculated a careful plan to lower Garnett's sodium levels slowly over a forty-eight-hour period while closely monitoring him. He would be kept on appropriate IV fluids, dextrose and potassium, and would no longer be given any sedatives to paralyze him.

"We wanted to see Garnett wake up," the doctor explained, "so we could remove him from [life support]."

Dr. Goltzman also issued an NPO order, meaning Garnett was to have nothing by mouth, so the staff could carefully control any kind of liquid going into Garnett's body. His mother was specifically told not to give Garnett anything to drink because it could kill him.

* * *

At 11:25 P.M., Lacey took a photograph of her son, lying intubated, with an endotracheal tube down his throat, and posted it on Facebook.

"Garnett's stable on life support," she wrote. "Keep praying!!!"

When Mallory McWhorter saw Lacey's social media postings back in Decatur, she asked all her Facebook friends to pray for Garnett.

"I went to school with his mommy," she wrote, "and have watched this baby grow up through fb! He is on life support and has been med flighted!! Please also pray for his mommy."

Lacey's old high school friend Rania Cottingham also was shocked by Lacey's postings.

"I saw 'Everybody pray for Garnett. He had seizures,'" she said. "So we were all very concerned and commenting on it. And then it just progressed and got worse and worse."

When Rania showed her husband Lacey's photographs of Garnett on life support, he told her something was wrong.

"I would read him the updates and show him the pictures," said Rania, "and he was like, 'She's smiling. How is she smiling? That's weird.'"

Monday was Martin Luther King Jr. Day, and in the early hours, Lacey began updating friends and family about Garnett's condition. Someone asked her why his sodium would go up from the 140s to the 180s in such a brief period.

"I'm not really sure," she replied at 1:32 A.M. "But the seizures he had coulda been from the sodium levels."

Another friend wanted to know if the excess sodium could have been caused by diabetes or diarrhea.

"He's had a lot of diarrhea," replied Lacey, "but the doctor doesn't think that's the cause."

"Does he have any renal issues?" asked the friend.

"Not that I know of," she replied.

At 6:05 Monday morning, Lacey Spears posted an update on Facebook.

"Still no answers," she wrote. "His fever is down & his labs are still off. Sodium levels dropped from 180's to 177, still very high. He's still on life support. Keep praying."

One hour later, Dr. Goltzman checked in on his young patient before going off shift. With him was his deputy, Dr. Alan Pinto, who would be taking over Garnett's care.

Although the little boy was still intubated, with restraints on his hands, his sodium level was beginning to fall, in line with Dr. Goltzman's calculations.

"At 7:20 A.M. his sodium was 172," said Dr. Goltzman, "but it was coming down appropriately."

All through the morning, Garnett's sodium level continued to drop, and by the early afternoon, Garnett started waking up.

"He was doing fine," said Dr. Pinto. "He was nodding his head to questions, and he was breathing on his own."

But when Dr. Pinto told Lacey the good news, that they would soon be removing the endotracheal tube, she tried to stop them.

"His mother did not want us to extubate him," said Dr. Pinto. "She said she did not want him to be uncomfortable."

Dr. Pinto explained the dangers of keeping Garnett intubated, such as the risk of infection or of the endotracheal tube getting dislodged. Then, despite Lacey's objection, the breathing tube was removed at 3:30 in the afternoon.

As the sedatives wore off, Garnett kept saying that he wanted to go home.

"He was awake," said the doctor. "He was alert. He was talking. He was following commands."

Although Garnett was now out of danger, the NPO order remained in effect while doctors continued to work on lowering his sodium back to normal. Nellie Grossenbacher, who had been at Westchester Medical Center most of the day, saw Garnett soon after the endotracheal tube was removed.

"He was groggy," she remembered, "but you could see his personality coming through. He was asking for water . . . but they said we were not to give him any fluid."

At around 5:00 P.M., when Nellie was satisfied that Garnett was okay, she told him she had to go home.

"And he said, 'Don't go. I want you to stay,'" Nellie remembered. "I said, 'I have to go home to your friends.'

"Lacey and I both looked at each other and smiled. Like, 'All right. This is going to be good.'"

Back in Decatur, April Chambers and another school friend, Rachel Landers, set up a PayPal account to raise money for Garnett's hospital fees through the First Bible Church. The church, which Lacey had once attended, donated $500 directly into her Wachovia bank account, and over the next several days they would raise a further $800 from well-wishers who were closely following Garnett's progress on Facebook.

Many other people, touched by Lacey's emotive postings, began sending gifts to Garnett's hospital room.

Although his doctors were delighted with Garnett's good progress, his mother was posting increasingly dramatic Facebook updates about her son's condition.

"My heart is broken," she wrote at 4:23 on Monday afternoon, alongside a new hospital photograph of Garnett.

"He's my world. He is 'Garnett the Great' and he will pull through."

At 7:17 P.M., Garnett's labs were drawn again, and the results showed his sodium was now down to 161 and his chloride was 131. These were still "grossly high," but far better than twenty-four hours earlier.

At 7:31 P.M., Lacey went on Facebook, posting a new photograph of Garnett lying in his hospital bed.

"Keep the prayers coming," she wrote. "He's still critical but off the vent!"

That evening, several friends from the Fellowship Community visited, and after they left, Garnett fell asleep. At around 9:00 P.M., Lacey woke up to find him thrashing around in his bed, entangled in his IV tubes and machine wires. She summoned a nurse, who said everything appeared normal, speculating that the sedatives wearing off could have made him uncomfortable.

During the evening, Lacey spoke to Meka Taulbee, her holistic nutritionist in Clearwater. Taulbee would later tell detectives that Lacey said that Blake's family was at the hospital to support her and their grandson.

Lacey's next Facebook update, together with a new photograph, came at 9:36 P.M.

"He's still in the PICU," she wrote. "Maintaining his oxygen off the ventilator. Very sleepy, is also alert & responding. Sodium level 165 at 3 pm, so they are still dropping to a more normal range. Let's hope for a great night with some much needed rest for him."

When Dr. Pinto did his night round, he was pleased to see Garnett stable and resting comfortably.

"There were no issues," he recalled. "He was still saying he wanted to go home. He asked for some water. We gave him some sips, just to wet his lips."

Soon after the doctor left, Lacey posted on Facebook.

"G is screaming in pain," she wrote. "Screaming his

head hurts. We laid his bed flat & just wait to see what happens."

After reading this, Oona Younger replied on Lacey's timeline.

"I am so sorry this is happening," she wrote. "He was so peaceful a few hours ago. I will be back tomorrow. I love you guys so much. Praying super hard."

At midnight, Dr. Ariel Sherbany arrived at the Maria Fareri Children's Hospital to carry out a neurological exam on Garnett Spears. Although the doctor found him "lethargic," the little boy was otherwise completely normal.

"I didn't see anything that concerned me," said Dr. Sherbany. "It seemed like he was coming along as one would expect, having been sedated with medications."

23

"THE REALM OF BRAIN DEATH"

On Tuesday morning, the East Coast was hit by another heavy snowstorm. Terry and Tina Spears were still almost three hundred miles away from New York, and at 5:25 A.M., Lacey began checking Google to see how long it would take them to reach the hospital.

"Still hours away," she texted a friend. "14 hours without stopping."

Although Garnett's PICU nurses would later remember him "having a pretty restful night," his mother's Facebook posts said otherwise.

"It's 6 am," she wrote. "There has been very little sleep going on for G through the night. Both his IV's blew, a new one was placed in the early hours. He's no longer sedated, he can respond when asked questions, just not always clear enough to understand what he's saying. The most disturbing symptom is he's in pain & won't hold his head up & roll over without SCREAMING out in pain. He's been thrashing around most of the night. No stomach pains so far!!! No retching!!! No abnormal eye movement. Just the concern of the head pain & the inability to hold his head up. No update on his labs. Sodium was 165 last night."

Then Lacey took three more photographs of Garnett in bed, which she duly posted on Facebook. This elicited twenty-nine responses, including one from Nellie Grossenbacher, who asked what Lacey needed her to bring when she came to visit later.

"Nellie," Lacey replied. "That asshole of a doctor is the doctor today. He's already been outside [the] door ranting!!!"

A few minutes earlier, Dr. Goltzman had started his shift and had done the rounds with Dr. Pinto, who had briefed him on Garnett's overnight progress. Garnett's most recent labs, at 6:45 A.M., had shown that his sodium level was now almost back to normal, at 146, and his chloride was 114.

"His sodium was coming down nice and slowly," said Dr. Goltzman, "as I calculated and expected."

When the two doctors walked past Garnett's room, they looked through the glass doors and saw him "sleeping comfortably."

"He was stable," said Dr. Pinto. "No concern."

At 7:15 A.M., Lacey sent an instant message: "Two of the nasty doctors are on call today."

Then she called Nellie Grossenbacher, saying that Garnett had had a bad night and not slept. She said she had told the nurses but they had not done anything.

"She felt like they were disregarding her," said Nellie. "I told her that I would be coming to the hospital, and hung up the phone."

A few minutes later, Dr. Carey Goltzman was having a meeting in his office when a code bell sounded, signaling an emergency in Garnett Spears's room.

"I shot out of that office like a bat out of hell," said Dr. Goltzman, "and I ran straight into the room."

The doctor saw Lacey leaning over the bed.

"I looked at Garnett, and looked at the mom," he said. "Under the bed I saw an empty bottle of Poland Spring water. And the first thing I said to the nurse was, 'Get that bottle!'"

The doctor already had his suspicions that Lacey had fed her son salt. Now he wondered if she had defied his orders by giving him water, which would cause irreversible brain damage.

Dr. Goltzman then ordered Lacey out of the room before turning his attention to Garnett, who had stopped breathing.

"I looked at his eyes very quickly," said Goltzman, "and both pupils were blown and dilated. They weren't reacting to light. He was having a brain stem problem."

After checking Garnett's airway, breathing, and circulation, the doctor ordered a bag valve mask to help him breathe. As he was putting the mask over Garnett's face, Dr. Alan Pinto, who had heard the code bell as he was leaving the hospital, rushed in to help.

"I went ahead and I intubated him," said Dr. Pinto. "I put back the endotracheal tube to breathe for him."

Then Dr. Goltzman ordered a brain CAT scan as well as new blood work.

While doctors and nurses attended to her son, Lacey Spears was busy making calls and posting on Facebook. She called Nellie Grossenbacher at around 7:30 A.M., screaming that Garnett had stopped breathing and had coded.

"She was hysterical and crying," said Nellie. "She said, 'Are you coming? You need to come now.'"

Then, at 7:43 A.M., she posted on Facebook, "GAR-

NETT STOPPED BREATHING & is back on the vent!!!
Please pray!!!"

There were fifty responses to her post, offering sympathy, love, and prayers.

"Praying, praying and praying," wrote Oona Younger.

":(I'm so sorry Lacey," wrote another friend. "This is
so unfair, positive thoughts and lots of prayers."

"Praying my heart out," wrote Rania Cottingham, who
was now checking Facebook every few minutes for updates on Garnett.

Nellie Grossenbacher arrived at Westchester Medical
Center to find Garnett on life support. When asked what
had happened, Lacey seemed more concerned that she
was under suspicion than about Garnett.

"She felt like the hospital was accusing her," said Nellie. "She said they had taken a bottle of water out of the
room."

A few minutes later, Terry and Tina Spears arrived at
the hospital after spending almost two days driving from
Kentucky. Lacey had a quiet word with Nellie, asking her
not to tell Lacey's parents that she was under suspicion.

"She didn't want people to really talk in front of her
mother," said Nellie, "about her lifestyle or Garnett's
health."

A brain scan performed at 10:38 A.M. revealed that Garnett Spears was brain dead. The high concentration of salt
in his body had shifted water into his brain cells, causing
them to swell. This had led to a build-up of pressure in
the intracranial cavity, and as his brain expanded, it had
nowhere to go in his skull. It had then started herniating
as it pushed downward, crushing the vital centers in the
brain that control respiration and blood pressure.

A normal CAT scan of the brain would show scalloping all around the inside of the skull. But Garnett's brain was now completely flat, pressed up against the skull.

"There was marked acute cerebral edema," explained Dr. Goltzman, "and there was herniation of the brain stem. The brain had swollen . . . and there was nothing I could do about it at that time."

A few minutes later, Dr. Goltzman discussed the CAT scan results with Lacey and her parents. On a monitor in a small waiting area next to the doctor's station, he showed them the images of Garnett's brain.

"I explained . . . there was a good chance that he was going to enter the realm of brain death," remembered Dr. Goltzman, "the way that the CAT scan looked, and the . . . herniating was probably secondary to . . . this high sodium level. And despite the fact that we were appropriately lowering it very slowly, he was succumbing to the insult that had been received."

The doctor promised to keep them updated as the day progressed, in case there were any changes. Then Lacey fell to the floor and wept uncontrollably. Her son, who had been steadily improving until just hours before, was now effectively dead.

At around 11:00 P.M., Garnett "dumped" his urine through his Foley catheter, getting rid of all the free water he had in his body. Lacey, her parents, Nellie Grossenbacher, Carol Grieder, and Oona Younger were all at his bedside when this happened. Someone asked if he would ever recover.

The neurologist examining him replied that, based on the massive amount of fluid coming through the catheter from his kidneys, he would not survive. There was no brain activity.

"And it was at that point that she realized that [he was dead]," said Nellie. "She ran out of the room and down the hallway and just [started] crying. She was flopping around on the floor, yelling, 'My baby! My baby!'"

For the next hour and a half, Lacey lay on the ground in the hallway outside, distraught. Nellie and Garnett's teacher came out to comfort her.

"She was crying," said Grieder. "Calling out."

Finally, Lacey's mother came out of Garnett's room to talk to Lacey.

"She said, 'I'm sorry you're going through this,'" said Nellie, "'but this is not about you. This is about your child. And your child is going to die, and you need to spend whatever minutes you have left with him. So pull yourself together and get in your kid's hospital room.' And Lacey went."

At around 11:45 A.M., Dr. Goltzman met with Dr. Jennifer Canter, the director of the child abuse pediatric program at Westchester Medical Center. He briefed her on Garnett Spears's unexplainable brain death and revealed his suspicion that Garnett's mother had poisoned the boy with salt.

On Dr. Canter's recommendation, Dr. Goltzman then telephoned the New York State Child Abuse Hotline in Albany, New York, calling in a child protective services (CPS) report on Lacey Spears. He told them that he suspected Lacey had fed salt through her son's G-tube, causing his brain death.

Right after receiving the call, the abuse hotline notified child protective services in both Westchester County and Rockland County. Normally, a Westchester CPS worker would be dispatched to investigate, but a severe snow advisory had grounded the agency's cars. So they referred the matter to the Westchester County District Attorney's office, which alerted the Westchester County Police.

At midday, an EEG showed no activity in Garnett Spears's brain, so Dr. Goltzman ordered a brain death protocol. Before the Westchester Medical Center could officially declare Garnett dead, there would have to be two clinical brain death exams by two different doctors, twenty-four hours apart.

In the meantime, to make certain there was no medical explanation for Garnett's massive rise in sodium, Dr. Goltzman called in almost a dozen specialists, from various medical fields, to examine the boy. These included a neurosurgeon, a renal specialist, and even a genetic expert. They all confirmed that there was absolutely no medical explanation for the fatal rise in Garnett's sodium.

Shortly after the EEG result, Dr. Goltzman summoned Lacey Spears into a conference room. He informed her that nothing could medically account for such a huge rise in her son's sodium level.

"I said to Miss Spears," Dr. Goltzman later testified, "that this was going to be an unfortunate negative outcome for this youngster. I did not have a really good explanation as to why his sodium had risen so precipitously and . . . hypernatremia was the cause of his problem."

He told her that he was obligated to call in child protective services because he suspected that this was not an accident. On hearing this, Lacey did not register any reaction whatsoever.

PART THREE

24

UNDER SUSPICION

At 2:15 P.M. on Tuesday, January 21, Detective Dan Carfi of the Westchester County Police Department was ordered to Maria Fareri Children's Hospital to investigate a possible child abuse case. The fifty-year-old seasoned investigator grabbed a notebook, pens, and statement forms. Then he drove to Westchester County Police headquarters, at 1 Saw Mill River Parkway, Hawthorne, New York, where he collected Detective George Ruiz and headed to the Westchester Medical Center.

They arrived at 2:50 P.M. and met Westchester County assistant district attorneys Christine Hatfield and Christine Cervasio in the lobby. They all took the elevator to the second floor to meet Dr. Jennifer Canter in a conference room.

"She gave us an overview of what's happening," said Detective Carfi. "There's a young man, Garnett Spears, who was airlifted two nights prior with high sodium. She starts going through the whole case."

Dr. Canter told them that Garnett's sodium level had

been normal on Sunday morning but within a few hours had risen to 182. He was now brain dead, on life support, and she was certain that his mother had poured salt into his G-tube.

"She kept drilling that this is medically impossible," recalled Carfi. "This is just not explainable. And at some point she said, 'If you're going to search her house, you're looking for salt—household salt.'"

Meanwhile, the Ramapo Police Department, across the Hudson River in Rockland County, also was notified by its local child protective services. Detective Kirk Budnick, age fifty, was at his desk when he received a call about a mother giving her child "foreign substances causing a fatal reaction."

He then contacted Rockland County CPS caseworker Vanessa Torres, who wanted to first check Lacey Spears's house and make sure no other children were there. A few minutes later, Detective Budnick collected Torres from her office, and they drove to the Fellowship Community in Chestnut Ridge. They went straight to Tulip House, where they spoke to Lacey's upstairs neighbors, Shaiya and Charisse Baer, who confirmed that Lacey and Garnett lived in the basement and that there were no other children.

"They report that Garnett is an active little boy," Detective Budnick later wrote in his case notes, "and that Lacey is a loving doting mother."

After meeting with Dr. Canter, Detective Carfi walked past room 2108, where he saw Garnett Spears lying on the bed, surrounded by Lacey and her parents.

"Machines are all hooked up, and he's on life support," recalled Detective Carfi. "He's still and very pale, lying straight in the bed. I didn't go in. Sometimes, having a policeman come right in is a little overwhelming."

Then he walked down the hall, to interview Dr. Carey Goltzman in his office.

"Dr. Goltzman believed that these injuries were as a result of Garnett being given a foreign substance by his mother," said Detective Carfi. "[It] raised Garnett's sodium levels to a potentially dangerous level."

At the end of the interview, the doctor handed the detective the Poland Spring water bottle that he had ordered seized after Garnett coded.

A few minutes later, Detective Carfi and the two Westchester County assistant district attorneys met Detective Kirk Budnick of the Ramapo Police, who had just arrived. It was decided that this would be a joint investigation between the Westchester County and Ramapo police because the case spanned both jurisdictions. It was the first time the two detectives had ever met, and for the next year they would work closely together, piecing together what had happened to Garnett.

Their first move was to get a search warrant for Lacey Spears's apartment. Detective Budnick had his partner, Detective Gregory Dunn, age fifty-four, then went straight over to the Fellowship Community and secure Lacey's residence until a search warrant could be prepared and signed by a judge.

At 4:10 that afternoon, Lacey Spears was interviewed by Detective Dan Carfi in a conference room at Westchester Medical Center. Also present were Dr. Jennifer Canter and Westchester County assistant district attorneys Christine Hatfield and Christine Cervasio.

Lacey recounted Garnett's medical history as well as her version of the events leading up to the present afternoon. She first told the detectives that Garnett's father had been a police officer who had been killed in a traffic accident. She also said that she treated Garnett with holistic medicines, but when Carfi asked which ones, Lacey could not remember. She then handed him her black iPhone 4 in a red case, so he could copy down all the names of the herbal medications.

Detective Carfi took careful notes, wondering why Lacey was so talkative at such a stressful time. She appeared in no hurry to rejoin her parents and friends, who were keeping a vigil at her dying son's bedside.

"She appeared to be troubled," said Detective Carfi. "But she was in no hurry to leave us and wanted to hang out."

The detective was also surprised at Lacey's obvious familiarity with medical terminology.

"That raised my eyebrows," he recalled. "She would refer to nurses taking care of her child as 'the nurses on the floor.' And little words that she used were triggers to me."

The detective, who has two grandchildren the same age as Garnett, was also struck by her apparent lack of emotion. Throughout the interview, Lacey sat stiffly at the conference table with her arms crossed. Occasionally she appeared to cry, but he saw no tears. Then, as soon as someone asked her a question, she had an answer ready, without missing a beat.

"Everybody was kind of taken aback," recalled Detective Carfi. "That change of emotion, from crying to 'Well, I can answer that question.' It was so smooth. It was remarkable."

After the interview, Lacey returned to room 2108, where Garnett was lying brain dead on life support. Since arriving that morning, Tina Spears had never once left her grandson's side, but Lacey was constantly flitting in and out of the room, texting and making calls on her iPhone.

"I was with Lacey in the room," remembered Nellie Grossenbacher, "and she was crying and very upset. And then her phone rang, and she was, 'Hello.' She just snapped out of it."

Nellie also noticed how little interaction there was between Tina Spears and her daughter.

"Her mother was very distant from her," she said. "I mean, very distant. If it was me, and I was in the hospital with one of my children sick, my family would hug and kiss me. At no point did her mother lay a hand on her. There was no physical contact, which makes me think that her mother probably thought that she did hurt him."

That night, Nellie Grossenbacher became concerned about the continuing police presence in the hospital, as Detective Carfi interviewed several of Garnett's nurses and his nursery school teacher, Carol Grieder. She called a hospital therapist she knew, asking about the significance of having detectives and social workers there.

"And my friend said, 'They believe [Lacey] killed her kid,'" said Nellie. "'If it was nothing, they'd send one member from social services. But if they have police there, they believe that she harmed her child.'"

Then Nellie realized that if the doctors believed Lacey really had harmed Garnett, then she probably had. Nellie became so upset that she left the hospital and drove home.

Over the next several days, Lacey posted a succession of photographs of Garnett on life support, shocking Nellie and many of her other friends.

"She posted pictures of him brain dead in the hospital," said Nellie, "and writing, 'Pray for my son.'"

* * *

Late that night, Rebecca Thompson spoke to Lacey on the phone. Then she posted a poignant message to Lacey's 105 Facebook friends.

> Lacey asked me to update you all because they really need prayers right now. She said that they need a miracle and asked you all please to pray for one. The doctors say that there isn't anything they can do for Garnett. He's on life support and that's the only thing that is keeping him here. The swelling that he has in his brain is not something they can do anything about. It came on very suddenly (within 3 minutes) and they've done all they can do. Please pray for Lacey and her sweet little boy. They need it right now.

Back in Decatur, Alabama, Shawna Lynch was horrified to learn that Garnett was brain dead and on life support. She immediately told his father, Chris Hill.

"I messaged him," said Shawna, "and I said, 'I don't know if you've heard, but Garnett's in the hospital. He's not doing well.'"

Garnett's grief-stricken father desperately tried to reach out to Lacey on Facebook, but she refused to answer.

"He couldn't see anything [on Facebook]," said Shawna, "so I would keep him updated on how everything was going."

At around midnight, Kenwood Paulen drove Peggy Florence to the airport, where she met her granddaughter, Rebecca Spears, who had flown in from Huntsville, Alabama.

"I picked up my grandmother," said Rebecca, "and then we got on a plane to New York [to go to the hospi-

tal]. It was very scary. Just confusing times, not understanding what was going on. My parents were already
there, and we were all going to support Lacey."

At 12:45 A.M. on Wednesday, Ramapo Police detectives
Kirk Budnick and Dennis Procter arrived at the Fellow-
ship Community to search Lacey Spears's apartment.
They carried a search warrant signed by a Rockland
County judge.

"We were looking for sodium, salt, and medications,"
said Detective Budnick. "We didn't know [exactly what],
because she said they were on a holistic diet. So I knew
the child was most likely poisoned by something, but
what it was, nobody could tell us."

There was at least a foot of snow on the ground as they
collected Detective Greg Dunn, who had been waiting
outside. Then the three Ramapo Police officers walked
to the back of Tulip House to go inside.

"Rockland Police! Search warrant!" shouted Detective
Budnick. When there was no answer, they all entered
through a small vestibule, leading straight into Lacey's
living room.

"The living room was pristine," recalled Detective
Dunn. "It was extremely neat, and everything appeared
to be in its place."

The three detectives immediately saw the feeding machine, the Kangaroo pump, and a plastic feeding bag full
of white liquid hanging from an IV pole. There also was a
blue canvas bag attached to it, bearing Garnett's initials,
GPTS. Hanging on the wall were several photographs of
the little boy as well as his paintings from school. Pictures
of owls, and stuffed owls, were everywhere.

"She would tell people," said Detective Budnick, "that
the owls were the reincarnated Blake."

Then the detectives walked into the kitchen and

stopped in their tracks. There, on the kitchen table, Lacey had made a shrine. It consisted of Garnett's photograph next to several candles, some medications, and a large box of sea salt.

"It was surreal," recalled Detective Dunn. "Why a box of salt and his photograph behind it? And there were candles."

They then looked in the garbage can in the kitchen and found a second plastic feeding bag. It contained whitish liquid, similar to the liquid in the bag hanging from the feeding machine. When they opened the hallway closet, they saw hundreds of different holistic medications, vitamins, and compounds.

Every room in the small apartment was scrupulously tidy, except the bedroom.

"It didn't match the rest of the apartment," explained Detective Budnick. "There was a mattress on the floor, unmade, and just one double-size bed. They co-slept."

Detective Dunn photographed the apartment and its contents from every angle. While he was doing this, Budnick and Procter collected 174 herbal medications and various compounds. These included fourteen herbal medications prescribed by Dr. Holly Johantgen. They also took two open twenty-six-ounce containers of salt and a syringe found in a box on the couch.

On the way out, they discussed seizing the feeding bag with the whitish liquid, too, but decided against it.

"I just had granddaughters who were less than a year old," explained Budnick. "My daughter was breast-feeding. When we walked in, I looked at the bag and said, 'She's breast-feeding.' It looked like breast milk in a bag, so we took pictures of it and moved along."

As Lacey's apartment was being searched, she posted on Facebook.

"Tonight I sit at the bedside of my beautiful, amazing, lively, one of a kind sons [sic] bed, Garnett the Great," she wrote, "knowing his soul is already with the angels . . . There's just no words to describe this horrible nightmare. Please pray Garnett's journey into his next life is nothing short of amazing."

Her post elicited sixty-three responses, all expressing sympathy for Garnett and applauding her courage.

"I am at a loss for words," wrote one friend. "You are an amazing person and Garnett is lucky to have you as his mom!"

At 4:12 A.M., Lacey sent a text message to her sister, Rebecca, who was on the way to New York with their grandmother.

"G's beautiful soul left to join the angels yesterday morning," she wrote. "He's still in [sic] life support & will remain that way until you and gramma get here. Then I'll decide when it's time to turn the machine off. G's gone!!!!!"

25

"I NEED A FAVOR"

At 8:20 A.M., Garnett Spears had the first of the two clinical brain death examinations needed before he could be officially pronounced dead. It was performed by the hospital's neurosurgical chief resident, who found that the five-year-old was in fact brain dead. An EEG also showed electrocerebral silence, the absence of any electrical activity in the brain.

"Lacey [was] told that Garnett had met the criteria of the initial clinical brain death exam," said Dr. Goltzman, "and that we have between two to twenty-four hours to perform the next clinical brain death exam."

Right after hearing this terrible news, Lacey telephoned her friend Valerie Plauché at the Fellowship Community. Like everyone else at the Fellowship, Valerie had been monitoring Garnett Spears's progress on Facebook.

"I was on the edge of my seat for news," Plauché explained, "and I was waiting and worrying about Garnett."

After a sleepless night, she had woken up at 5:30 A.M., immediately checking Facebook for news of Garnett.

"I saw something that Lacey had posted about Garnett having passed over."

After reading it, Plauché posted her condolences.

"A great light is passing," she wrote. "So grateful to have known and loved this radiant being . . . to have witnessed him blast open every heart with his gentle, irresistible joy . . . Please let's surround [Lacey] and Garnett with Love & Light . . . "

Three minutes later, Lacey instant messaged her to call as soon as possible.

"We didn't connect right away," said Plauché. "But then we finally did, and we both cried. It was just a shared moment of grief."

Valerie asked if there was anything she could do, and Lacey said she would let her know.

At 10:18 A.M., Valerie Plauché's cell phone rang, and Lacey's name came up on the caller ID. It was such a bad connection that Valerie had to go up on the roof for better reception.

"She wanted me to go to her house," Valerie would later testify, "and get a feeding bag in the middle of her living room and throw it away and not tell anybody. She [sounded] serious: 'Can you do it now? Can you do it now? I don't want you to tell anybody.' "

Valerie agreed to do it, saying she would call back later. But, after hanging up the phone, she felt confused by Lacey's "odd" request. So she asked her friend Chloe McKenna to help her do something for Lacey.

"Lacey had emphasized 'Don't tell anybody,' " explained Plauché. "And a little something clicked in my head, that it was just something that I didn't want to do alone."

Then the two women put on heavy overcoats and boots, and Chloe found a black garbage bag to put the feeding bag in. It was still snowing heavily as they started walking toward Tulip House, and progress was slow because Valerie had a twisted ankle.

Five minutes later, they arrived at Tulip House and knocked on the front door. Shaiya Baer and his six-year-old daughter, Lizzie, answered, and Valerie told him they had to get something for Lacey.

"Shaiya was very nervous," Valerie recalled. "And he said, 'I wouldn't do that. The police were here and they took pictures of everything and took three bags of stuff out of her apartment.' He was concerned and really didn't want me to go downstairs."

Despite his objections, the two women entered Lacey's basement apartment, followed by Baer and Lizzie. They walked into the living room and saw the feeding bag, full of what looked like infant formula, hanging from an IV pole.

"I was very focused on the mission," said Valerie, "so I walked over to the stand and observed it. And it was a bag with liquid in it, [and] it was attached to this whole stand and tubes."

As she tried to unhook the feeding bag from the machine, Shaiya warned her again to leave it alone.

"It was a little complicated," said Valerie. "It wasn't that easy to just take off. And we spent a couple of minutes trying to figure out . . . how to remove it."

After finally disconnecting it, Plauché put the feeding bag in the black garbage bag they had brought with them and left the apartment. But after learning the police had been there earlier, she decided not to throw the bag away as Lacey had asked. She brought it to her apartment and put it in a closet, without taking it out of the garbage bag.

At 10:52 A.M., Valerie Plauché called Lacey, saying she had gone to Lacey's apartment with Chloe McKenna and Shaiya Baer and had taken the feeding bag as asked. Valerie also mentioned that the police had been there, taking photographs and leaving with three bags of her stuff.

"She said she would never do anything to hurt Garnett," said Plauché. "It was a quick call because I was late for work."

Over the next hour, Valerie Plauché became increasingly uncomfortable about what she had done. The Fellowship was abuzz about the police searching Lacey's apartment while Garnett was on life support. And Shaiya Baer's warning not to remove possible evidence still rang in her ears.

At around 11:30 A.M., Valerie told a coworker about Lacey's request, saying that "something odd had happened" and that it was not "sitting well" with her. The coworker advised her to tell the Fellowship's director of nursing, Nancy Leopold, immediately. Valerie went off to find her at Hilltop House.

"She was somewhat upset," Leopold later testified. "Her voice was shaking . . . and she asked to speak to me privately."

Then Valerie told her how Lacey had asked her to remove a feeding bag from her apartment and get rid of it, without telling anyone.

Leopold then called Bob Scherer of the executive circle, which at the time was meeting about Lacey Spears and previous night's police search. After hearing this new information, Scherer said he would call her back later.

After learning from Valerie Plauché that police had searched her apartment, Lacey Spears made nine calls to

Oona Younger in quick succession, demanding to know who had said the police were arresting her.

"Lacey became very angry," Oona later told detectives.

At 12:37 P.M., Lacey posted an update on Facebook.

"My sweet baby Garnett has been declared brain dead!!!" she wrote. "THAT'S MY BABY BOY. I'M NOT READY TO LET HIM GO!!!"

Her posting elicited fifty replies, including one from April Chambers, whose fund for Garnett's medical expenses was now receiving substantial donations.

"I love you Lacey," she wrote. "I am so sorry."

Lacey's aunt, Sandra Newkoop, who lives in Texas, also posted a heartfelt comment.

"For what Ever [sic] reason Garnett's short journey is over here on Earth, But just beginning in Heaven! So Garnett the Great put on your wings and soar!"

Shawna Lynch appealed for prayers.

"Please say a prayer for Lacey Spears," she wrote on Lacey's timeline. "Her son Garnett is now an angel in heaven. Lord please be with Lacey. Lord give her the strength to be able to make it through this."

After sending it, Shawna called her mother-in-law, Jeannine Lynch, telling her that Garnett was near death on life support.

"Shawna called me and said, 'Lacey and Garnett need your prayers,'" recalled Jeannine. "I'm a praying woman, but I wanted to go one step closer."

So Jeannine immediately sent Lacey a friend request on Facebook, saying she was praying for her and Garnett.

"And within three or four minutes," she said, "Lacey accepted my friend request."

At 12:45 P.M., Lacey Spears was interviewed by the hospital's child abuse advocate, Dr. Jennifer Canter, in the presence of Detective Dan Carfi. Less than an hour earlier, Detective Carfi had taken the Poland Spring water bottle that Dr. Goltzman had ordered seized, and a plastic cup, to the Westchester County Police laboratory for analysis.

Once again, Lacey was asked about the days leading up to Garnett coding, and what exactly she fed her son through his G-tube.

Lacey told Dr. Canter that Garnett was given "elderberry care, breast milk, and a new diet of blended fruits and veggies" through his feeding tube. She added that she liked to add "a pinch of salt" for flavor.

She also speculated about Garnett accidentally causing his own death.

"Spears stated that Garnett once in a while would play with the syringe used for the GI feedings," Detective Carfi later wrote in his police report, "and it's possible he could have put something in the GI feeding tube."

At 3:00 that afternoon, Ramapo Police detectives Kirk Budnick and Greg Dunn arrived at the Maria Fareri Children's Hospital. They walked past Garnett's room and saw Lacey, her parents, and several friends inside.

Then they met with Dr. Jennifer Canter and Detective Carfi, who updated them on their interview with Lacey Spears. Dr. Canter told them that, based on Lacey's "demeanor" and on Garnett's medical history as reported by his mother, Lacey displayed distinct signs of Munchausen syndrome by proxy.

At 4:40 P.M., the three detectives commandeered a large conference room and began interviewing Lacey's parents and friends, to get a better idea of what had happened. Lacey was more than cooperative in facilitating the interviews.

"It was very strange," recalled Detective Budnick. "She was trying to run the show and say, 'You need to talk to this person. You need to talk to that one.' She was doing it, I felt, to get more attention. I don't think she was too concerned about us being there."

They first interviewed Oona Younger, who knew all about Garnett's G-tube and his medical problems. She told them that Lacey had called her the previous Friday, saying Garnett was having seizures and that she needed a car to take him to the hospital.

The detectives next interviewed Terry Spears, who asked them to speak up, because he was hard of hearing. Lacey's father said he had had a liver transplant and suffered from celiac and Crohn's diseases. He said he and his wife had driven to New York from Kentucky as soon as they heard how sick their grandson was.

At the beginning of the interview, Detective Carfi told Terry how sorry he was to hear from Lacey that Garnett's father, Blake, had died in a traffic accident.

"And he said, 'What are you talking about?'" said Carfi. "'Who's Blake?' I said, 'Garnett's father.' He goes, 'No, Garnett's father is Chris Hill. He's fine and lives in Alabama.'"

Then Carfi told Lacey's father that an investigation had been initiated into his grandson's present condition because a call had come in from child protective services and was being routinely followed up.

"I said to him that if at any time I thought his daughter was to become a target of this investigation, I would tell him."

At 6:44 P.M., as detectives interviewed her parents across the corridor, Lacey Spears informed her Facebook followers that she would soon be deciding when to turn off Garnett's life support.

"I don't even know what to say," she began. "The out pouring & support is so much appreciated. I never realized just how many love my little boy. However, at [this] time I would like for the hours we have left with G to be spent with his family. Sometime tomorrow I will make the decision to remove his life support. Please hold him close, send him love & just know he's going to fly high. Loving Garnett the Great!!!"

That night another fifty friends sent their tearful condolences, and there was an online candlelight vigil for Garnett.

"My candle is lit for you tonight," wrote Danielle Jolly, "in hopes you find peace and strength."

At 7:00 P.M., Nellie Grossenbacher, who had returned to the hospital, was summoned to the conference room for an interview.

"And they said, right from the beginning, 'We're here for Garnett. We don't care about Lacey,'" she said. "'We're here to find out what happened to this child.' And I still defended her."

Nellie told the detectives she knew all about Garnett's eating problems and his numerous hospital stays. But detectives made a special note when she mentioned that whenever Garnett was at her house, he ate everything without any problems.

After the interview, Nellie warned Lacey that she was definitely under investigation and needed to get a lawyer immediately.

"And she said, 'I didn't kill my kid,'" recalled Nellie. "I said, 'That's wonderful that you didn't kill your kid, but they believe you did, and you need to get a lawyer. You need to represent yourself and have yourself protected.'"

She also advised Lacey not to take Garnett off life support for the time being.

"And she asked why," recalled Nellie. "I said, 'You need to get a lawyer and figure this out, because if you take him off life support it's going to be a murder investigation. If you feel that the hospital did something, get every single record and don't take him off life support. And don't leave the hospital without all the records.'"

Nellie now suspected that Lacey had poisoned Garnett because she seemed unconcerned about collecting any medical evidence.

"If you didn't kill your kid, and you think the hospital did something," reasoned Nellie, "you are going to take every goddamn record from the hospital. And if your kid is legitimately sick, and you're not keeping him sick, you're going to have information to provide hospitals and say, 'Here's his medical history.' At least, I would."

At around 7:00 P.M., after getting off work, Valerie Plauché drove to Westchester Medical Center to see Garnett. She walked into his room and saw the little boy brain dead, on life support.

"He was lying in bed," she said, "with a lot of tubes hooked up, and he didn't have any life in him."

On the way out, she saw Lacey Spears.

"I just said hi and gave her a hug," said Valerie. "And that was all."

Shortly after arriving back at the Fellowship, Plauché received a call from Nancy Leopold, who had just spoken to Bob Scherer of the Fellowship's executive circle. She asked Valerie to type out a full account of Lacey's conversation that morning in an e-mail, and to send it to her.

When Leopold arrived at Valerie's Hilltop House apartment soon afterwards, Valerie was still working on it.

"She was sitting there while I typed it up," said Plauché, "and [sent it] to her e-mail address."

Her e-mail, which was sent at 7:53 P.M., gave her account of what happened:

> I received a call from Lacey at around 10:15 am. on Wednesday, January 22, 2014. She said she needed me to do something for her and that I could not tell anyone. I said ok. She asked me to go to her house and take the feeding bag off the machine in the living room and take it out and throw it away. I said ok. She asked if I could do it right now and I said I will try. She asked that I call her afterwards. I ran downstairs and asked Chloe to please come with me. Together we walked over to her house and went to the door, Shaiya & Lizzie were there. We said we had to get something for Lacey and Shaiya explained that the police had been there the night before which alarmed me. We all went downstairs and it took some time to figure out how to remove the bag from the machine. We took the bag and left and I said this is supposed to be a secret. I came home and stashed the bag away, thinking if the police were involved it might not be a good idea to throw it away. I called Lacey and said that Chloe came with me and Shaiya was there and the police had been there and taken pictures of everything and that I had gotten the bag.
> That is how I remember it.
> Valerie Plauché

Then Nancy Leopold asked Valerie for the feeding bag taken from Lacey's apartment, and Valerie went into her study, retrieved it from the closet, and handed it over.

Leopold then took the plastic garbage bag with the feeding bag inside to the Fellowship's offices in a nearby lodge. It was late and the medical office was closed, but Leopold had her own key. After letting herself in, she met

Dr. Gerald Karnow, who was working late. Then they both went into a small back room known as "the lab" and opened the combination lock to a storage room behind it.

Leopold took the garbage bag and opened the twist top, taking a quick glance inside. She saw what appeared to be "a plastic pouch and tubing," and closed it again.

She then placed it in a brown cardboard box, sealed it with tape, and wrote in large letters, "LEAVE FOR NANCY. DO NOT MOVE."

Then she called Bob Scherer, to let him know that Lacey's feeding bag was now safely under lock and key.

As Nancy Leopold carefully locked away the feeding bag, Lacey Spears had her third police interview. She was called into the conference room at 8:10 P.M., and came in crying. She kept asking what had happened to Garnett and why he was brain dead, repeatedly breaking down in tears, with her face buried in her folded arms.

When Detective Carfi asked her a question, Lacey suddenly "popped her head up," calmly replying, without any signs of distress. All three detectives were amazed by the transformation.

"That was super strange," explained Detective Budnick. "When she first came in the room, she's crying, 'Oh my child! Oh my child!' Dan asked her a question, and then no tears, nothing."

Detective Carfi told Lacey that they were investigating what had caused Garnett's medical condition. Once again, Lacey outlined Garnett's numerous medical problems and his inability to eat normally. She told them how she and Garnett had converted to their organic lifestyle and diet in Florida. And she pointed out that his sodium level had risen to two hundred when he was a baby and doctors could not explain why.

"I asked Lacey if she used salt during her preparation

17-year-old Lacey Spears in her 2004 Decatur High School Yearbook.

(Photo courtesy of the Spears family)

Decatur High School.

(Photo courtesy of John Glatt)

Growing up, Lacey was known to everyone as Lacey Bug.

(Photo courtesy of the Spears family)

In November 2007, 20-year-old Lacey proudly showed her friend Shawna Lynch her "baby bump." She later claimed to have had an abortion in Florida.

(Photo courtesy of Shawna Lynch)

Lacey's parents took out this ad in the Decatur High School yearbook in Lacey's senior year.

(Photo courtesy of the Spears family)

Lacey and JonJon, who she claimed was her son, at the nursery where she worked.

(Photo courtesy of Shawna Lynch)

The Cedar Key Apartments where Lacey and Rebecca shared an apartment.

(Photo courtesy of John Glatt)

At one point, Lacey and Shawna Lynch were inseparable until her mother-in-law, Jeannine Lynch, staged an intervention, as she was so concerned about Lacey's influence.

(Photo courtesy of Shawna Lynch)

Chris Hill had a short-lived affair with Lacey, before she dumped him. Later she would refuse to acknowledge him as Garnett's father, threatening him with the police.

(Photo courtesy of John Glatt)

Little Garnett playing with his toys at the Cedar Key Apartments.

(Photo courtesy of the Spears family)

Lacey posted this stock photograph on Facebook, claiming it was Garnett's father, Blake, who had died tragically in a traffic accident.

(Photo courtesy of Getty Images)

Lacey loved posing with Garnett for her Facebook friends all over America.

(Photo courtesy of the Spears family)

Lacey and Garnett in Clearwater, Florida, where his health seemed to improve for a time.

(Photo courtesy of the Spears family)

Garnett loved playing in the street outside his grandmother's house in Clearwater.

(Photo courtesy of the Spears family)

Lacey was proud of the strictly vegan diet she fed Garnett.

(Photo courtesy of the Spears family)

Lacey could be very moody and seemed depressed during her short visit to Decatur, Georgia from Florida.

(Photo courtesy of Shawna Lynch)

Lacey and Garnett joined the Fellowship Community in New York in November, 2012.

(Photo courtesy of John Glatt)

Garnett was much loved in the Fellowship Community where he was fondly known as the Little Mayor.

(Photo courtesy of the Spears family)

Lacey's living room in Tulip House, with Garnett's feeding machine to the right.

(Photo courtesy of the Ramapo Police Department)

The damning EEG video which prosecutors claimed showed Lacey carrying a connector tube and cup into the bathroom at Nyack Hospital to poison Garnett with salt.

(Photo courtesy of the Court Video Pool)

Lacey and Garnett lived at Tulip House in the Fellowship Community.

(Photo courtesy of the Ramapo Police Department)

Veteran detectives were speechless when they discovered this bizarre shrine to Garnett complete with salt on Lacey's kitchen table.

(Photo courtesy of the Ramapo Police Department)

Nyack Hospital doctors were baffled by Garnett's inexplicable rise in sodium, which would prove lethal.

(Photo courtesy of John Glatt)

Unconscious and on life-support, little Garnett Spears was air-lifted to Westchester Medical Center in the middle of a snowstorm in early January, 2014.

(Photo courtesy of John Glatt)

One of the dozens of photos of Garnett in Nyack Hospital that Lacey would constantly post on Facebook.

(Photo courtesy of Nellie Grossenbacher)

Lacey's mug shot after her arrest on June 17, 2014.

(Photo courtesy of the Westchester County Police)

The first day of Lacey's murder trial during the prosecution's opening statements.

(Photo courtesy of the Court Video Pool)

Terry and Rebecca Spears on the opening day of Lacey's trial at Westchester County Court.

(Photo courtesy of the Court Video Pool)

Westchester County Assistant District Attorney Doreen Lloyd delivered a powerful opening statement, where she branded Lacey as "a calculating child killer."

(Photo courtesy of the Court Video Pool)

Minutes before the prosecution's opening statement, Lacey broke down in tears at the defense table.

(Photo courtesy of the Court Video Pool)

Westchester County Court in White Plains, New York.

(Photo courtesy of John Glatt)

The lead prosecutor, Westchester County Assistant District Attorney Patricia Murphy.

(Photo courtesy of John Glatt)

Lacey's defense team of Stephen Riebling (left) and David Sachs (right).

(Photo courtesy of Gail Freund)

Lacey looks apprehensive during closing statements.

(Photo courtesy of the Court Video Pool)

Patricia Murphy delivered the prosecution's closing statements calling for the maximum sentence.

(Photo courtesy of the Court Video Pool)

At her sentencing, Judge Robert Neary told Lacey Spears that her crime was "unfathomable in its cruelty," before sentencing her to serve twenty years to life for the depraved indifference murder of her son, Garnett.

(Photo courtesy of the Court Video Pool)

Rebecca Spears comforts her father, Terry, after Lacey was sentenced to twenty years to life.

(Photo courtesy of the Court Video Pool)

The three main detectives on the case (from left to right), Kirk Budnick, Dan Carfi, and Greg Dunn at the commendation ceremony recognizing their success in bringing Lacey Spears to justice.

(Photo courtesy of Christine Carfi)

The Waldorf School's Memorial Card tribute to Garnett Spears.

(Photo courtesy of Nellie Grossenbacher)

of foods for Garnett," wrote Detective Dunn in his police report. "Lacey responded that she used very little salt and . . . only Himalayan salt. She would feed Garnett clear broths . . . and give him breast milk."

She then blamed the medical treatment he had received for causing his brain death. She told the investigators that on Monday afternoon, after being extubated, he was alert and talking to Nellie Grossenbacher and other friends from the Fellowship. Then, at around 9:00 Monday night, Garnett began thrashing around in his bed, complaining of headaches.

"I told Nurse Collette. I told Nurse Collette," she kept repeating to the detectives.

26

THE SMOKING GUN

At 9:00 A.M. on Thursday, Bob Scherer of the Fellowship Community's executive circle called the Ramapo Police Department. Detectives Kirk Budnick and Greg Dunn had been out all night, working on the case, and had just arrived back at their headquarters when the phone rang.

"He said, 'I think we need to talk,'" recalled Detective Budnick. "And then told me exactly how Valerie Plauché had got the phone call [from Lacey], and what happened."

As they were leaving for the Fellowship to pick up the feeding bag, Detective Budnick received another call, from White Plains attorney David Sachs, which went to voice mail. Sachs left a message saying that his firm, Riebling, Proto & Sachs, had been retained by Lacey Spears, and asking Detective Budnick to call him as soon as possible.

On the way to the Fellowship, Budnick called Detective Carfi, who had now been appointed lead detective in the case, with news of a possible breakthrough.

After hearing how Lacey had asked Valerie Plauché to secretly dispose of the feeding bag, Carfi wanted to bring Lacey Spears to the police station immediately, put her in an interview room, and interrogate her.

"He goes, 'We can't,'" recalled Carfi. "I said, 'What do you mean, we can't?'"

Then Budnick explained that he had just received a call from Lacey Spears's new attorney.

"I'm like, 'Oh shit,'" said Carfi. "So there goes that opportunity."

At 9:30 A.M., the two Ramapo detectives arrived at the Fellowship Community and met Matt Uppenbrink, who took them to the health center. There, they took possession of the eighteen-by-twelve-inch box, sealed by Nancy Leopold, that contained Lacey's feeding bag.

They then interviewed Valerie Plauché, who gave them a written statement about Lacey's call and what she had done.

The two detectives brought the box back to Ramapo Police headquarters, where it was put in an evidence locker.

"That was the smoking gun," explained Detective Carfi. "That was the thing that convinced the investigators, their bosses, and the D.A.'s office that this young lady had harmed her child. Now we could really focus on Lacey. We've got to get into her life and see what's going on. Why did she do this?"

Just after 10:00 A.M., Dr. Carey Goltzman performed the second clinical brain death examination on Garnett Spears. The little boy now met all the criteria for brain death.

"I made the call," said the doctor, "and I declared this youngster, Garnett Spears, brain dead as of 10:20 A.M. on the twenty-third of January 2014."

Dr. Goltzman then called the Westchester County medical examiner, to inform him, as well as the organ donor network, to determine which organs could be procured for transplantation purposes.

Two minutes after her son had been declared legally dead, Lacey Spears posted a photograph of him on Facebook. Underneath it she wrote, "Garnett the Great journeyed onward today at 10:20 am."

She then put dozens of candles on her home page in his memory.

Her dramatic post unleashed a torrent of heartfelt condolences from her friends, offering love and support in her hour of need.

"Words cannot express how heartbroken I am for you," wrote one. "Garnett was so full of life and you could tell in his smile just how much he loved you."

"Heaven received a beautiful angel today," wrote another. "Please pray for Lacey Spears as she needs love and strength to deal with the passing of her beautiful baby boy today."

"Fly high Garnett ♥" wrote another. "Your Mama gave you as much love in your 5 years that the rest of us could only hope to feel in a million lifetimes. Hopefully she feels all the love we have for her."

On Friday morning, frustrated that Lacey Spears had ignored his repeated attempts to contact her, Chris Hill posted a photograph of his smiling son on Facebook. Underneath it, he wrote:

This is my other son Garnett and he is 5 years old. I never get to see him because his mom just up, and moved to New York. Well, Friday he had some severe seizures that caused his brain to swell, and now is brain dead and on life support. Even though I don't get to see him, I feel like he's been with me this hole [sic] time. IM not going to lie. I cried for hours when I found this out, and it will continue to hurt till the day I die. Our children aren't supposed to go before us, but if it does happen, it's the worst feeling in the world.

Then, after Shawna Lynch told him that Garnett had been taken off life support, he sent Lacey a barrage of Facebook messages.

"What happened?" he asked her.

I can't read any of your newsfeed, but I heard about Garnett last night . . . I can't stop crying . . . I know I wasn't part of his life, but I was waiting for the day when he would try and find me :(IM so sorry Lacey. I know you must be in a really bad place right now . . . I know I am. I know IM the last person you wanted to hear from, and IM sorry if I made things worse on you, because that's not my intentions. Even though I wasn't in Garnett's life, I still love him, and miss him like I was. I looked at your photos about once every 2 weeks just to see him grow. You can respond if you want. If you don't . . . that's ok too. I know he was your life . . . IM so sorry.

Over the next few hours, Hill's posts became increasingly angry.

I know he's my son. IM 100% positive. He looked exactly like me when I was a kid . . . EXACTLY. This hurts me too. I cried all night and day. I keep staring at his pic, and it's killing me inside. Only reason I wasn't a part of his life, is because you wouldn't let me! I tried, and you know I did . . . I just

want you to acknowledge that. I Begged you! . . . I'm
not trying to make you feel bad. I know you have
enough on your mind, but if you want to talk about
him, I would like to know how smart, and fun he
was . . . don't make this awkward, because it's not,
and IM not going to be mean to you. I just want to
know him.

At 12:15 P.M., detectives Carfi, Budnick, and Dunn met
with Dr. Jennifer Canter and renal specialist Dr. Robin
Matloff in a conference room at Westchester Medical
Center. Dr. Matloff had now reviewed Garnett's medical
records and told the investigators that although hypernatremia can be caused by diabetes insipidus, that cause
had now been ruled out.

He told them that all of Garnett's organs had been
working perfectly, and he agreed with Dr. Canter that "no
medical condition" could have caused Garnett's lethal rise
in sodium. It had to have come from an outside source.

Rockland County Child Protective Services investigator Vanessa Torres, who was also at the meeting, said her
agency would begin tracking down all Garnett Spears's
medical and CPS records from Alabama, Florida, and
Tennessee.

At 3:30 P.M., Lacey Spears set up a PayPal account so
that well-wishers could send her donations. She made a
Google search for PayPal, and then typed in "Send
Money. Pay Online or Set Up a Merchant's Account—
PayPal."

She signed up for a PayPal account and logged in.

That afternoon, Lacey Spears's sister and grandmother finally arrived at Westchester Medical Center.

"She was really devastated," said Rebecca Spears,

"and distraught that her child had passed away. It was very scary. Just confusing times, not understanding what was going on."

At 4:35 P.M., investigators called Rebecca into the conference room for an interview.

"I thought this was normal," she said. "A child has become ill, nobody really knows why, and unfortunately he's passed away. And so yeah, it only made sense that they would be investigating. None of us realized that they were looking at Lacey, that they were thinking she had done something."

Rebecca told the detectives that her nephew Garnett and been in and out of hospitals since birth. She said that his father was a man named Chris, who had denied Garnett was his and wanted nothing to do with him.

She said that the last time she had seen Lacey and Garnett was in Clearwater at Christmas, and he had been fine. She also stated that Lacey had had a "falling out" with her grandmother, resulting in Lacey taking Garnett to New York. She said that Lacey was a "good mother," and she did not understand why the police were involved.

At 6:38 P.M., after more than a dozen Facebook messages from Chris Hill, alternating between anger and conciliatoriness, Lacey finally answered him.

"I need a number to reach you at!" she wrote him.

After Hill typed in his number, Lacey replied, "I'll call you [when] I can. Right now I just can't. Soon, very soon."

"It's OK," he replied. "I understand. I'm just glad you said something . . . I know he was your world."

"My heart & soul," she answered.

Then she stopped replying to his messages, as he begged her not to shut him out. It would be another two weeks before he heard from Lacey again.

* * *

At 7:35 P.M., the detectives gathered the entire Spears family in the conference room to explain why they were investigating Garnett's death. Detective Budnick began by saying that whenever a young child dies, there's a hospital and police protocol to try to find out what happened. He added that it was quite possible that they might never know what had happened to Garnett.

"I'll never forget the look on Lacey's face," said Detective Greg Dunn, who was sitting directly across the table from her. "It was like a look of relief. A smile came over her face, like, 'I'm okay. This is something that's never going to be found.'"

During the interview, Lacey's grandmother, Peggy Florence, was crying. When detectives began asking her questions, Tina Spears said her mother was too upset to talk to investigators.

Then, suddenly, Lacey stunned the investigators by declaring, "If I mixed something that killed Garnett, it's not my fault. I didn't murder him."

After the interview, Detective Budnick took Terry Spears outside for a quiet word. He told Terry how Lacey had phoned Valerie Plauché and asked her to go secretly into Lacey's apartment and get rid of Garnett's feeding bag.

"I don't think he could comprehend what I was saying to him," recalled Budnick. "I was trying to keep Terry in touch with what was going on."

At 8:00 Thursday night, the three investigators entered Lacey's apartment with a new search warrant. This time they were looking for the second feeding bag with milky liquid in it, which was in the kitchen garbage can. They also wanted all the equipment for the gastrostomy feeding machine.

"The residence was in the same condition as it was when we had left," said Detective Dunn, "other than the clear bag that had been hanging from the apparatus was gone."

It was the first time Detective Carfi had been inside, and he was immediately struck by all the stuffed and ceramic owls lining the bookshelves.

"The rest of the home was very neat," he remembered. "Everything seemed to have its place. There was a toy box on the floor that was open, but all the toys were in it."

As Detective Dunn took more photographs, his colleagues seized the IV pole and feeding machine. They took the feeding bag containing milk-colored liquid from the kitchen garbage and a white box sitting on the couch that contained everything needed to work the feeding machine. They also seized the blue canvas bag with Garnett's initials on it, which had been attached to the IV pole. Inside it, they found a ten-milliliter syringe, three feeding bags, and two empty MIC-KEY extension bags, which were missing the connector tubing.

After leaving Lacey's apartment, the detectives drove across the Fellowship to Hilltop House, to reinterview Oona Younger, who had called earlier and said she had new information. She told the detectives that Lacey had given Dr. Goltzman an incomplete picture of Garnett's medical issues when Garnett had first arrived at Westchester Medical Center.

"She was being untruthful and not telling him everything," Oona said, adding that, when Oona had tried to interrupt, Lacey had given her "the most evil face you could imagine."

On Friday night, Lacey's Facebook friends held another online candlelight vigil for Garnett. Back in Decatur, Rania Cottingham was so worried about Lacey that she instant messaged Rebecca Spears to see if she could do anything.

"I'm at a loss for words," she wrote. "Do you know anything about arrangements? If you guys need anything at all, please don't hesitate to ask me . . . Lacey and G inspired me more than I can ever explain."

A few hours later, Rebecca replied.

"Knowing that people are surrounding us is helpful right now!" she wrote. "G is going to save other children's lives. He is an organ donor. [Lacey] wants to have him cremated and a mark placed on the Spears family plot. [The Fellowship Community] is going to throw him a celebration of life party. Outside of that I don't know of any definite plans."

Late that night, Lacey did a Google search for the exact number of days Garnett had lived. She typed in a search for "days between December 3, 2008 through January 23, 2014." The answer was 1,877 days.

Soon afterwards, Lacey uploaded a video of Garnett on Facebook, together with a new message.

"My baby! My baby!" she wrote. "Give me my baby back!!! My Heart!!! My soul!!!"

27

"THEY THINK I HURT HIM!"

Early Friday morning, January 24, attorney David Sachs sent Detective Budnick a fax after getting no reply to his voice message the previous day.

"Dear Detective Budnick," he wrote. "I am writing to advise you that my office is being retained by Lacey Spears with regard to your department's investigation into circumstances concerning the recent passing of her son. I would like to speak to you as soon as possible on this matter. I'd appreciate it very much if you return my call as soon as you have the chance to do so."

Later that morning, Detective Budnick gave the feeding bag that Valerie Plauché had taken from Lacey Spears's apartment, as well as the second bag found in Lacey's kitchen garbage, to Detective Dan Carfi. Carfi immediately brought them, together with the feeding machine and all its accessories, to the Westchester County Police Department's laboratory for testing.

Because it was now a joint investigation between the Ramapo Police Department and the Westchester County

Department of Public Safety of a possible homicide, it was decided to use the Westchester County laboratory to expedite things.

"We use the New York State Police lab in Albany," explained Detective Budnick. "Westchester was a much faster analysis."

For the next year, lead detective Dan Carfi would work closely with the two Ramapo detectives on what would become an increasingly complex investigation.

A few hours later, after testing both feeding bags, forensic toxicologist Christopher Cording reported back that both contained high concentrations of sodium.

The case had now become a murder investigation, with Lacey Spears as the prime suspect.

On Friday afternoon, the Fellowship Community asked Lacey to move out, citing misrepresentations in her original application to join. Later, Lacey would say she felt betrayed.

"I thought Matt Uppenbrink was my friend," she explained, "and then he told me to move out in a week. They never asked for my side of what had happened."

That day, a Fellowship Community administrator sent out a cryptic memo to all residents, informing them of Garnett Spears's death.

"While [Garnett] was in intensive care," it read, "there were circumstances surrounding his condition that were of concern to the medical staff, which prompted them to notify the police, and also child protective services."

At around 6:00 P.M., Lacey Spears researched different ways to commit suicide by using her diabetic mother's supply of insulin. Among her thirty Google searches over the next half hour were "Insulin overdose for non-diabetic," "What happens if a non-diabetic injects insulin," and "How much insulin would kill you?" She also searched for "Kenneth Barlow: the first documented case of murder by insulin."

At 7:33 P.M., she instant messaged a friend back in Decatur.

"These fucking people believe I hurt him!!!" she wrote. "Never!!!!"

"I know you would never hurt him," came the reply. "You gave him a great life in his short years, he was a lucky little boy to have you for his mommy."

A few minutes later, Lacey called April Chambers, whose fund for Lacey and Garnett now had $1,300 in it. Lacey asked her to change the name of the fund from Garnett's Medical Expenses to just Expenses.

"I didn't feel comfortable with that," said Chambers, "because that money was supposed to be for Garnett and not for her to get a lawyer. So I closed the account and refunded everyone their money."

When Lacey tried unsuccessfully to access the PayPal account, she was livid. She then sent April a furious instant message.

"These mother fuckers think I hurt him!!!!" she wrote. "I had to get a lawyer!!!! Lost my job and home too."

"I'm so sorry, Lacey," Chambers replied. "Why do they think that?"

"That's my son," Lacey wrote back. "My son that's brain dead."

"Like, at that point, I just knew in my heart that she had done it," said April. "And I didn't ever actually confront her because I didn't want her to stop talking to me. If she admitted something to me, I wanted to be able to tell the police."

That evening, Detective Dan Carfi managed to access Lacey's Hippy-HappyMomma Facebook account. He saw numerous photographs of Garnett in hospital rooms and Lacey's postings to friends while he was lying brain dead in the Westchester Medical Center.

He then began making arrangements to subpoena all of Lacey's various social media accounts as evidence.

"After she got her lawyer," said Carfi, "Lacey started deleting stuff. She tried to cover her tracks."

Late Friday night, Lacey began another series of Internet searches, this time about overdosing on sleeping pills. She asked, "Is taking an overdose of sleeping pills an effective way of committing suicide?"

28

IT'S HOMICIDE

At 9:40 A.M. on Saturday, the three detectives went to Westchester Medical Center to reinterview the Spears family and were told that the family had left several hours earlier. Lacey and her sister had checked into the Comfort Inn in Hawthorne, New York, in a room being paid for by the Fellowship. Her parents and grandmother were in a nearby Super 8 motel in Nanuet, New York. Detective Dan Carfi sent a plainclothes officer in to stake out the Comfort Inn and watch Lacey.

The detectives then went to the Westchester County Medical Examiner's office for Garnett Spears's autopsy. Several hours earlier, the deputy medical examiner, Dr. Aleksandar Milovanovic, had taken possession of Garnett's body after his heart, liver, kidneys, and spleen had been removed for transplantation.

Dr. Milovanovic had already been briefed about the case by Westchester County Assistant District Attorney Christine Hatfield, who asked him to check for any of the medical conditions his mother had reported. She also told the medical examiner that Garnett's sodium level had inexplicably soared from 144 to 182.

After Detective Carfi had formally identified the body, Dr. Milovanovic began the autopsy. He began with a preliminary external examination, photographing Garnett's body and taking X-rays to check for any bone fractures or other injuries.

Then he carried out an internal examination, opening up the body's cavities to check the remaining organs, finding nothing wrong with them. He then examined the child's brain, which had been swollen and compressed in the skull.

"So there was no evidence of trauma to the brain," explained Dr. Milovanovic. "There was no contusion. There was no tumor. There were no hemorrhages."

Then, as the three investigators and the assistant district attorney looked on, the forensic pathologist examined Garnett's gastrointestinal tract. He inspected the esophagus, stomach, and small and large intestines, looking for any evidence of disease, as reported by his mother.

"Everything was normal," said Dr. Milovanovic, who could find no signs that Garnett suffered from Crohn's disease or celiac disease.

He also submitted cultures of Garnett's stool to the Westchester County microbiology laboratory to see whether there was any bacteria that would cause infection of the intestine and diarrhea.

"All the results came back as negative, and that was verified by my histology," he said. "There was no inflammation to cells in the tissue. So there were no infections."

After reviewing all the records from Nyack Hospital and the Westchester Medical Center and his own thorough examination of Garnett's body, Dr. Milovanovic determined that Garnett Spears had died from hypernatremia caused by being fed sodium from an outside source. And the manner of death was homicide.

Lacey Spears was busy that morning. After driving out to the Fellowship Community to pack up her and Garnett's belongings, she returned to her room at the Comfort Inn. At 2:00 P.M., she drove to the George M. Holt Funeral Home in Haverstraw, New York, to discuss Garnett's cremation and funeral arrangements.

Over the previous several days, April Chambers had been texting Lacey, asking if there was anything she could do to help.

"I was trying to fish for information," she explained. "I would send her three or four messages and she wouldn't say anything. Like she wouldn't give me information at all."

Then, on Saturday morning, which happened to be April's young daughter Priscilla's birthday, Lacey sent her an instant message.

"Please light a special candle in memory of Garnett at Priscilla's party," she wrote. "Don't have to say why just burn a candle for him. He's [sic] be so thrilled to special [sic] with your bug!"

Just after 4:00 P.M., the three detectives arrived at the Comfort Inn with a search warrant to seize Lacey Spears's iPhone, iPad, and laptop computer. First, Detective Dan Carfi went into the hotel and informed the manager that he was there to execute a search warrant.

"I told her that it was going to be a very quiet thing," recalled Detective Carfi. "We're not going to bust doors down or anything like that."

Then, with detectives Budnick and Dunn, he waited in the parking area for the Spears family to return. Soon afterwards, Terry Spears pulled up with his wife and mother-in-law and went into the hotel to join his two daughters, who were already there.

At 4:50 P.M., the investigators went to room 129 and knocked on the door. When the door opened, Detective Carfi went in.

"I remember seeing mom sitting on the bed," he said. "Lacey's right in front of me, and Rebecca's standing next to mom."

He then asked Lacey's father to step outside, where detectives Budnick and Dunn were waiting.

"We wanted to separate Terry," explained Detective Carfi, "because we told him, when we had first met him, that we would let him know if things changed."

Then Carfi informed Terry Spears that this was now a murder investigation and that it was focusing on Lacey. On hearing that, Spears collapsed to the ground, on one knee, holding his head.

"He was visibly upset," said Detective Carfi. "He knew something was terribly wrong."

Carfi then went back into the room and told Lacey that he needed her iPhone, her iPad, and the laptop that she had been using in the hospital. He said he was aware that she now had a lawyer and that he had not come to question her.

"She hands me the phone," said Carfi, "and all her chargers, too. She won't speak to me at all. Nothing. Not a word."

Then Rebecca said that her sister had been using Rebecca's iPad at the hospital, and that he could take it, too.

"We were all really shocked when they turned up at the motel," Rebecca recalled. "We really didn't understand why, and we were all just very confused and scared. It's not normal for us to have the police show up [with] a warrant."

Then Terry Spears went out to his car to collect Lacey's laptop, which he handed over.

After giving Terry a copy of the search warrant, the detectives left.

"Lacey never said a word," said Carfi. "We weren't going to question her."

Later, Rebecca would say that this was the first time her family realized that police suspected Lacey of harming Garnett.

"That's when it finally really hit me," she said. "You really think that she's done something wrong."

Late Sunday morning, *Journal News* crime reporter Shawn Cohen arrived at the Fellowship Community. The previous night, a routine check with the Westchester County Medical Examiner's office had revealed that a five-year-old child had died at the Maria Fareri Children's Hospital under unexplained circumstances.

"There was no name," said Cohen. "I don't even think there was an age. There was a child's death, and they weren't even calling it suspicious at that time."

That morning, Cohen worked his police sources, learning that the victim was a young boy who lived with his mother at the Fellowship Community in Chestnut Ridge. Cohen then drove over to the Fellowship's grounds and started snooping around, discovering that the dead boy's name was Garnett Spears and that he had lived there with his mother, Lacey.

"I also found out that the police had visited the Fellowship and were asking questions," said Cohen. "I got the sense that there is a lot more."

When Matt Uppenbrink heard that a reporter was asking questions about Garnett, he ordered Cohen to leave.

"It's a very private place," said Cohen, "so they were instantly suspicious of me. Matt Uppenbrink confirmed the names and that he didn't believe anything was suspicious."

On his way out, Uppenbrink told Cohen that everyone there was "grieving" for Garnett, who had not been feeling well for some time.

"He was a lively kid, a sweetheart," said Uppenbrink. "He was loved and is loved."

Juani Tantillo, whose mother, Linda, had died at the Fellowship Community a day after Garnett, said everyone had already been instructed not to discuss Garnett's death with reporters.

"The people at the Fellowship are private," she said. "It's such a sensitive issue."

29

THE WAR ROOM

On Monday, January 27, at 10:00 A.M., detectives Dan Carfi, Kirk Budnick, and Greg Dunn met in a large conference room at the Westchester County Police headquarters in Hawthorne, New York. It would be the first of many status meetings in what they dubbed the "War Room." Over the next year, they would see more of each other than their families, working together on the Lacey Spears investigation.

Although the Westchester County Police Department had been appointed the lead agency, it would work hand in glove with the Ramapo Police.

The three detectives complemented each other, making a formidable team. A self-confessed type A personality, Dan Carfi was wiry, compact, and detail oriented. He also was a weekend biker with a shaved head and two full sleeves of tattoos. Deceptively easygoing, with a smartly clipped mustache, Kirk Budnick was thoughtful, methodical, and didn't miss a thing. Meanwhile, the debonair Greg Dunn, who had snow-white hair and a mustache, often lurked in the background, quietly observing—the perfect foil for his longtime partner.

That morning, they were joined by several Westchester County assistant district attorneys as they reviewed all the evidence so far, dividing up future interviews and groundwork between them. Now six days into the investigation, all the investigators had worked around the clock and had hardly slept. It would be a huge undertaking, spanning three states and hundreds of interviews.

"We're going to have to do this kid's timeline," explained Detective Carfi. "From when he was born till today. We'll have to get every hospital record and look at everything."

From now on, the three detectives from the two police departments on either side of the Hudson would bond into one tight unit. Their motto became "Justice for Garnett," and they would end up becoming close friends.

In the beginning, they met in the War Room every couple of days for progress reports and exchange of information. They posted numerous photographs, to-do lists, notes, and other snippets on chalkboards mounted on half a dozen easels spread out everywhere. There also was a large monitor screen at the front for PowerPoint presentations.

"We really started living it," said Carfi, "to the point where I would be working on things at four o'clock in the morning and text Kirk, 'Are you up?' 'Yeah, I'm up, let's talk.'"

After that first meeting, Detective Carfi brought Lacey's iPhone, iPad, and laptop to the Westchester County computer forensic unit for analysis. Lacey's father had provided her passwords. Then he began working on another search warrant, allowing a computer forensics expert to download evidence from Lacey's iPhone, which contained thousands of photographs, videos, texts, and so-cial media postings.

As the investigators convened in the War Room, Lacey Spears and her family met their new criminal attorneys, David Sachs and Stephen Riebling, for the first time, in their law offices in White Plains, New York. They all sat around a large table in the conference room, and for the next several hours Lacey told them her story.

"We discussed a lot," recalled David Sachs. "Just a general background of Lacey's life, including what had happened in the hospital."

Later, Sachs would describe it as an "emotional" meeting with their new client, who was still recovering from her son's death.

"Lacey [had] the appearance of a mother who was shell-shocked," he remembered. "Her son passes away [and] at the same time she's told . . . that she's a murder suspect in his own death. I'm no psychologist, but to say the weight of the world is on your shoulders at that point is probably an understatement."

Then the attorneys drafted a strategy to protect Lacey's rights until they had a clearer picture of what the West-chester County District Attorney's office planned to do.

"The advice is always don't talk to the police any-more," said Stephen Riebling, "because you're under investigation. If there's going to be any communication, it has to go through your attorney."

The high-powered attorneys also came to a financial arrangement with Terry Spears, which has never been dis-closed.

"These aren't wealthy people," said Sachs. "These are people of modest means . . . who have invested a lot of money in our legal defense because they believe in her innocence."

* * *

After the meeting, the Spears family went back to the Super 8 in Nanuet, where they were all now staying to save money. Detective Dan Carfi arrived shortly afterwards to bring Lacey to the medical examiner's office and formally identify Garnett's body. When she refused to go, her father went instead.

"And so we bring dad over," remembered Carfi, "and they set up Garnett in a viewing window inside a glass enclosure, with a little light on him, and he's covered."

Then Terry Spears stood outside the glass for a few minutes, saying good-bye to Garnett.

"It was very sad," said Carfi. "That's his only grandson, and he seemed like a good guy. So we totally understood, but we also knew we had a job to do. And that Garnett needed some kind of help, some kind of justice. No question."

While her father was identifying Garnett's body, Lacey Spears tried to access funds collected by well-wishers for his medical treatment. At 3:49 P.M., the fund's co-organizer, Rachel Landers, called the Westchester County Police tips hotline to report Lacey's suspicious activity.

30

"GET THOSE TAPES"

On Tuesday, January 28, the *Journal News* printed its first story about Garnett Spears's mysterious death. Under the headline "Police Investigate Death of Chestnut Ridge 5-Year-Old," the brief story revealed that the Westchester County Police were probing Garnett's death, with the assistance of the Ramapo Police.

"However, they noted," wrote reporter Shawn Cohen, "there were no obvious signs of foul play, such as bruising or broken bones."

It quoted Rebecca Spears saying that Lacey had brought Garnett to Nyack Hospital with a stomach virus, and he had died several days later.

Rebecca explained that her nephew had suffered "chronic ear infections and dietary problems" and had been "in and out of hospitals for years." She said it was "standard protocol" for the police to investigate an unexplained death of a child and that she was confident that "no wrongdoing" would be found.

"Lacey was a wonderful mother," Rebecca said. "She

loved her son and still loves her son very much. He was her whole life. She's mourning a terrible loss here."

As soon as the *Journal News* story was published on-line, the Westchester County Police tip line was inundated with calls from Lacey's friends.

"My phone was blowing up," recalled Detective Dan Carfi, "as soon as her friends started seeing [the newspaper] stuff. They would say, 'I think you should know about this.' And then they would start telling us all this crazy stuff."

At 10:00 A.M., detectives Budnick and Dunn drove to the Green Meadow Waldorf School to reinterview Carol Grieder, who besides being a kindergarten teacher is also a registered nurse. They were discussing how Lacey could have fed Garnett salt in the Nyack Hospital room when Grieder suddenly asked if they had seen the video from the EEG machine. It was something no one had even thought of.

"And we were like, 'What video?'" said Detective Budnick. "And she said EEGs have video and audio. And that's when I called up the D.A.'s office and said, 'We need a subpoena immediately. Get those tapes.'"

That morning, Nellie Grossenbacher went to the Super 8 motel in Nanuet to collect a sweater and a Lego set from Lacey. She walked into the motel room where Lacey was huddled with her family.

"She was waiting for his ashes," Nellie recalled. "And as soon as I got there, she said, 'Did you see the papers? What's everyone saying at the school? What are they thinking?'"

During their brief meeting, Lacey never mentioned Garnett or how sorry she was about losing him.

"It's all about her," said Nellie, "and I think that she loved the limelight that she got out of this."

Late that afternoon, Rebecca Spears flew back to Alabama, leaving Lacey, her parents, and her grandmother behind in New York. A few hours later, Lacey's aunt, uncle, and two cousins arrived to help her pack up her stuff and arrange shipping to Lacey's parents' farm in Kentucky, where she had decided to live.

The police investigation now began to focus on Decatur, Alabama. Detective Carfi contacted the Decatur Police Department, asking them to interview Garnett's real father, Chris Hill, and several of Lacey's friends who had called with promising tips.

That afternoon, detectives Budnick and Dunn began interviewing some of Garnett's pediatric doctors. They first met with Dr. Kenneth Zatz in his Nyack office. Dr. Zatz told them Garnett had been his office eight times since March 2013. He described Garnett as "a happy, healthy boy" and completely normal except for his gastrostomy tube and a perforated left ear.

Lacey had told him that she tube-fed Garnett nightly with pumped breast milk and had him on the Gut and Psychology Syndrome diet, an intense nutritional program to heal the gut lining with various broths and other soothing foods.

"Lacey accompanied Garnett by herself to all the office visits," Dr. Zatz told the police. "She stood out among mothers as being very respectful to me. Many questions were answered as 'Yes, sir' or 'No, sir.' I remember thinking that she must have come from a military family, or it was her Southern upbringing."

The two detectives then drove to Princeton, New Jersey,

to meet Garnett's pediatric gastroenterologist, Dr. Ivan Darenkov. He told them he had first seen Garnett in April 2013, when his mother complained that he was not eating well and had been diagnosed with celiac disease. He told detectives that he had repeatedly asked Lacey to send him records of previous evaluations and surgeries, but she never had.

"It was not clear to me what the reason for the [G-tube] surgery was," he said. "I recommended a feeding evaluation to see what could be the problem. Mom never followed my advice."

Dr. Darenkov said Lacey had "a very flat affect" and was often evasive.

"Lots of time, she would respond with long pauses or silences," he said. "I did think [it was] due to the trauma of her late husband's death, as she relayed to me [at] the first appointment."

At 8:46 A.M. Wednesday, after not seeing any Facebook postings from Lacey Spears for several days, Rania Cottingham sent Lacey's sister, Rebecca, an instant message. She wrote that she had been online, looking for Garnett's obituary, and had come across the *Journal News* story about some kind of police investigation.

"I was just curious," she wrote. "Investigating what?!?! What the hell do they think? What is going on? I'm scared and hurting for Lacey, I'm worried about her . . ."

Rebecca replied a half hour later, explaining that, under New York law, all deaths must be investigated, whatever the person's age.

"It's also to help determine what happened," Rebecca wrote. "There may have been a mistake made by one of the hospitals. It is unclear at this time."

"Oh I was getting worried," Rania replied. "I hope they

find out what was wrong, but I hate she's having to go through that . . . Is she doing okay? I mean I know she can't be doing great, but my heart hurts for her . . . Are you there with her?"

"She's holding up the best she can," Rebecca answered. "She no longer wishes to live in New York. She wants to be closer to family. She is unsure if [she] wants to live in Kentucky with our parents or in Florida with our grandmother at this time."

Rania then asked Rebecca to send Lacey her love, saying she didn't expect her to be on Facebook at such a difficult time.

"No problem," replied Rebecca. "I'm sure in time she will reach out to you and others. Right now she [is] still in a hazed shock from everything."

Early on Thursday afternoon, reporter Shawn Cohen called Rebecca Spears's cell phone to speak to Lacey. Rebecca said that Lacey was asleep and asked him to give her sister time to mourn the death of her son.

Now, concerned about what people were saying about her, Lacey began blocking many of her friends on Facebook. She also started deleting as many of her past social media postings as she could.

"She blocked me on Facebook," said Mallory McWhorter. "It was random people. Lacey didn't know if they thought she had murdered her son or not."

At 2:15 Thursday afternoon, a week after Garnett Spears had been officially declared dead, Ramapo detectives Kirk Budnick and Greg Dunn were back at the Fellowship to interview administrator Bob Scherer. Scherer told them that Lacey had now been "terminated" from her job there and had removed all her personal property.

He then gave them permission to search Lacey's basement apartment and to take anything relating to their investigation of Garnett's death.

"The furniture was gone," said Detective Dunn. "There
were some boxes that had been left behind, and some food
items, specifically a couple of containers of salt."

After the search, they seized the salt, some bags of garbage, and more feeding bags found in the basement garbage. All the property was then brought back to Ramapo
Police headquarters to be analyzed later.

On Friday, January 31, the *Journal News* ran a second
story, under the headline "Chestnut Ridge Case: Mother
Mourns Her Little Prince." Reporter Shawn Cohen had
now accessed Lacey Spears's Twitter account, revealing
a whole new dimension to the story.

"The mother of a 5-year-old child," it began, "used social media to document her years-long struggle to care
for her often sickly child, whose recent death is being investigated by police."

The story included Twitter extracts, such as Lacey's
November 2009 posting: "My Sweet Angel Is In The
Hospital For The 23rd Time :(Please Pray He Gets To
Come Home Soon." Another read "Please Pray 4 My Lit-
tle Prince. He Has Another Bad Ear Infection :) Poor
Baby Boy."

The story also printed the Fellowship Community
memorandum, circulated after Garnett's death, which
mentioned that concerned doctors had called in police
and child protective services.

A spokesperson from the Westchester County District
Attorney's office was quoted as saying that they were still
awaiting toxicology results from the medical examiner
before deciding whether to pursue criminal charges.

Once again, Rebecca Spears was quoted, saying Garnett "meant everything to Lacey." This would be the last interview she would ever give the *Journal News*, as the whole Spears family battened down the hatches.

A few hours after the story appeared, Detective Joseph Callero of the Westchester County Department of Public Safety's Forensic Investigations Unit began an in-depth analysis of Lacey Spears's iPhone 4. It ultimately would take him two weeks to physically extract everything on it, including deleted texts and phone calls. There also were twenty-three thousand photographs and videos, including 215 photographs taken between January 11 and January 24—the day after doctors officially declared Garnett dead.

The eventual extraction report would run to almost eighteen hundred pages.

Later they would obtain her complete social media records by subpoena. These contained almost fifty thousand pages from her various Facebook accounts alone as well as from her MySpace, Instagram, and Twitter accounts.

Late that afternoon, the George M. Holt Funeral Home informed Lacey that Garnett's ashes were ready for collection.

"Hi Lacey," wrote a funeral home employee. "I wasn't sure if you knew that everything is ready for you to come in and sign? I will be at the front desk and the front door is open."

Soon after collecting her son's ashes, Lacey flew to Scottsville, Kentucky, moving into the Spears family farm with her parents and brother, Daniel. The garage would be converted into a room where she would live for the next few months. She felt certain that that the police investigation would soon fizzle out, and then she could move back to Florida and have another baby.

31

On Saturday, February 1, Lacey once again tried unsuccessfully to log into the PayPal account to access Garnett's Medical Expenses. When she couldn't, she immediately texted April Chambers.

"I can't get logged in," Lacey wrote. "Can you see if you can log in? I haven't changed anything."

Soon afterwards, April informed Lacey that the account was now closed.

"Lacey," she wrote, "I have no idea what is going on currently. I do know this, I don't want to be in the middle of it anymore. I have refunded everyone their money. If you would like to set up your own accounts to have donations sent to then please by all means go for it, but Rachel and I decided at this point the best thing to do is delete the accounts and step away from the situation."

Right after receiving her text, Lacey unfriended April, and Rachel Landers, on Facebook and never spoke to them again.

* * *

A few hours later, Lacey Spears was back on Facebook for the first time in more than a week. She had a new cell phone and a special message for the dwindling number of friends who had stayed loyal to her.

"Thank you all for the love, light and support," she wrote. "There will be a service for Garnett. I will inform you all when I know more. Hold my little boy close to your hearts."

There were twenty-eight responses, and a couple of days later a group calling itself Friends of Lacey Spears launched a new appeal to raise money for her.

"[We] have set up this fund," wrote the anonymous Clearwater-based organizer on Facebook, "to have a memorial for Garnett and a sweet memory that his Mama can visit when she is back in Florida on Honeymoon Island. Please share and help us meet this goal."

On Sunday, detectives Budnick and Dunn interviewed Dr. Kevin McSherry, who had been the attending physician at Nyack Hospital when Lacey brought Garnett in. The doctor said Garnett had been stable when he arrived at the hospital and that he did not believe the boy had suffered any seizures, as reported by his mother.

"Dr. McSherry . . . decided to admit Garnett for observation," wrote Detective Dunn in his subsequent police report. "He suspected the possibility of Munchausen by proxy syndrome."

At 7:40 P.M. on Tuesday, Lacey Spears posted on Facebook a photograph of Garnett, with his wide, gap-toothed smile, playing on the beach in Clearwater.

"There are no words," she wrote underneath. "I can't fathom living without without [sic] my son, my heart, my soul, my very reason for living. Garnett was & is the greatest gift I have ever received! He knew nothing but joy, happiness & that he was & is deeply loved! I love you Garnett, G, Garnett the Great, Gster, Baby G!!!"

The next day, Lacey wrote that she had gone to the store to buy shampoo and had "broken down," seeing Garnett's car seat empty.

"I don't really know how I'll live without my son, my soul, my heart," she wrote, "but I do know Garnett never wanted to see me sad, crying or anything but happy. I am hollow, angry, sad and lost without him. Life has no purpose."

On Thursday morning, the three detectives met in the War Room at Westchester County Police headquarters to review their progress. People at the Fellowship and other social media friends had already given them some of Lacey's various Facebook and MySpace postings. There also was a string of e-mails supplied by Carol Grieder.

At the meeting, the team decided to enlist a forensic computer expert to prepare a detailed search warrant to serve on Facebook, MySpace, and other social networking companies. The goal was to obtain everything about Garnett, and all his illnesses, that Lacey Spears had ever posted on social media over the years.

Lacey Spears marked the two-week anniversary of her son's death by posting on Facebook. It would be the first of several lengthy accounts she would give of his death and the torturous heartbreak she was now suffering.

"2 weeks ago today at 10:20 am Garnett was declared brain dead. 2 damn weeks ago I sat holding the hand of my son knowing he would never say, 'I love you momma' again."

Lacey wrote that she still didn't understand why it had happened.

"I sat by his bedside until 2 am on the 25th of January

when he was wheeled into the OR and a team of doctors harvested his organs giving life to other children. I remember holding his hand for the very last time, the smell of his hair and the warmth of his tiny 35lb body. I miss him, I keep hoping he will come bouncing around the corner and his joy and smile will fill the room. I love you Garnett the Great, always and forever."

Now living with her family in Kentucky, Lacey helped out on the family farm, which was run by her father after he got off work as a metal fabricator. And she was in regular contact with her new legal team back in New York.

"We just maintained communications the best we could," explained David Sachs. "That was the extent of our representation at that time."

For the next few months, Lacey tried to keep a low profile as the investigation into her continued up north.

"She was still just grieving the loss of a child," said her sister, Rebecca, "and [knowing] you're being looked at is hard in itself."

Lacey was now posting daily updates on Facebook, chronicling her grief and describing how Garnett was now trying to make contact from the other side. One day, her brother, Daniel, accidentally bought one of Garnett's favorite drinks from a store. To Lacey, this was full of significance.

"I never would have thought a store in KY," she wrote, "would have an organic tea my son so often asked for. I just know Garnett was telling me he is here with us. I held that bottle of tea crying. My Garnett. My sweet Garnett the Great!!!"

In another posting, she wrote of waking up to "a fresh blanket of snow" and then realizing that Garnett would not be playing outside in his sled.

On Sunday, February 9, Lacey relived the final minutes before Garnett coded, squarely blaming the West-chester Medical Center for her son's death.

I sat at the bedside of Garnett on Tuesday, January 21st. I sat there having just seen the doctors caring for him. I was confident Garnett was improving, he was off life support. I knew he wasn't out of the woods, he had however greatly improved.

I sat there holding his leg, feeling his warmth, watching him sleep and longing to pick him up, hold him, snuggle his little body against mine . . . I sat watching my son, Garnett's heart began to beat out of his chest. I could see it. I watched with my own two eyes. I watched and held my son as he took his last earthly breath. I will never forget. Never. May [sic] sweet baby boy died from sever [sic] brain swelling. I watched as he struggled, was in pain and there was nothing I could do. NOTHING! I had been lead [sic] to believe he was improving, stable and just needed to be monitored. Less than 5 minutes after the doctor walked out of his PICU room he was gone. Garnett had left this earth and began [sic] his journey elsewhere. I never got to hold him. I did crawl in his bed numerous times . . . but I NEVER GOT TO HOLD HIM!!! I want my baby boy, Garnett, G, Garnett the Great!!! I WANT HIM BACK!!!!

A couple of hours later she wrote, "I am nothing with-out you Garnett!!! Nothing!!! I need your smile again!!!" Soon afterwards, she took a more philosophical view.

"Garnett was one of a kind," she wrote. "He was wise beyond his year [sic] and was pour [sic], whole, joyful and my heart! I dreamed of having G when I was just a little girl, 5 or 6."

Her postings, fondly recounting their idyllic life together, were read by her Facebook friends all over the world. And although most of them had never met Lacey Spears or Garnett in real life, they felt personally involved in her tragedy.

"So many hugs heading your way, Lacey," wrote one. "Garnett was a joy to read about on your Facebook from hundreds of miles away. Cherish the time you had with him for his journey is not over, it has just began[sic]! He is with you in everything you do!!! All my love and prayers!!"

At 7:00 A.M., Monday, February 10, detectives Kirk Budnick and Greg Dunn began interviewing all Nyack Hospital medical staff who had any contact with Lacey and Garnett. An attorney representing the hospital sat in on all the interviews, in case of any possible medical malpractice suits.

Pediatric Care Associate Jessica Shields told the detectives that she had seen Garnett several times on the day after he was admitted. He was walking around his room, hooked up to the EEG machine. Garnett had asked her name and what she was doing. She described the little boy as "joyous and happy," saying he told her he wanted to be "a daddy" one day.

Nurse Whitney Buford Bisland had helped intubate Garnett when he started having seizures, remaining with him until he was airlifted to Westchester Medical Center. She told the investigators that Lacey had said this was not the first time Garnett's high sodium had caused seizures.

"Lacey told her Garnett had seizures when he was 9–10 months old," noted Detective Dunn in his report. "Lacey said sodium level was 200."

* * *

That day, Lacey Spears posted two dozen photos of Garnett and more than a thousand words on her Garnett's Journey Facebook page.

"This morning I took a shower," she wrote. "I don't remember if I even used shampoo but I stood in the shower and cried."

She then went on to detail their life in the Fellowship Community, and Garnett starting kindergarten.

"His teacher was so warm, loving, comforting," she wrote, "and the best part for myself was she was a pediatric nurse. I knew in the depths of my soul he was safe."

A few hours later, she wrote about Garnett's fear of monsters.

"He was terrified of monsters. Night time and the dark brought intense emotions for him. I always went to bed with him, every night. 7:15 you could find us snuggled in bed, Garnett's head on my heart so he could hear my heart beating."

Garnett's "nights of monsters" had made her feel "worried and helpless," so she conjured up some "monster spray," with which they would spray the bedroom before going to sleep. She wrote that her son had finally overcome his fear of monsters by telling them to go back to their mommas to sleep.

"I would then hear him sweetly say every night or when he felt scared, 'Now monsters this is my momma time and you need to go and have your momma time.' My sweet little boy was wise beyond his years and as I tried to teach him about life I often learned from him."

The response to her postings was ecstatic, as her Facebook followers requested more and more Garnett stories.

"Lacey, you have a gift with words!" wrote one. "I love the stories you are choosing to share with us, I hope you are keeping a journal as well."

But the next day, after receiving a letter from the

Supplemental Security Income program informing her that she was no longer eligible for Gannett's monthly disability payment, she was furious.

"Today had broken me, more than I already am," she posted. "Seems impossible, yet true. I received a piece of mail from the SSI office. The notice you receive when your disabled child DIES and there [sic] funds need to end. The one I received because my Garnett is DEAD. Do you hear me!!! My baby, my heart, my soul, is DEAD!!! I certainly hope the letter can be replaced for I ripped it up and threw it away. I am not ready to read it, fill it out or send it in."

Lead Detective Dan Carfi was now busy researching Munchausen syndrome by proxy. He was especially interested in the case of Amber Brewington, a Pittsburgh mother who had poisoned her two-year-old child with salt through his feeding tube. Carfi contacted Detective Tom Leheny of the Pittsburgh Police Department, who sent him the complete case file. It bore an uncanny resemblance to the Lacey Spears case.

Nine months older than Garnett, Noah King had been born a healthy baby but was hospitalized at four months with critically high sodium levels. While he was at Children's Hospital in Pittsburgh, a nurse had seen his mother, Amber Brewington, tampering with his feeding tube. But it was too late. Noah had a stroke that left him paralyzed on one side of his body, and he will never recover.

After being arrested, his twenty-three-year-old mother admitted using a syringe to inject salt water through Noah's feeding tube, blaming postpartum depression. In August 2010, Brewington, who had been diagnosed with borderline personality disorder, severe depression, and mild mental retardation, pleaded guilty to aggravated assault and endangering the welfare of a child. Allegheny

County Court of Common Pleas judge Joseph K. Williams III sentenced Brewington to five to fifteen years in prison, where she is receiving mental health treatment.

After reading the Amber Brewington case file and several other criminal cases involving Munchausen syndrome by proxy, Detective Carfi was convinced that Lacey Spears suffered from the syndrome.

"There are apparently nine or ten criteria that fit people who suffer from this disorder," explained Detective Carfi. "Lacey hit all nine, and then an extra one. I mean, it was textbook how she met the criteria for Munchausen syndrome by proxy."

On Wednesday, February 12, a flash drive containing forty-plus hours of Garnett Spears's EEG video was delivered to the Ramapo Police Department. As soon as it arrived, Detective Budnick started viewing it at his desk. He was mesmerized when he saw a clip of Lacey taking Garnett to the bathroom at 10:25 A.M. on Sunday, January 19, with a feeding tube and cup in her hands.

"I just called everybody," recalled Budnick, "and said, 'Hey come and look it this. What do you think?'"

32

As the Ramapo Police detectives viewed the EEG video, Lacey Spears messaged Chris Hill on Facebook. It was the first time she had been in contact in almost three weeks.

"Hey," she wrote him at 11:46 A.M. that Wednesday.

"I didn't expect to hear from you," Hill replied a minute later. "[How] are you?"

"Not ok. just here," she answered. "Do you want to come to a celebration I am planning in G's honor?"

"Yes. Where?" he asked.

Lacey told him her celebration for Garnett would be held on Saturday.

"I will get you the details," she promised. "There will be a service in KY and FL. Garnett was cremated and will have a headstone in KY. Just haven't finished the details."

"That's what I heard," he replied. "Would have been very hard to see him laying in a casket. I couldn't handle that."

"No casket," she wrote. "Just a headstone."

Then Lacey told him how she had donated their son's organs to help other sick people.

"G was a giver," she explained. "I felt he would want to help others."

Then Lacey asked if he wanted some of Garnett's things, so he could get to know him a little bit. And she sent him a photograph of their son on his way to school, wearing his winter anorak, woolen hat, and jeans.

"That's a good picture :)" wrote Hill. "Are you staying by yourself or do you at least have people there to talk to you?"

"Garnett started school back in sept.," she told him. "He and I cried every morning when I had to leave him. He never wanted to be apart."

Lacey then sent him a photo of Garnett on his fifth birthday.

"One reason I'm still standing is because I didn't know him like you did," replied Hill, "but it still hurts a lot. I always thought there would be a day that you told him about me [and] later on he would try and find me."

"His favorite color was red," wrote Lacey, "and he lived in a tie dyed shirt. Garnett's most prized possession was [his] bobo [pacifier]. He had been through so much I just couldn't take it away."

"I love the pictures," Hill replied. "Red huh lol :)"

"I died that morning when I sat holding his leg as he took his last unassisted earthly breath. I didn't know he was gone until later that afternoon."

"I wish I could hold him," wrote his father.

"He was fine hours earlier and then DIED. The hospital fucked up!!! I swear to you if I ever see that nurse again I will hurt her. Garnett was in pain all night and I begged to see a doctor. I will hurt her. I promise you that."

Then Lacey assured him Garnett knew he was deeply loved and the center of her world.

"If they didn't do something about his pain," wrote Hill, "I would have shown my ass big time."

"I BEGGED TO SEE A DOCTOR, HAVE TEST DONE. MEDS!!! She wouldn't listen."

"I know you did."

"It happened so fast," Lacey continued. "Too fast. I can't accept he's gone."

"I know this isn't your fault," he reassured her, "and don't think it is."

"It's not my fault. I loved him. I gave him everything I had."

"I know he was your world," said Hill. "I looked at his photos quite a bit . . . whenever it would let me see them anyway."

Then Lacey agreed to allow him back into her Facebook world.

"I will add you as a friend," she told him, "but PLEASE don't share his pictures. NOT YET. IN TIME."

Over the next hour, Lacey told Chris Hill various details about his son, saying he loved Lego and his model John Deere tractor.

"I should call you sometime," she wrote, "so you can ask all the questions you have about him. I don't know when but I would want you to at least hear about him."

"That would be nice," he replied.

Then Lacey suggested that maybe "we could meet and talk," as she was now only about three hours away. But, she added, at the moment she was too upset to even get off the couch.

"I want to fucking die," she wrote. "I need to be with him."

Lacey said she understood that he must be angry after she cut him out of their son's life, but he had to accept that.

"I do want to share the memories I have with you," she wrote. "I can't bring him back. I want to."

"I'm not angry with you," he replied. "Just sad."

Lacey then sent him another set of photographs of Garnett, happily playing with his toys. The final one was of him lying in his hospital bed, brain dead on life support.

"The very last time I saw him," she wrote. "2am on Saturday the 25th. Moments later he went to the OR to have his organs harvested. I promise you Chris, I loved him with [every] part of my being. I promise you I will never be the same. NEVER."

When Chris Hill asked what she had told Garnett about him, Lacey ignored his question.

"My life," she wrote. "I just don't know if I can go on without him. I don't eat or sleep or do anything. Just hold down this couch. No matter how many people are around me I feel so alone. I'm not an angry person but I want to hurt that fucking nurse. I want to hurt someone."

Lacey then sent a photograph of a smiling Garnett sitting on her lap on Christmas morning.

"Children should never go before their parents," Hill wrote. ""It's just not right."

"No they shouldn't," she agreed.

He then told her that he was running out of data on his phone. He asked her to text him instead.

"I can tell you need to talk," he told her. "I won't blow your phone up. You talk when you want."

Lacey then gave him her cell phone number and invited him to call.

Several days later, Chris Hill called Lacey's phone while he was out walking his dog in the snow.

"I was trying to sympathize with her," he later explained. "Tell her to keep her head, because she says she hasn't got out of bed."

Concerned about her welfare, Hill told her to pull

herself together, get out of bed, have a shower, and go for a walk.

"I said, 'You need to stay active or you're going to die,'" he remembered. "And she said, 'I'll try but I can't think of anything else but Garnett right now.'"

On Thursday, February 13, the *Journal News* revealed that investigators had seized "food items" from Garnett's mother's apartment and were still awaiting toxicology results. Shawn Cohen wrote that detectives had already interviewed Lacey Spears and members of the Fellowship but were being "tight-lipped" about their investigation.

"They've asked everyone questions about how things were with Lacey," Matt Uppenbrink was quoted as saying. "I don't know if there's a pattern of anything that could rise to the level of questionable."

David Sachs told the *Journal News* that his new client was "absolutely devastated" by Garnett's death.

"There's no indication," he said, "that Lacey has ever been anything other than a loving, caring, and devoted parent."

Rebecca Spears refused to comment other than to say that Lacey had done nothing to harm Garnett.

"She's having a really hard time," she said. "She loved him and did everything she could to care [for] and protect him."

Cohen had also accessed some of Lacey's Facebook postings through one of her friends, who had read them over the phone to him. These included Lacey's September 2012 postings about her "soul mate," Blake, being "Garnett's Daddy."

Soon after the story came out, Cohen got a tip that investigators believed Lacey Spears had poisoned Garnett with salt.

"Finally I found a police source who was sharing some

hunches about what was going on in the hospital," Cohen said. "That his sodium level had spiked, and it had caused him to have all these seizures."

On February 14, Lacey Spears instant messaged Autumn Hunt and asked her to sing "Happy Birthday" to JonJon, who turned seven that day. It was the first time Lacey had been in touch since Garnett's death.

"I asked her how she was coping," said Hunt, "and she seemed like a mother in mourning. I asked if she was talking to a counselor, and she said she was but she wanted her baby back."

The next day, a memorial service was held for Garnett at the Mount Union General Baptist Church in Scottsville, Kentucky. Close family and several friends attended, including Jessica Kyle, who drove in from Decatur. Lacey had arranged numerous photographs of Garnett on a table in the church. But Chris Hill was not there because she had never followed through with her invitation.

Rebecca Spears attended with their parents and their brother, Daniel. After the service, a marker was placed on the Spears family plot in a cemetery four miles from the Spears farm.

"Garnett was cremated," said Rebecca, "and he sits at present in an urn on top of my father's dresser."

On Sunday, February 16, Shawn Cohen revealed that the Maria Fareri Children's Hospital had called the police to report suspiciously high sodium levels in Garnett's blood.

"Sources said the sodium level sent up a red flag," reported Cohen, "but would not speculate on what caused the spike in the chemical compound that can cause neurological problems and, in extreme cases, death."

Two days later, he reported that Lacey had posted many photographs of Garnett on life support, asking for prayers. The story also contained half a dozen of her Facebook postings, which discussed Garnett's "dangerously high" sodium levels.

On Thursday, February 20, the *Journal News* revealed that Chris Hill was Garnett's real father. After being contacted at his home in Athens, Alabama, Hill sent Shawn Cohen a brief statement.

"I Facebooked Lacey until she responded," he wrote. "I could tell by her photos . . . that she loved Garnett. There is no reason to be investigating her. She would never have harmed Garnett."

Several days later, Matt Uppenbrink told the *Journal News* that Garnett's death and the subsequent police investigation had plunged the Fellowship Community into grief.

"It's like an open wound," he explained.

Then, reacting to the recent revelation that Garnett's real father was alive and well in Alabama, Uppenbrink said, "If it's true, there's going to be a lot of hurt people. [Lacey] had told us that Garnett's father had passed away early on in his life."

The Fellowship Community's cofounder, Ann Scharff, described Lacey Spears as a typical single parent, struggling to make a life for herself and Garnett.

"She was responsible," Scharff was quoted as saying. "She tried to care for her son well, and she did her work here well. I mean, any young mother struggles . . . It's not easy raising children."

Detectives and *Journal News* reporter Shawn Cohen were now running down Lacey Spears's history in parallel investigations. They interviewed the same friends and acquaintances back in Decatur and Clearwater.

During the last week of February, Cohen called Shawna

Lynch for some background information. She gave him a telephone interview, staunchly defending Lacey.

After hanging up the phone, Shawna left a message on Lacey's phone, saying that a reporter had just called.

"So Lacey called me back," said Shawna, "and said, 'What did you say to him? What is he asking?' She was in a panic mode. Then real quickly she's like, 'I've got to go.'"

A few hours later, Lacey unfriended Shawna on Facebook and stopped returning her calls.

"I had been defending her," said Shawna. "So you're going to treat me like that when I'm defending you and everybody else is talking all kind of bad stuff? So the person that she turned out to be is not the person that I knew."

During the last week of February, Detective Greg Dunn began calling Lacey's friends in Alabama and Florida, using phone numbers recovered from her iPhone. Her school friend April Chambers told him that she and Lacey had reconnected on Facebook, sharing a common interest in natural foods. She said Lacey had told her that Garnett had undergone open-heart surgery and had had many ear infections. She had also read Lacey's posts about Blake being killed in a car accident in 2011 but had discovered that the supposed picture of him she was posting was from a stock photo agency.

"After she had heard about Garnett passing away," Detective Dunn wrote in his report, "she and her husband developed a pay pal [sic] account to help Lacey but . . . discontinued this when she heard about the investigation."

The detective also interviewed Lacey's holistic nutritionist, Meka Taulbee, in Clearwater, who said she had devised a vegan, plant-based diet plan for Garnett.

"Lacey used to call her multiple times a day, at any hour, including the middle of the night," Dunn reported. "Lacey told her she did not get along with her father and was afraid of him."

Meka said she had been in Facebook contact with Lacey after Garnett's death.

"Lacey mentioned that there was a police investigation," wrote Dunn, "[that] could take up to a year. She was in Kentucky but moving back to Florida."

Several days later, Dunn spoke to Pam Hamilton, who had met Lacey on a Facebook group for mothers who have lost children. The nurse from Mesa, Arizona, said Lacey, whom she had never met in person, had claimed that two of her children had died at birth.

"Lacey had told her that [a family member] had sexually abused her," wrote Dunn, "and Garnett's father was killed in an accident."

Another Ramapo detective telephoned Jessica Kyle, who was still standing by Lacey. After putting down the phone, Jessica duly reported back to Lacey.

"He was trying to get the story of your life together," she messaged Lacey on Facebook. "I told him that you loved Garnett, and you would never do anything to hurt anyone. He asked some specific questions, and I answered them the best I could."

"What questions did he ask?" wrote Lacey. "Do you remember?"

Jessica replied that the detective had specifically asked who Blake was, if she knew a guy called Chris, and which of them was Garnett's father.

"I told him that I had never met the dad," Jessica told Lacey, "so I couldn't answer that. That when we were in middle school there was a guy named Blake that you talked about a little bit, but never got into detail."

The detective had also asked if she thought Lacey "had potential" to deliberately harm anyone.

"Of course I said no," Jessica wrote, "and that you loved G too much to put him in harm's way."

"Ok, thank you," wrote Lacey. "This shouldn't even be happening. I love my son and did not hurt him."

"I read the articles," replied Jessica, "and get so mad the way that you are being portrayed. It's wrong on every level. Everyone that we went to school with just keeps sharing the articles. These people around here need to get a LIFE."

After a three-week absence, Lacey Spears returned to Facebook, updating her remaining friends on how she was coping with Garnett's loss.

"Days turn into night and night into days," she wrote. "Weeks come and go . . . Time is of no relevance . . . I am hollow, empty and lost."

Writing that there were no words to describe "the depths of my pain," she felt consumed by anger because she would never see Garnett grow up.

"No one can walk this journey for me or take my pain," she wrote. "Only I do that and I WILL . . . Moment by moment, step by step I will carry on for Garnett."

Her aunt, Sandra Newkoop, offered words of support.

"Lacey no one can imagine what you have went threw [sic]," she wrote on her niece's timeline. "A living nightmare sweetheart . . . Lacey you are one strong lady and you have kept on with your journey for Garnett. You have to hold on. Lacey your baby is watching you from Heaven and he Loves his Mommy so very much."

Despite her anguished Facebook postings, Lacey had now settled down in Scottsville. Most days, she went for long runs in the woods near the farm. She had a new puppy named Remington, and she and her brother, Daniel, were often seen at the local Walmart.

Lacey also attended the Open Door Outreach Church in Scottsville until, according to detectives, she was asked to leave following a confrontation with another church member.

Almost every day, she would post long, self-pitying accounts of her grieving for Garnett. But they were always mostly about her, with her dead son as a supporting player.

"At 26 I never imagined my life would be here as it is now," she wrote on March 7, the six-week anniversary of Garnett's death. "I never thought I would be standing at the bedside of my 5 year old son, holding his tiny leg as he took his last breath . . . I will never forget hearing the doctor pronounce Garnett brain dead . . . Those words haunt me, they run through my thoughts endlessly."

She then described the ordeal of dealing with the organ donor process, funeral arrangements, and organizing a celebration of Garnett's life.

"Stacks of papers to be completed," she explained, "countless phone calls to be made and the endless questions. All of which I had to take care of. No, you can't imagine what I have experienced the last 6 weeks and I hope no one ever does."

33

LOSING GARNETT THE GREAT

In mid-March, the *Journal News* dispatched Shawn Cohen to Alabama, Kentucky, and Florida to dig into Lacey Spears's past. A source had tipped him off that investigators suspected Lacey Spears suffered from Munchausen syndrome by proxy. His editors believed the story had great potential.

"The word was Munchausen," recalled Cohen, "and there was a lot of armchair speculation as [my editors] started reading the stuff I was bringing in [from] Facebook. She was posting these pictures of Garnett with bandages and essentially dying in the hospital. It was sick."

Over the previous several weeks, Cohen had begun cultivating many of Lacey's old friends as they were being questioned by detectives.

"It got a little uncomfortable," he explained. "I'd covered crime for more than a decade and had relationships with people in law enforcement. So when I start to learn information on my own, often investigators want to hear what I have."

So there was a tacit understanding that each side would help the other as they started uncovering more information about Lacey Spears.

"There was some communication both ways," said the reporter, "because I didn't want to screw up things for them."

In Scottsville, Kentucky, Lacey also was keeping close tabs on his progress, trying to control things as well as she could.

"Lacey was paying attention," said Cohen. "In fact, half the people I spoke with were getting admonishments not to speak with me."

After landing in Alabama, he first interviewed Lacey's childhood friend Jessica Kyle. Initially, Jessica did not want to talk, but Cohen won her over by saying someone needed to say something positive about Lacey.

Jessica then opened up, telling him how her mother, Lisa, had once contacted Alabama child protective services after Lacey complained of sexual abuse by a family member. Lacey had then moved into the Kyle home for a while, though it was only many years later that Jessica discovered why.

"She spilled her guts to me," said Cohen, "and then we were going to meet the next day at nine in the morning [to carry on]."

Right after he left, Jessica reported back to Lacey via Facebook.

"So I had a reporter show up at my house today from the *Journal News*," she told Lacey. "They are looking for support stories. I know I said I wouldn't talk, but he told me he wants to make sure that they show support stories too. Love you and I hope this doesn't make you upset with me."

When there was no immediate reply, Jessica assured

her that she had not discussed anything they had recently talked about.

"Please don't be upset with me," she wrote. "He insured that my words would not be strewed."

"I'm not," Lacey replied several minutes later. "Just scared of what lays ahead. Missing G pretty bad today."

":(I'm so sorry for you sweetheart. I cried during the interview."

Then Jessica mentioned that Shawn Cohen was coming back in the morning to continue the interview.

"I have a feeling he is going to ask me about your past home life," she told Lacey. "What do you want me to tell him? I know it's a sensitive subject. All I've talked about so far is growing up with you."

"Nothing," came Lacey's terse reply. "I don't want my life shared. It's not helping only hurt my situation. Do not share my home life as a child!!!!! PLEASE."

"I had a feeling that's what you would say," Jessica replied. "That's why I refused to make any comments on that."

"Just tell him to speak to my lawyer," wrote Lacey. "You didn't share anything off my Facebook page?"

At 4:30 A.M. the next day, Jessica telephoned Shawn Cohen and asked him to drive straight over to her house. It was still dark outside when he arrived. He was greeted by Jessica and her boyfriend.

"She's in full panic mode and threatening to sue me," Cohen remembered. "And she's like, 'Everything I told you, you can't use it.' It turns out that she had communicated with Lacey after I spoke to her. Lacey went nuts."

The seasoned crime reporter explained that, unfortunately, it was too late, because he had already filed his interview with his editors.

After Cohen left, Jessica updated Lacey via Facebook.

"I called the reporter over and told him I do not want to be a part of this report," she told her. "He said that this has happened before and he will have to speak with his editor."

There was no reply from Lacey.

Several days later, Shawn Cohen took Chris Hill to lunch at Logan's Roadhouse, Hill's favorite restaurant, in Athens, Alabama. Hill immediately told him that Lacey had already been in touch, asking that he not talk to the *Journal News* reporter.

Then, over a steak and a succession of twenty-two-ounce beers, Chris Hill opened up about his relationship with Lacey and how she had dropped him right after she became pregnant with Garnett. Toward the end of the interview, Hill pulled out his phone, which had some of Lacey's texts on it.

"I handed him my phone," recalled Hill, "and he wrote everything down."

It was during lunch that Hill learned for the first time that Garnett might have been poisoned with salt. When he got home later, he immediately texted Lacey, asking about it.

"She said, 'What are you talking about?'" said Hill. "'How's that even possible?' That's what she said."

During his five days in Decatur, Shawn Cohen also spoke to Ginger Dabbs-Anderson, Shawna Lynch, Paula Sandlin, Autumn Hunt, Kathy Hammack, Christy Burnham, and Riley Vaughn. He also made the five-hour drive to Scottsville, Kentucky, but Rebecca Spears refused to talk to him.

Then he flew to Clearwater, Florida, for the second leg of his nine-day trip. There, he interviewed Peggy Florence's neighbors, Ken and Rebecca Paulen, who spoke about Lacey and Garnett's life in Florida. He also interviewed Jak and Nicole Plihal, who told him that Lacey had found out about the Fellowship Community through contacts she had made at various parenting groups. He also learned that many people had become wary of Lacey because her stories were not adding up.

While Shawn Cohen was running down her life in Alabama and Florida, Lacey took to Facebook to attack anyone who had dared to speak to him.

"Today I hurt," she wrote on March 21, "for someone felt necessary to judge how I lived and raised my son. I don't regret how I chose to parent Garnett and I don't look back in my life and wish I had done something different. I followed my heart, I listened to my soul, I healed myself as I loved my son! I miss Garnett."

On Sunday, March 23, the *Journal News* printed the first in a five-part series called *Losing Garnett the Great*. A week earlier, Shawn Cohen's first story had appeared, under the headline "Truth, Lies and Lacey Spears." It had also run in the Gannett Company's national flagship publication *USA Today* and had been so well received that a complete in-depth series on Lacey Spears had been ordered.

The five-part series, spanning Lacey's childhood in Decatur, her life in Clearwater with Garnett, and their subsequent move to New York, made for riveting reading. It took the story to a national level, with Lacey branded as the "Mommy Blogger."

Her attorneys refused to comment on any part of it and ordered their client to avoid reading it.

"We strongly encouraged her not to read what's reported in the papers," explained David Sachs. "But as you might imagine, it would be very difficult advice to follow."

Sachs said he and his partner, Stephen Riebling, were

still in daily contact with Lacey, who was now receiving grief counseling.

"[She's] staring down the barrel of an indictment," he said, "with police investigating you for murdering your son. And you're afraid to do anything to appropriately grieve."

In the wake of the *Journal News* series, the story was picked up in the *Decatur Daily*. On March 26, it ran a front-page article with a photograph of Lacey next to Garnett in a frog outfit, under the headline "Boy's Death Puts Decatur Native in Spotlight."

Reporter Seth Burkett interviewed Lacey's friends Rania Cottingham and Autumn Hunt.

"Lacey's not crazy," Hunt told him, "under any circumstances."

After reading the story, Jessica Kyle contacted Lacey.

"I hate to be the one to tell you," she wrote, "but the news has hit the newspapers down here."

"Don't talk to anyone," came Lacey's reply.

Jessica also told her that an advance production team from ABC's prime-time show *20/20*, as well as several other news reporters, were now in Decatur.

"I am so sorry," said Lacey. "What does your [family] think of all of this?"

On Thursday, March 27, Nancy Grace ran a segment on Lacey Spears on her top-rated HLN cable news show. It revealed, for the first time, some of Lacey's Facebook postings.

"When a beautiful five-year-old little boy dies in the hospital," Grace told her thousands of viewers, "heartbreak for a grieving mother who chronicles the child's final days over social media. But tonight police are asking, Did Mommy inject a lethal dose of salt into her own little boy's feeding tube?"

After showing a brief clip from "The Good Mother," a 2013 Lifetime TV movie about Munchausen syndrome by proxy, Grace read out a selection of Lacey's postings, written as Garnett began seizing in Nyack Hospital. Then she interviewed children's advocate Marc Klaas, whose twelve-year-old daughter, Polly, was murdered in 1993.

"Look at the pictures of this little child," Grace told him. "And to think someone was systematically injecting him with salt?"

"It wasn't 'someone' who was injecting him, Nancy," said Klaas. "It was his mother. There is something terribly wrong with this woman, and she should . . . most definitely be spending the rest of her life behind bars, if she's convicted of murdering this child."

Back in Alabama, Chris Hill watched the Nancy Grace show, recording it on his DVR. After reading the *Journal News* series and assimilating all the new information about Lacey, he was in total shock.

"I don't even know what to say to this," he wrote on Facebook. "But if she did in fact kill my son, I hope she goes to prison for the rest of her life . . . and then to hell."

That same night, Lacey posted a new photograph of Garnett during happier times in her new Facebook album, "Garnett the Great's Legacy."

"This picture speaks volumes!" she wrote. "Captures the essences of who G really was . . . A free spirit, a lover of tie dye and journeyed to the beat of his own liking . . . I love you. I am certain that you are shining your light in the hearts of all you now know!"

On Friday, April 4, the Westchester County Medical Examiner's office quietly ruled Garnett Spears's death a homicide based on the autopsy. The cause of death was "hypernatremia from exogenous source resulting in

cerebral edema." The ruling was not made public because of the ongoing police investigation.

A few hours later, Ramapo detectives Kirk Budnick
and Gregory Dunn returned to the Fellowship Community to interview Lacey's upstairs neighbors, Shaiya and
Charisse Baer. The detectives asked the couple if Lacey
had ever discussed wanting to have another child.

Charisse said that Lacey had often spoken about it,
even suggesting that Shaiya be the father.

"They were shocked by the thought," Detective Dunn
wrote in his report. "Lacey never brought that idea to
them again."

Then Shaiya told the investigators that Lacey had developed a personal relationship with Oona Younger's husband, Howard Friedman.

"Lacey had been observed sitting on his lap in public
locations at the Fellowship," wrote Dunn. "Shaiya . . . had
also heard that Lacey may have approached Friedman
about having a child."

Four days later, the two detectives returned to the Fellowship to interview Friedman, who knew that they
wanted to speak to him about the idea of fathering Lacey's child. He said it had first come up after Lacey told
Oona that she wanted another child.

"She mentioned going to a bar to find someone to con-
ceive a child with her," Detective Dunn later reported.
"Howard described his wife as having a loving care for
Lacey and that she even suggested allowing him to father
a child. Howard stated that he never had any sexual rela-
tion with Lacey."

34

As the murder investigation moved into high gear, Lacey Spears fought back. According to her Facebook postings, she was now running seven miles a day, doing yoga, and watching sunrises from a hayloft overlooking the farm.

"If I know one thing," she told her few remaining Facebook friends, "I know I'm strong! I'm stronger than I realize . . . I'm not giving up! You better believe I'm gonna fight . . . I'm gonna fight until the end. I'm gonna hold my head up."

Almost every day, Lacey was on Facebook, posting picture after picture in her "Garnett the Great's Legacy" album and reminiscing about their idyllic life together.

"Remembering all our trips to the beach," she wrote. "The countless sunsets we watched as you drifted off to sleep in my arms."

A few days later, she contemplated Garnett being in heaven.

"I don't know much about heaven," she wrote. "I do know there are no g tubes! I know Heaven must have some incredible Vegan, Veggie, Gluten Free Pancakes with lots of 'Golden Syrup.' I also know that there is one amazing little boy up there."

She also pondered Garnett's place in the universal master plan.

"Things happen in our life for a reason," she wrote. "We all are here to serve a purpose, to for fill [sic] a calling. I never imagined my little boy would only grace this earth for 5 years. Those are the greatest 5 years of my life. I miss him. I hurt to hold him. I know that Garnett is in the greatest place possible. I love you Garnett. Love & Light."

On April 20, Lacey marked Easter by posting a photograph of Garnett alongside a special message to him.

"Happy 1st Easter in Heaven," it read. "May my heartfelt letter reach you in the sky . . . Love & Light."

She also uploaded a photo of Garnett, with his G-tube visible, in support of the Feeding Tube Awareness Foundation.

"Support children with feeding tubes," she wrote. "Order a tubie t-shirt! Many children have feeding tubes we are unaware of. My Garnett the Great was a Tubie Baby!!! Pink one headed my way."

The next day—the three-month anniversary of Garnett's death—Lacey reposted a photo of him in the hospital.

"3 months ago this morning my little boy slipped into a coma. His time here on earth was finished . . . Seeing him in such pain was dreadful, horrifying. He bore it bravely, with no complaint. How I wish the pain could have been given to me instead."

In late April, the Green Meadow Waldorf School held a special memorial service for Garnett Spears. The school sent his mother a memorial card with Garnett's photograph on one side, a quote from Rudolf Steiner, and a short tribute to him.

> There is no footprint
> Too small to leave
> An imprint on this world.
> Garnett had a special sparkle and
> Fiery spirit that made us all smile.
> He was joyful, inquisitive, funny and
> Charming—a loving star child.

After receiving the memorial card, Lacey proudly posted a picture of it on Facebook.

> This is the memorial card from the service held in his honor. I was also given an amazing painting of a child reaching for a star high in the sky. Garnett was known to all from school: children, parents, teachers & staff members as the 'star child.' I was gladden [sic] to know that not one day has passed without his name & memory being brought up in his nursery class . . . Today 3 months ago I walked out of his PICU room leaving his tiny body behind . . . Today I cry tears of sorrow for I miss him . . . I also cry knowing he lives on in all who knew him.

On May 7, the *Huffington Post* ran a story with the headline "Did Mommy Blogger Lacey Spears Poison Her 5-Year-Old Son for Attention?" The article said that, although she still had not been charged, Lacey Spears was at the center of a criminal investigation after suspiciously high levels of sodium had been found in her son's blood before he died. It also revealed that Lacey had asked a friend to get rid of a bag used to feed Garnett through his G-tube, which was later found to contain a high concentration of salt.

David Sachs told the Web site his client was totally innocent.

"Lacey is completely devastated by the loss of her son," he said, "and absolutely denies harming [him] in any way."

Communications Director for the Westchester County District Attorney's Office Lucian Chalfen was quoted as saying that "a shoe will drop" in the case in a month or so.

Four days later, the London-based *Mail Online* branded Lacey Spears a "sick blogger mom." Reporter Will Payne had spent several days in Decatur, researching the story.

"A whole web of lies she had told has now unraveled," read the story, "including how she claimed Garnett's father was a hero cop called Blake who tragically died."

Autumn Hunt told Payne that she desperately wanted to believe Lacey was innocent, since Lacey had spent so much time taking care of her son.

"She had my child," said Hunt, "so that could have been my Jonathon. It's so hard for me to think she did it. When I read some of the information about her, she sounds like a different person."

On Monday, May 12, a team of six New York detectives flew to Huntsville, Alabama, to conduct around forty interviews with Lacey Spears's friends and the medical staff who had treated Garnett. The night before leaving, they met in the War Room to finalize logistics.

"We wrote down on pieces of paper everybody's assignment in Alabama," recalled Detective Dunn. "And listed it like a schedule. We had sticky notes all over the television as to what we were doing there."

In preparation for the trip, the detectives had recruited Johnny Coker, an investigator for the Morgan County District Attorney's office in Decatur, as point man. Within half an hour of landing, detectives Dan Carfi and Greg Dunn met with Coker in his office.

"Johnny laid out a plan to interview all these people," said Detective Carfi. "Most of the interviews took place in his D.A.'s office."

The investigators split up into three groups to cover the most ground possible in the limited time they had. Each night they would meet back at the Huntsville hotel where they were all staying, to compare notes.

At 2:00 P.M. that Monday, detectives Budnick and Dunn drove to Ginger Dabbs-Anderson's home in Athens, Alabama. The one-time nurse at Decatur General Hospital had already been interviewed by phone and was viewed as a potential key witness for the prosecution. Unfortunately, she had some baggage: she had reportedly lost her state nursing license for a year after helping a friend falsify a prescription for painkillers. That mishap could harm her credibility, and it was ultimately decided not to call her as a witness.

Dabbs-Anderson told the detectives that she had first met Lacey in the spring of 2009, after Lacey brought Garnett in complaining that he couldn't hold down food. At first, staff tried to teach Lacey how to feed him properly, but she always complained that he vomited.

Eventually, the staff was instructed to feed Garnett away from his mother, to see whether he was sick.

"I would take him to the nurse's station," Dabbs-Anderson told the detectives, "hold Garnett, and feed him formula from a bottle. [I would] keep him there for two hours to allow his formula to digest. He never vomited."

Dabbs-Anderson told the investigators that, after she and Lacey became friends, Garnett often spent nights over at her house and always ate normally. She also spent time at the apartment Lacey shared with her sister, where Dabbs-Anderson once witnessed something shocking.

"Lacey [was] holding Garnett down in the bathtub because he was crying," she said. "I grabbed Garnett out of the tub, dried him off, and took him out of the house for a little while to give Lacey time to calm down."

Dabbs-Anderson said she didn't report Lacey to child protective services because she felt Lacey was just "overwhelmed," and Dabbs-Anderson never saw Lacey mistreat Garnett again.

She also recounted that Lacey had arrived at her house in tears one day, claiming a family member had raped her in Garnett's presence.

"I encouraged her to call the cops," said Dabbs-Anderson, "and even told her that I would. She wouldn't, and started crying and screaming hysterically and begged me not to do so."

In addition to talking to medical staff in half a dozen hospitals spread out over Alabama and Tennessee, the detectives also talked to Lacey's childhood friends.

"We were getting her whole life, from a child," said Detective Carfi, "all kinds of crazy stories. When Lacey was in middle school, she had a doll that she carried around all the time, and [she] pretended it was real. Then, as she went into high school . . . she was babysitting all these kids. So there were all kinds of stories coming in, left and right. They were outrageous . . . kind of nutty."

On Thursday, May 15, detectives Carfi and Dunn interviewed the real Blake Robinson, who is a deputy sergeant with the Morgan County Sheriff's Office. Robinson was astonished to learn that Lacey had told everyone that he was Garnett's father.

"He had met Lacey Spears prior to 2007," wrote Dunn, "and had only seen her on three occasions. He never had any personal relations with her."

Coincidentally, Morgan County District Attorney investigator Johnny Coker was an administrator at one of the Decatur churches. He had known Lacey and Rebecca Spears years earlier, when his church had given them charity.

"We started to see a pattern of church abuse," explained Detective Carfi. "Lacey and Rebecca were taking advantage of several churches and would go in and get free things from them."

Lacey reportedly claimed to have lost a previous child, even using a fictitious death certificate to get additional help.

While the detectives were in Alabama, Facebook's corporate office in Manhattan complied with a search warrant for all four of Lacey's accounts: Lacey Spears 16, Lacey Spears 33, HippyHappyMomma, and Garnett's Journey. The files were so huge that they had to be sent to Westchester County's forensics division to be converted into a manageable size.

As they scoured through the fifty thousand or so pages, detectives noticed how Lacey strictly compartmentalized each of the accounts for different levels of friends and family.

"It was very interesting," said Detective Carfi. "On each of the four sites, which were going at the same time, she would have a group of friends, but none of them knew each other. Site one talks about Daddy Blake and having memorial services for him. But site two is maybe more for her family, and has nothing about Blake, so she couldn't tell that lie to them. And then there was site three and four, with people that didn't know each other. She had friends online she'd never met, who were really into her."

The Facebook material generated many new leads for the investigation.

"So we needed to go and talk to these people," said Detective Carfi. "Was I interested in any more lies? No. I wanted some facts. The facts that we would be learning would be the medical records and talking to medical professionals."

On their return to New York, the detectives met with the Westchester County District Attorney's office. After reviewing all the new evidence, the decision was made to convene a grand jury and go for a murder indictment against Lacey Spears.

On Tuesday, June 3, the Westchester County grand jury met for the first time. Over the next two weeks, it convened on five more occasions, hearing evidence from detectives, doctors, and several members of the Fellowship Community.

On the first day, Detective Carfi contacted the U.S. Marshals office in Bowling Green, Kentucky. He briefed a marshal that an indictment charging Lacey with murder could soon be handed down by the grand jury, and that they might be needed to help arrest her. He also requested around-the-clock surveillance of Lacey, in case she tried to flee.

The marshals set up a command center a half mile away from the Spears's farm, with high-powered binoculars trained on the house 24–7.

"Down there is cornfields, then a private road and a house," said Carfi. "It's not like you blend in easily. So it was a pretty big undertaking to get this surveillance."

On Tuesday, June 10, the Westchester County District Attorney's office sent Lacey Spears a grand jury notice, inviting her to testify. The following day, her attorney David Sachs informed the office that his client had declined.

35

"JUSTICE FOR GARNETT"

Late on Monday night, June 15, Lacey Spears and her father flew to New York and checked into a hotel. David Sachs had warned that an indictment was imminent and that it would be in Lacey's best interest to be close by and to avoid extradition.

"We knew that it was coming," said Rebecca Spears. "David asked us to come back to New York. He said, 'I can't tell you one hundred percent if they are going to press charges, but there's a good chance that they will.' He made sure that nothing totally caught us by surprise."

The next morning, a Westchester County grand jury indicted Lacey Spears for the second-degree murder and first-degree manslaughter of her son, Garnett. The two charges carried a maximum sentence of twenty-five years to life.

After the indictment was signed by a judge, an arrest warrant was issued for Lacey Spears. Copies were posted on the Web site of the New York Statewide Police Information Network and e-mailed to the U.S. Marshals office in Bowling Green, Kentucky.

David Sachs then called the Westchester County Police to tell them that his client would surrender at 2:45 that afternoon.

Word of Lacey Spears's imminent arrest leaked to the press. Soon, half a dozen TV news crews and reporters were encamped outside the front door of Westchester County Police headquarters.

At 2:45 P.M., David Sachs and Stephen Riebling pulled up at the back door of police headquarters. They escorted Lacey and her father, Terry, who had his arm around her, inside. Several photographers photographed Lacey, with her head bowed, as she entered the building.

"I took custody of Lacey right there," said Detective Carfi. "I led her by the arm into the booking area, where I fingerprinted and photographed her. She looked nervous because we were in a jail cell area."

An hour and a half later, after Lacey had been processed, Detective Carfi and another officer brought Lacey outside, walking her past reporters to an unmarked black car. He then drove her to the Westchester County courthouse in White Plains to be arraigned.

They entered through an underground basement, and a few minutes later, Detective Carfi led Lacey upstairs in handcuffs to Judge Barry Warhit's courtroom.

As she entered, Lacey looked at her father, who was sitting alone in the public gallery. On the opposite side of the courtroom were detectives Carfi, Budnick, and Dunn. Behind them were print and TV reporters. The arraignment was being filmed for the six o'clock news.

"Are you Lacey Spears?" asked Judge Warhit.

"Yes, sir," she replied meekly.

David Sachs told the judge that his client was pleading

not guilty to both counts of the indictment. He asked for bail, saying that although Lacey had no family in New York, she was not a flight risk.

"She resided at the Waldorf community," he said, "in an effort to better her son's life. She took care of the elderly. She took care of the garden, and it was her ability—unique ability—to get a great education for her son."

He said that although she had lived in several states, she did not have a "transient lifestyle" and had only moved around to improve her son's life. He told the judge that his law firm had been retained by Lacey back in January after several police searches of her apartment.

"She did so," said Sachs, "not out of some consciousness of guilt . . . but because the hospital [and] police detectives start questioning her."

Sachs noted that the case had already received "widespread media scrutiny and coverage," and Lacey had known for months that she was the "lone suspect" in her son's death and that she faced arrest.

"She was always ready, willing, and able to address it," he told the judge, "if it came to a head."

Sachs denied Lacey went into hiding in Kentucky after Garnett's death, saying she had wanted to mourn with family around her.

"Besides the nature and seriousness of the charge," Sachs continued, "all indications are that my client is not a flight risk. And her parents have great money needs [and] her mother is on disability. Her father has an income of $44,000 a year [and] it took them great expense just to get here. So I'm asking this court to use its discretion in setting a reasonable amount of bail."

"And what would that be, in your mind?" asked Judge Warhit.

"Even bail in the range of $150,000 to $200,000 would

be the equivalent to this family of one or two million dollars," Sachs told him.

"So what's warranted?" asked the judge.

"Bail not to exceed $150,000," replied Sachs.

Westchester County Assistant District Attorney Doreen Lloyd stood up to oppose bail, outlining the events leading up to Garnett's death. She said the defendant's son was about to be released from Nyack Hospital on Sunday, January 19, when his mother had taken him into the bathroom. Everything had been captured on video from the EEG machine.

"And what you can see in her hand on this video," said Lloyd, "is a connector tube that is generally used for the G-tube, and a cup with liquid. He is healthy. He appears normal. He does not appear in distress."

But soon afterwards, she told the judge, Garnett started retching in pain and becoming visibly ill. And because of a surgical procedure he had had at nine weeks, he was unable to vomit out whatever she had put in his system. As the morning progressed, Garnett became increasingly sick. Labs were drawn at 1:20 P.M., and his sodium was at 144, which was within the normal range.

"This defendant then asks the medical staff there," said Lloyd, " 'Are you going to be repeating the blood work?' And she keeps asking about the sodium level."

Throughout the afternoon, Lloyd continued, Lacey Spears repeatedly brought Garnett into the bathroom, even though at times he was unable to stand up. And when she brought him out, he was clearly in distress.

"She does it over and over and over again," said Lloyd, "resulting in, at 5:30, this child, this five-year-old boy, her son, ends up having a severe event. He cannot breathe. He is intubated, his entire extremities . . . are shaking."

She told the judge that more lab work was then done,

showing that Garnett's sodium level had risen from 144 to 182 in a short period of time.

"There's absolutely no medical explanation for that rise in sodium," Lloyd told the judge. "And as the defendant is taking her son into that bathroom . . . with that connector tube in her hand and that cup, that coincides with evidence on the EEG machine that shows . . . that child goes from moderate to severe cerebral dysfunction."

She explained how Garnett had then been airlifted to the Westchester Medical Center for specialized pediatric treatment.

"Unfortunately, he does not survive the events," she said, "and on January twenty-one of 2014, he codes in the early morning hours and suffers severe brain damage and trauma and swelling, which he will not recover from."

She then told Judge Warhit that, within minutes of being told her son was brain dead, the defendant had phoned a friend at the Fellowship Community, asking the friend to throw away the bag from her feeding machine without telling anyone.

"Now, luckily for us," said Lloyd, "the Fellowship Community provided that to detectives from the Town of Ramapo Police Department. A search warrant was executed on that home, and another feeding bag was recovered from the garbage of the Spears's residence. Those two bags had massive amounts of sodium. This mother was intentionally feeding her child salt at toxic levels."

Lloyd also revealed that Lacey had searched Google for the effects of sodium on children while at Nyack Hospital.

"The evidence is quite clear," said the assistant district attorney. "It is a very strong case. It shows that this defendant researched, planned, and executed her crime against her own son in a wanton and depraved manner."

Asking Judge Warhit to deny bail, Lloyd said although

the defendant had surrendered, she had no idea what the charges would be until a few minutes previous.

"It is murder in the second degree, and she is facing life in prison," said Lloyd. "She travels from state to state . . . and has absolutely no reason to return to New York. We're recommending she be held without bail, pending the indictment."

Judge Warhit agreed, remanding Lacey Spears to custody and setting the next court date for July 2.

After the arraignment, Commissioner George Longworth and Captain Christopher Calabrese of the Westchester County Police, and Detective Lieutenant Mark Emma of the Ramapo Police Department, held a joint press conference on the steps of the courthouse.

"Today we concluded a five-month investigation into a tragic death of a young child," Commissioner Longworth told reporters. "It took us across five different states, hundreds of interviews, examination of thousands of documents, and a significant manpower commitment by a number of different agencies."

He was then asked how the investigators had coped with the "emotional baggage" that came with the death of a child.

"I think any homicide is taken very seriously by law enforcement," he replied, "but there's a special emphasis when a child is involved. Certainly."

"How would you characterize this crime?" asked a female TV reporter.

"I think it's tragic," he replied, "when a caregiver of any child does anything but protecting."

Another reporter then asked how it felt to be able to move forward with an indictment.

"This is a very sad day for everyone," said Captain Calabrese, "but it is a day for justice. Justice for the betrayal of the intimate trust between a mother and child, justice for a mother's continual abuse and death of her innocent child for her own selfish psychological needs and financial gain. Justice for Garnett."

Back in Decatur, Alabama, many of Lacey's former friends applauded her being brought to justice.

"Thank God they're finally going to get justice for G," said Shawna Lynch. "I just hope she gets what she deserves."

Mallory McWhorter had mixed feelings after Lacey's arrest.

"Do I feel sorry for her or do I hate her?" she asked. "And I think a lot of people here are stuck in the middle of that."

Christine O'Brien watched the arraignment on television and recognized the heavy sweater Lacey was wearing as the one Lacey had stolen after first arriving at the Fellowship.

"She was actually wearing my father's sweater when she turned herself in," said O'Brien. "She stole that from me."

That night, Matt Uppenbrink released an official statement on behalf of the Fellowship Community.

"We hope that there will be a swift resolution to these proceedings," it read, "and that our young friend Garnett Spears is remembered with the same love he so freely gave to all of us in life."

The Green Meadow Waldorf School released its own statement: "We are deeply, deeply saddened at Garnett's passing and continue to mourn the loss of this child. This is an unspeakable tragedy and we will continue to keep Garnett in our thoughts and prayers."

After leaving the courtroom in handcuffs, Lacey Spears was driven to the Westchester County jail in Valhalla,

New York, to spend her first night behind bars. She was immediately placed on suicide watch and was not allowed any blankets, sheets, or shoelaces. She also had no access to the Internet or any personal belongings, including her pictures of Garnett.

"I was not suicidal," Lacey would later maintain.

On Wednesday morning, Lacey Spears's arrest made headlines all over the world. "Mother Charged with Fatal Poisoning of 5-Year-Old Boy," ran the headline in the *New York Times*. "NY Mom Accused of Poisoning Son with Salt," trumpeted the New York *Daily News*.

"For years, a doting woman paraded her motherly instincts on social media," read the *Daily News* story. "But on Tuesday, Lacey Spears kept her head bowed low as she surrendered to the justice system for allegedly torturing her son in secret."

"Pictured in Handcuffs, the Mommy Blogger Accused of 'Depraved Murder' of Her Son, Five, With Salt Overdose," was the banner headline for the *Mail Online* story.

Later that day, Ginger Dabbs-Anderson posted a photograph of herself and Garnett on her Facebook page.

"I just want justice for G," she wrote underneath it. "I love that little boy and can find peace in the way I loved him and treated him!!!"

A few hours later, she gave an exclusive interview to Jane Velez-Mitchell on the cable channel HLN. Identified only as "Anonymous," the former nurse called Lacey a "pathological liar," saying "Garnett was the sickest child" she had ever seen.

"I don't know that it was the salt," she told Velez-Mitchell, "but I really do believe . . . that she tried different things throughout his life to put him in danger."

"Was this woman an incredible actress?" asked

Velez-Mitchell. "She is obviously capable of getting a huge following on social media."

"Yes, in front of people," agreed Dabbs-Anderson, "she was the perfect-looking mother. You can see the pictures on Facebook. She bought him toys. She did take him to parks. But I think behind closed doors she did bad things."

Late Wednesday afternoon, David Sachs spent an hour with his client in Westchester County jail. Later, he described her as being "optimistic" and not suicidal at all.

"Lacey's always maintained her innocence," he said. "She's a person that holds out hope. But then again, you become indicted in the murder of your son, and you can't even believe that's happening. Like, how is this real? It's . . . a nightmare. If that can happen, then so [can] a conviction. So that was terrifying."

After the indictment, Chris Hill vented his feelings about Lacey Spears on his Facebook page.

"I don't understand how you could do something like this to your own child!?" he wrote. "I hope you rot in hell you crazy Bitch!!"

On July 7, Lacey Spears made the front page of *People* magazine. "Accused of Murder: Did a Mother Poison Her Son?" was the story teaser. Inside, a four-page spread focused on the possibility that Lacey could suffer from Munchausen syndrome by proxy.

"To any of Lacey Spears's hundreds of online followers," it began, "she seemed like the perfect mom, one whose life revolved around her 'little prince,' Garnett."

It went on to quote some of Lacey's social media postings about Garnett being in and out of the hospital since birth.

"When the 5-year-old went into the hospital yet again

in January after he began retching and having seizures," the story continued, "she chronicled her bedside vigil on Facebook, even posting photos of him on life support."

The article quotes psychiatrist Dr. Marc Feldman, an acknowledged expert in Munchausen syndrome by proxy, who described Lacey as a textbook case.

"For a very long time," he explained, "Lacey has been telling tall tales designed to make her appear admirable if not heroic. That's a cardinal sign."

Dr. Feldman said that Munchausen syndrome by proxy was not a mental illness but was criminal assault.

"They are forms of maltreatment and need to be assiduously prosecuted," he said. "These mothers tend to be psychopathic. They don't experience guilt and they lack empathy. The Lacey Spears case is likely to be taught for years to come as a quintessential [Munchausen syndrome by proxy] case because of the presence of so many indicators of this form of maltreatment."

But, Dr. Feldman added, it was highly unusual that Lacey had eventually killed her son.

"Most [Munchausen syndrome by proxy] perpetrators try to avoid a fatal outcome because death removes the opportunities for continued acclaim as a heroic, indefatigable mother," he explained.

At 10:15 A.M. on Wednesday, July 16, a procedural pretrial conference was held in front of Acting State Supreme Court Justice Robert Augustus Neary. The defendant was absent, but her sister, Rebecca, was present, sitting as far as she could from the half dozen reporters in the public gallery. Now living with her grandmother in Clearwater, Rebecca had arrived several days earlier and had already visited Lacey in jail.

At the ten-minute hearing, Lacey's two attorneys, David Sachs and Stephen Riebling, met to discuss the case calendar with the Westchester County assistant district attorneys, Patricia Murphy, Doreen Lloyd, and Christine Hatfield, in Judge Neary's chambers. After the conference, Judge Neary said the next case hearing would be held on October 13.

Outside the courthouse, Stephen Riebling spoke with reporters, saying that his client looked forward to her day in court.

"Despite the widespread attention the case has received over the past several months," he said, "we continue to trust that the people will keep an open mind and not judge Lacey . . . from what's been reported. The truth of the matter is that Lacey has pleaded not guilty and, with the support of her family, looks forward to her day in court and the opportunity to challenge the allegations and contest the charges. Going forward, the defense of this case will be focused on the relevant facts, not fiction."

The two attorneys refused to comment about whether a psychiatric defense was planned.

A few hours later, the New York State Office of Children and Family Services published a child fatality report on the death of Garnett Spears. It revealed that he had been diagnosed with elevated salt levels in Alabama well before his first birthday, and this had gone unreported to the authorities. The report was a result of Dr. Carey Goltzman's call to the New York State Child Abuse Hotline, alleging that Lacey Spears had poisoned her son with sodium through his G-tube.

"The cause of the child's death," stated the child fatality report, "was suspected to have been due to the mother's actions and possible Munchausen Syndrome by Proxy."

Since Garnett's death, the Rockland County Department of Social Services had received medical reports from Children's of Alabama in Birmingham, showing that Garnett had been critically ill with hypernatremia.

"These records also indicate there was concern for the mother's emotional stability," read the fatality report, "and it was presumed she suffered from Postpartum Depression and Munchausen by Proxy."

The 2009 Children's hospital records also revealed that Lacey had "verbalized . . . that she wanted to harm the subject child and was referred to Medical Social Services on 2/9/2009 for interpersonal conflict and dysfunction."

The fatality report further noted that there had been three complaints against Spears in Florida, alleging "inadequate Supervision and Lack of Medical Care." The complaints had all been investigated and were determined to be unfounded.

36

"A PINCH OF SALT"

On Monday, August 11, detectives Dan Carfi, Kirk Budnick, and Greg Dunn flew to Clearwater, Florida, to investigate Lacey and Garnett's life there. They spoke to the doctors who had treated Garnett as well as many of Lacey's friends from various attachment-parenting groups.

Soon after landing, the detectives interviewed Dr. Theresa Hohl, the pediatric chiropractor who had treated Garnett's ongoing ear infections for more than a year. Dr. Hohl told the detectives that Lacey had claimed that Garnett suffered from numerous ailments of which the doctor never saw any signs. Lacey never supplied any of Garnett's medical records, although she was repeatedly asked to do so. Lacey also told the doctor that she was being treated for a possible head tumor, and she complained of headaches.

At 3:00 P.M. that afternoon, the detectives interviewed Kimberly Philipson, who lived next door to Lacey's grandmother. She told them she had become friends with Lacey when Lacey came to care for her dying uncle, Bo.

Philipson said that, at first, Lacey appeared to be close to her grandmother, until they began arguing about how Garnett was being fed.

"Lacey had told [Kimberly] that she was sexually abused by [two family members] and [was] pregnant," wrote Detective Dunn in his police report. "[Kimberly] had arranged for Lacey to get medical help and counseling. [Then] Lacey claimed that she suffered a miscarriage. Kimberly advised she had spoken to Peggy Florence about the allegations and rape and sex abuse . . . [Lacey] became angry and they no longer spoke."

Philipson said Lacey constantly talked about Garnett's eating problems.

"Lacey indicated that she would breast-feed," reported Detective Dunn. "Kimberly . . . never saw Garnett breast-feed."

That evening, detectives Budnick and Dunn interviewed Kerri Alcott, who had met Lacey at a Clearwater women's group. Alcott described Lacey as very needy, saying Lacey wanted friends who she could call at all hours. She told the detectives that the members of the women's group where she had met Lacey all had young children they breast-fed at meetings.

"Lacey would never breast-feed Garnett," Detective Dunn noted, "even when she claimed he needed to feed every few hours."

Lacey also had spoken about her frequent arguments with her grandmother about Garnett's medical issues and the types of foods she was feeding him. Kerri said she finally ended the friendship because Lacey demanded too much attention.

The next morning, the two Ramapo detectives interviewed Lacey's holistic nutritionist, Meka Taulbee. Meka said she had first met Lacey in August 2011, after Florida child protective services asked to see Garnett's diet plan. Lacey had asked her to devise a vegan diet for him, and they soon became friends. Lacey had told her all about Garnett's medical problems and about him having celiac disease.

Then, after Lacey claimed to have financial problems, the nutritionist hired her to clean her house in exchange for Meka's services.

"Meka advised that Lacey had become very dependent on her," reported Detective Dunn, "and was calling her all hours of the day and night and disrupting her sleep. She felt Lacey was always looking for attention."

On Wednesday afternoon, the detectives interviewed Emma Bryant, who had first met Lacey through a mutual friend at a local women's group of breast-feeding mothers. She said Lacey claimed to use a breast pump every three hours, in addition to breast-feeding Garnett. But Emma never saw Lacey actually breast-feed.

"She recalled that Lacey would tell her very inconsistent stories about her having a miscarriage," reported Dunn, "but [Emma] did not believe [Lacey] was ever pregnant. She had heard that Lacey had sexual relations with one of the women's husbands from the women's group in an effort to get pregnant."

Bryant also said that although Lacey constantly complained about Garnett's eating problems, he always ate normally at McDonald's.

"Emma advised that Lacey was a compulsive liar," wrote Dunn, "and claimed she had a brain tumor. [Lacey] would listen to other people's stories and then use them as her own."

They next interviewed Jessica Wilson, who had hired Lacey to babysit her two children while Jessica was working. She had first met Lacey at a mother's group in Clearwater, and they became friends.

She also said that Lacey had told her that she had a brain tumor, as well as Crohn's disease and celiac disease. Wilson had eventually fired Lacey after her daughter had gotten Icy Hot back-pain ointment in her eyes and Lacey could not explain how.

"Jessica Wilson [said] Lacey had stolen a quantity of her clothing," reported Dunn, "and then returned [it] after [being] questioned."

On August 28, Lacey Spears's defense team went on the offensive, filing a thirty-two-page motion to suppress the prosecution's most damning evidence. David Sachs called for the indictment to be thrown out, on the grounds that it was "defective" and did not meet the legal standards for the offenses charged.

Sachs also wanted more than forty-three thousand pages of Lacey Spears's Facebook and MySpace records to be ruled inadmissible at trial.

"Such information is entirely and wholly irrelevant," he stated in his motion.

It also asked the judge to prohibit prosecutors from mentioning Munchausen syndrome by proxy at trial.

"Any expert witness testimony and arguments offered by the people," wrote Sachs, "relating to Defendant's alleged mental state would not be based upon facts but rather mere speculation and/or unsupported assumptions."

The defense also wanted any statements Lacey had made to law enforcement ruled inadmissible, since they had been taken "involuntarily" and "violated" her rights.

The motion further asked the judge to bar prosecutors from introducing the two feeding bags that had been found to contain high concentrations of sodium. It claimed there had been no probable cause for the search warrants and that police did not have the authority to seize them.

The motion asked the judge to rule that nothing found on Lacey's iPhone could be used at trial, claiming the search warrant for them was "defective."

Finally, the defense moved to suppress Garnett Spears's medical records from forty-three hospitals, doctors' offices, and other health-care providers because they did not cover the four-day period during which their client was accused of poisoning her son.

Still under suicide watch at Westchester County jail, Lacey Spears was now sharing a cell with accused child murderer Manuela Morgado. The forty-eight-year-old mother was charged with killing her four-year-old son, Jason, in October 2012. Prosecutors alleged that Morgado, of Mamaroneck, New York, first drugged the boy, intending to administer helium from a tank to suffocate him. When the child began to struggle, she taped his hands and feet and then suffocated him with a pillow.

The two accused child killers were finally split up in mid-September, when a tearful Morgado pleaded guilty to killing her son. She was sentenced to twenty years to life in the Bedford Hills maximum-security prison.

Detective Dan Carfi denied reports that Morgado had been put in the same cell as Lacey to try to get Lacey to confess to killing Garnett.

"We have no influence over the jail," he said. "They put these two women together because they're two women in the same predicament."

Nevertheless, the detectives did later question Morgado about whether Lacey had admitted anything.

"Lacey said she didn't do it," said Detective Kirk Budnick.

On Friday, September 26, Westchester County prosecutors responded to the defense motion with a forty-three-page motion of their own. It maintained there were no grounds for suppressing any of the evidence against the defendant.

The motion pointed out that, while being questioned at Westchester Medical Center, the defendant had answered all questions willingly and never requested a lawyer.

The prosecution's motion contained two items that Lacey had told detectives and that would later make national headlines: her comment about using "a pinch of salt for flavor" when feeding Garnett blended fruits and vegetables through his G-tube, and her speculation that he might accidentally have put something in his feeding tube to cause his own death.

On Wednesday, October 15, Judge Robert Neary handed prosecutors a major victory, ruling against all defense motions. In a written decision, the judge found no grounds to dismiss the indictment and ruled that all the search warrants were in order. This cleared the way for prosecutors to introduce their strongest evidence at trial.

Judge Neary also wrote that it was premature to exclude any evidence relating to Munchausen syndrome by proxy; the trial court judge could decide this matter at a later date.

Several hours after the ruling, a visibly upset Lacey Spears was back in Westchester County court for a pretrial status hearing. Once again, the courtroom was packed with detectives and reporters, who filled the public gallery.

Throughout the ninety-second hearing, Lacey, who had visibly put on weight since her arrest, looked grim, only nodding as her attorney whispered in her ear. She was handcuffed and wearing a loose-fitting white-and-black hooped top.

Judge Neary announced that the trial could now proceed, sending the case to an assignment judge to set a date.

Outside the courthouse, defense attorney Stephen Riebling addressed the press.

"One of the things we should always be careful about," he said, "is what the popular perception of things are. There's a lot of . . . speculation and rumor. Our job is to deal with the relevant facts."

One week later, Lacey Spears was in Judge Richard Molea's courtroom to schedule a trial date. Wearing a thin-striped white-and-blue top with long sleeves, Lacey, who was handcuffed, appeared more upbeat, bidding her two attorneys good morning. At the brief hearing, both sets of lawyers asked the judge to delay setting a trial date, due to another major case that lead prosecutor Patricia Murphy was working on.

"I understand that, at this point," said Judge Molea, "we're not ready to set a firm date."

He set the next hearing for December 11, to finalize a trial date.

Two days later, Tina Spears died of colon cancer at the age of forty-nine in a Kentucky hospice. It was the latest tragedy for the Spears family.

"It was definitely a rough year," said Rebecca Spears. "We lost Garnett in January and Lacey was charged in June. We found out that Mom had cancer in September, and then we lost her at the end of October. It was very hard."

In an online obituary, the Goad Funeral Home wrote that the Miami, Florida, native was preceded in death by her only grandson, Garnett-Paul Spears.

* * *

On December 3, Garnett Spears would have turned six, had he lived. One week later, his mother was led into Westchester County court in handcuffs, accused of his murder.

"Good morning, Miss Spears," said Judge Richard Molea. "We just had a conference and sidebar with your attorneys and the district attorney's office . . . and have identified a trial date to begin your case: Monday, January 26."

The judge then asked the prosecutors if they had any additional issues to discuss. Assistant District Attorney Doreen Lloyd announced that prosecutors would soon file a Molineux application to the court on the admissibility of several prior bad acts that could be used to attack the defendant's credibility. She said she wanted the jury to hear that an Alabama hospital had found high levels of sodium in Garnett's blood before his first birthday.

"In addition," she told the judge, "there is other Molineux information, pertaining to the defendant's contention that she was . . . engaged to an individual by the name of Blake, who has died. And it is our contention that that person never existed."

Murphy added that Spears had also claimed to have had two other children besides Garnett—a boy, prior to Garnett's birth, and a girl, afterwards.

"It is our belief," she told the judge, "that those children never existed."

On hearing this, Lacey visibly stiffened and bit her lip.

Then Judge Molea said a trial judge would soon been appointed, setting the next court date as January 15, 2015.

Outside the courthouse, defense attorney Stephen Riebling refused to discuss the prosecution's new revelations.

"We're not going to make any comments regarding

what happened today," he said, "other than we're happy to have a trial date."

On January 12, 2015, prosecutors filed a motion asking Judge Robert Neary—who had now been assigned the trial—to admit all of Garnett's medical records, beginning at birth. They especially wanted the jury to learn about Garnett's only other documented case of hypernatremia, when he was nine weeks old, at Children's of Alabama.

"[It] supplies probative evidence tending to exclude a natural medical cause for Garnett's high sodium level at the time of his death," stated the motion, "as the doctors treating Garnett in Alabama likewise excluded an internal or natural medical cause for his high sodium level."

They also wanted the jury to view Lacey's iPhone text messages, photographs, and Internet searches, especially ones about the dangers of sodium to a child.

Prosecutors also announced that they did not plan to introduce any expert testimony or evidence that Lacey suffered from Munchausen syndrome by proxy, believing they had a strong enough case without it.

Five days later, Lacey was back in court for a brief pre-trial conference. For the first time, she was wearing black horn-rimmed glasses, with her long hair tied back.

The *Journal News* and CBS's *48 Hours* had both requested permission to film the high-profile trial. Judge Neary said he had "no problems" with the media, within certain boundaries. They could film opening statements, closing arguments, and the verdict, but there would be no cameras allowed inside the courtroom during the trial, and no still photographs could be taken of any witnesses.

After the five-minute hearing, David Sachs refused to

comment except to say, "She's looking forward to her day in court."

On Wednesday, January 21—two days before the one-year anniversary of Garnett's death—Judge Neary ruled that prosecutors could introduce damning evidence that the defense had fought to suppress. He agreed to allow the jury to see Garnett's medical records as well as the incriminating Internet searches and texts from Lacey's iPhone. It was a major blow for the defense on the eve of the trial.

"The court finds that such evidence is relevant and material to central issues in this case," wrote Judge Neary in his decision. "Such records tend to exclude any natural cause for the death of the alleged victim . . . They are inextricably interwoven into the fabric of this case."

37

"LACEY SPEARS IS A CALCULATING CHILD KILLER"

At 9:40 A.M. on Monday, January 26, Lacey Spears was led into court for the first day of jury selection. She looked composed and confident, wearing a light-gray two-piece suit. She calmly answered routine questions from the silver-haired judge, saying "Yes, sir" when she was asked if she knew what a "sidebar" conference was.

Defender Stephen Riebling began by expressing concern that prosecutors still might raise the issue of Munchausen syndrome by proxy during the trial. Lead prosecutor Patricia Murphy told the judge she had redacted all mentions of Munchausen syndrome by proxy, or factitious disorder by proxy, as it is also known, from certain medical reports that would be seen by the jury.

At 10:25 A.M., more than seventy prospective jurors filed into courtroom 302, on the third floor of the courthouse. A list of the thirty-five witnesses due to be called was then read out, in case any prospective jurors knew them personally.

Judge Neary then asked if anyone was unable to serve

due to health or religious beliefs, or had read about the case. Twenty-four immediately stood up and were questioned by the judge, who did not accept most of their excuses. But he did dismiss one woman, who said she was an educator and couldn't serve because she had taken an "oath to protect children."

At noon, Judge Neary halted jury selection until the next morning because there was a major snowstorm on the way. For the next two days, Westchester County court was closed because of the heavy snow and bad weather conditions.

Jury selection resumed on Thursday morning, and by the end of the day, six men and four women had been selected. Several parents of young children were dismissed after expressing their difficulty in being objective.

On Friday, lawyers picked the final two jurors needed for the panel of twelve, as well as four alternates. The final makeup in the jury box would be six men and six women.

After warning them not to read any coverage of the case, Judge Neary dismissed the jury, telling them to be back in the jury box on Monday morning for opening arguments.

On Tuesday, February 3, Lacey Spears's trial finally began after yet another heavy snowstorm had closed the courthouse on Monday. It was a freezing cold morning, and there were several dozen print and TV reporters waiting outside while Kathleen O'Connell, a senior producer at *48 Hours,* was inside supervising a live video feed. Sitting alone on a bench outside were Rebecca Spears and her father, Terry, who had arrived from Kentucky the previous night.

At around 10:20 A.M., the courtroom doors opened and everybody filed in and took their seats. A few minutes later, two female bailiffs brought in Lacey Spears and re-moved her handcuffs. She was wearing her gray suit with a navy-blue shirt and looked distraught as she sat down next to David Sachs and Stephen Riebling at the defense table.

Then, as the judge called the court to order, she broke down in tears. Sachs put his arm around her to reassure her as her sobs filled the courtroom. After composing her-self, she took off her glasses, wiped her eyes with the inside of her jacket, and cleaned her glasses with tissues Sachs had given her.

On the other side of the courtroom, the three assistant district attorneys, Patricia Murphy, Doreen Lloyd, and Christine Hatfield, looked on dispassionately.

At 10:35 A.M., the jury filed in, taking their seats in the jury box.

"I hope everybody survived the storm yesterday," said Judge Neary. "You seem to be in good shape, nobody's wearing a cast or limping, so that's a good sign."

Then, Assistant District Attorney Doreen Lloyd walked over to a lectern in front of the jury box to start her opening statement. The blond assistant district attor-ney was wearing a somber black suit, and for the next hour and five minutes, she kept the jury enthralled.

"Lacey Spears is not an innocent mother grieving the death of her son," she began. "Lacey Spears is a calcu-lating child killer who researched, planned, and executed the intentional poisoning of her son, Garnett Spears, with salt. She is no longer the mother of Garnett Spears, be-cause she murdered him."

Lloyd told the jury that, as her son lay dying in the hos-pital with a critically high sodium level in his blood, Lacey had called a friend to get rid of a feeding bag in her living room and to not tell anyone.

"And that call and the bag that she asked her friend to

get rid of," said Lloyd, "tells you everything that you need to know about this case. Because that bag is proof positive that this defendant was feeding her son salt. Not just a pinch of salt, but a massive and deadly amount of salt, with only one purpose: to poison her son."

As Lacey sat at the defense table, writing notes on a legal pad, the prosecutor told the jury that they would hear much about the image Lacey tried to project to her family, her friends, and the world.

"That she was a single mother of a special needs, sick child," said Lloyd. "She seemed to relish in the attention and sympathy she got from having a sick little boy. The evidence will show that that was a facade. It was a false image created by her, because her son was . . . not sick until his mother made him sick."

Lloyd told the jury that Garnett was unique because he had a gastrostomy tube, which he no longer needed but Lacey did.

"By the time he was five years old," she said, "he could eat and he could eat. You name it, he could eat it by mouth without any difficulties. Hamburgers, Chinese food, pizza, ice cream, cookies, and even his vegetables. And have seconds."

And when a gastrointestinal doctor told Lacey that Garnett no longer needed the G-tube, and wanted to have Garnett undergo a feeding and nutritional evaluation, Lacey never went back to that doctor.

"Again, part of that facade," said Lloyd. "Her son has a G-tube. He is ill."

The prosecutor told the jury that the G-tube was the murder weapon and the instrument of Garnett's death.

"Because that G-tube allowed her to put whatever substance she wanted directly into the stomach . . . of her son," said Lloyd. "And her choice of substances was salt."

She described Garnett Spears as a healthy blond-haired

blue-eyed little boy who endeared himself to everyone at the Fellowship Community through his intelligence and curiosity.

"He had a knack . . . at the age of five," said the prosecutor, "of remembering the names of everybody he met. That's smart. He basically became the little mayor of that community."

She told the jury how Garnett had absolutely no medical problems when he was born, until his mother took him home. Then, after his mother complained he could not keep his food down, Garnett had undergone a procedure called a Nissen fundoplication, rendering him incapable of vomiting. A week later, Lacey had brought Garnett to the emergency room at Decatur General Hospital. He was shaking and having seizures. When tested, his blood was found to have dangerously high levels of sodium. His condition was so critical that he had to be airlifted to Children's hospital in Birmingham, Alabama, where he spent the next two weeks being treated for hypernatremia, or excess salt.

"And despite test after test," Lloyd told the jury, "doctors . . . could find no medical explanation that would cause that rise in sodium in Garnett's body."

Over the next few months, his mother brought him to various hospitals, on numerous occasions, complaining that Garnett was not gaining weight. After being diagnosed with failure to thrive, a gastrostomy tube was surgically placed in him when he was nine months old.

The prosecutor then described to the jury in some detail how a G-tube worked. She explained that Garnett had a little port in his stomach area, with a MIC-KEY button that snapped open and closed. When it's open, a connector tube is attached, and formula or anything else can be put into a feeding bag on the other end.

"Another way to use the G-tube is to use a syringe,"

she said. "And with the connector tube, you can put whatever liquid you want in a big syringe and shoot it right into the body of the person."

A key element of the prosecution's case, she said, would be electroencephalogram video taken on January 19, 2004, right after Lacey Spears learned that her son would soon be discharged from Nyack Hospital, seizure-free.

"Within an hour and fifteen minutes of being told her son is healthy and going home," said Lloyd, "she poisoned him. And you will see the inhuman brutality and torture that she puts her son through. Words cannot describe it. You will see it for yourself."

She explained how the EEG video showed the defendant bringing her son into the bathroom, at which point he was looking "healthy, smiling and happy." She comes out to collect a cup and a connector tube, going back inside the bathroom for a couple of minutes. She then brings Garnett out, places him on the bed, and waits.

"You will see how ill he gets," she said, "but I also want you to watch her when she comes out of that bathroom. You have to watch her watching him. She observed him like a scientific experiment . . . She's waiting for a result that she knows is going to come. She even takes the nurse's call button and moves it up onto the floor in the ready position. And she watches and she waits."

The prosecutor told the jury that, within minutes, Garnett started to keel over and retch in pain.

"Showtime. Boom," said Lloyd. "She hits the button and the nurse comes in. And she's like, 'Look, look at my sick child.'"

It was just the beginning of his explosive diarrhea, and such bad headaches and stomachaches that he was screaming in pain.

Over the next few hours, doctors tried to figure out

what was happening to Garnett. Blood work was drawn, and the defendant kept asking what her son's sodium level was.

"And she's told it was normal," said Lloyd. "But I submit, ladies and gentlemen, that's not what she wanted to hear. That's not going to keep her son in the hospital."

The prosecutor said that, after hearing that his sodium level was normal, Lacey hauled Garnett back into the bathroom and gave him more salt through his G-tube. Once again, she waited on the bed with him for the poison to take effect.

"And it comes," said Lloyd, "but it comes harder this time. This little boy goes through so much. He had explosive diarrhea. He's screaming in pain. You will see the progression and illness that he goes through."

But, unfortunately for the defendant, said Lloyd, she was careless, forgetting to close the MIC-KEY button. And when his nurse gave Garnett medication later, she noticed, and made a mental note of it.

"There is no reason whatsoever that G-tube site should be open at that time," Lloyd told the jury. "He was not being fed. The only conclusion that you will come to is that she had just done something with it in the bathroom."

Over the next hour, Garnett became so ill that arrangements were made to airlift him to Westchester Medical Center, the only hospital nearby with a pediatric intensive care unit.

"Now Garnett gets extremely, extremely ill," said the assistant district attorney. "His entire body is shaking, and it's very disturbing to see this little boy suffer. But she stood by and watched it. Her work. What she had done."

Garnett's condition then deteriorated to the point where he could no longer breathe and had to be intubated.

"The defendant had reached her goal," said Lloyd.

"Garnett Spears is having seizure activity. Mission accomplished."

As doctors prepared Garnett to be helicoptered across the Hudson River, his mother seemed obsessed with his sodium levels.

"You know what the defendant says? 'Are you going to be repeating his blood work, because [the] last time this happened, his sodium level was elevated.' Well, she must be clairvoyant, because guess what? They run that blood work . . . and she seemed to know already what the blood work would show. That it was indeed elevated. She got it up to 182."

Lloyd told the jury that doctors at Westchester Medical Center were confounded when they heard the child's sodium level was 182, because it was "metabolically impossible" for it to go from 144 to 182 in just a few hours. But when the director of the Maria Fareri PICU, Dr. Carey Goltzman, examined Garnett on arrival, he immediately noticed the boy's G-tube.

"And the impossible just became possible," Lloyd said, while Lacey took copious notes at the defense table.

Over the next day or so, doctors carefully lowered Garnett's sodium level until he started to wake up and the breathing tube was removed. Everything went well until Tuesday morning, January 21, when his condition suddenly worsened.

"As a result of the poisoning inflicted upon him by his mother," Lloyd told the jury, "he coded. Garnett's pupils are blown, indicative of [him] having a brain injury."

A CAT scan was taken of Garnett's brain, which showed that he had suffered irreparable brain damage. After telling the boy's mother that Garnett would not be going home, Dr. Goltzman explained that there was no medical explanation for his rise in sodium, so he was calling in child protective services to investigate.

"It was then," said the prosecutor, "that the defendant called Valerie Plauché to get rid of the feeding bag in her living room without telling anyone. Because at that point the defendant knows the doctors were onto her, and the police were at the hospital investigating what had happened to her son. And the defendant knows what's in that bag, because she used it. Salt. That bag is proof positive this defendant was feeding her son salt."

Finally, Lloyd told the jury that, even after hearing all the evidence, they still might not understand why a mother would deliberately poison and kill her child.

"It seems to go against nature, that a parent would harm a child," she said. "It seems unthinkable. But, you see, Lacey Spears is not like most people, because she thought about it. She researches it. She planned it. She executed it and then she tried to cover it up. She sits here no longer a mother but . . . a murderer.

"And at the conclusion of the presentation of evidence in this case, we're going to ask that you return a verdict consistent with that evidence: that she is guilty of the murder of her son, Garnett Spears."

After a short recess, Stephen Riebling strolled over to the lectern to address the jury. At the end of the front row of the public gallery sat Lacey Spears's father and sister, watching closely.

"Throughout Garnett's life," Riebling began, "he had a great ability to touch the hearts of the people around him. And it didn't matter if you were a family member or a friend or even an acquaintance. And that's why his death, a sudden and unexplained loss of his life, is such a tragedy."

The defense attorney told the jury that he wanted them to know about "the joy and happiness" Garnett brought into people's lives, because the trial would only focus on his tragic final hours.

"And it's likely," he said, "that what we see and hear will touch each one of our hearts in one way or another. We will feel and react emotionally. It's okay for us to grieve for Garnett. It's okay for us to shed tears for him. That's what makes us human."

Then Riebling reminded the jurors that they had made a promise to not let emotions or feelings cloud their judgment and to focus solely on the relevant facts of this case.

"In talking about the facts," he said, spinning around and pointing to the empty witness chair, "now I'm going to ask that we all turn our attention to the witness stand. Please listen to the following."

Riebling then stood in front of the empty witness stand for fifteen seconds, without saying a word.

"Members of the jury," he finally said, "what you just heard—that deafening silence—represents the sum total of the direct evidence in this case against Lacey Spears."

The youthful attorney with a crew cut told the jury that not a single witness would testify to seeing Lacey Spears feed her son anything that would have caused his death.

"Why would Lacey," he asked, "suddenly and inexplicably take the life of her son? To murder her only child? [There's] no eyewitness on the day of this alleged crime. No forensic evidence from the scene of this alleged crime. And no answer to the question why. In their place, all you will hear is a deafening silence."

Riebling said that at Nyack Hospital, his client had been an exemplary mother, doing everything a parent in her position could be expected to do.

"And through her actions," he said, "you will see . . . how much she loved Garnett. And, most importantly, the very, very deep regard that she had for the value of his life."

The defense attorney—who specializes in medical malpractice suits—told the jury that Garnett's sodium levels had surged while he was at Nyack Hospital.

"It was normal when he entered the hospital on January 17, 2014," he said, "and we know this because Nyack Hospital drew his blood. They tested his sodium and [it] was normal. The entire week that Garnett was sick, before he went to Nyack Hospital, when he was having complaints of pain and headache and stomach problems and the rolling of his eyes, his sodium level was normal. He had no issues with sodium, and that's significant, because [when] Garnett was under the care of his mother he never had a sodium problem."

The defender said he welcomed the EEG video because it showed how Lacey had attended to Garnett's every need, comforting and playing with him. He conceded that the video did show Lacey with a feeding tube connector in her hand.

"But she unrolls, furls it right in front of the camera," he told the jury. "She takes it into the bathroom with Garnett, [but] there is a reasonable explanation as to why she had that tube. But what you won't see on that videotape . . . is that Lacey Spears does anything to Garnett. Despite their allegations, there is no evidence that she ever connected that tube to him. That she ever administered anything down the tube. They want you to speculate and they want you to assume."

Riebling told the jury that the Westchester Medical Center's discharge summary had listed Garnett's cause of death as "undetermined," failing to mention that an autopsy several days later would brand it "homicide."

"With all their expertise," he said, "they didn't know what caused his death. But the prosecution stands before you now and they say, 'It's Lacey Spears that caused his death.' That doesn't seem to make sense."

Riebling finished by promising the jury that he and David Sachs would analyze each and every fact in this case to see if it was credible or not.

"The prosecution's case is riddled with reasonable doubt," he said. "And based on that, I'm going to ask you to return a verdict in favor of Lacey and find her not guilty."

At 12:35 P.M., Judge Neary broke for lunch, telling the jury to be back at 2:00 P.M., when the first witness for the prosecution would take the stand.

38

"SHE WAS FRANTIC"

Just after 2:20 P.M., Oona Younger was sworn in and took the stand. Lead prosecutor Patricia Murphy asked her to describe the Fellowship Community.

"The Fellowship is an eldercare community," Oona replied. "We have a farm and craft studios. People that work there often live there."

"Is this a religious organization?" asked Murphy.

"No, not at all," she said.

"What is your role in the Fellowship?"

"I do a lot of different things," she answered. "I am a day planner, so I try to help in coordinating what happens in Hilltop House. I'm on the Care Circle, which is a group of day planners . . . who do alternative care of people at the Fellowship."

Then Murphy asked how Oona had first met Lacey Spears in the fall of 2012.

"I met her in the dining room," said Younger, "and she and Garnett were sitting in front of the fire. I came up and introduced myself. It was the day after the lights came on after Hurricane Sandy."

She and Lacey had soon become good friends, and Oona said she had considered Lacey and Garnett as close family.

"What sort of things would you do with just Garnett?" asked the prosecutor.

"Sometime we'd go to Barnes and Noble . . . in Paramus," she replied. "Sometimes we would go to Starbucks and we'd get a little lime drink. We would go to restaurants."

"What type of restaurants would you go to?"

"We went to the Nanuet Diner a number of times, [and] Temptations Cafe in Nyack."

"What kind of food did Garnett eat in your presence?"

"He used to eat a lot of chicken," said Younger. "Sometimes hamburgers. Everything. There wasn't anything that he would refuse to eat."

"And was he able to swallow that food?"

"Yes."

Then Murphy asked whether Garnett's mother had spoken about his "dietary limitations."

"Yes, she did," Younger replied.

"And did you ever see an example of his inability to eat?"

"The only thing I saw was, once he was eating broccoli and it took him a long, long, long time to chew one bite . . . and get it down."

"But he was able to?" asked Murphy.

"Yes."

Then the assistant district attorney asked about Garnett's energy level.

"He was very, very energetic," Oona replied. "He was always on the go."

"Did she ever talk to you about the need for Garnett's G-tube?" asked Murphy.

"Yes, she said he had failure to thrive and it was difficult for him to eat [as] his esophagus was a quarter of the size of what it should be."

Oona said that the only reason that Garnett might not eat at meals was if he "jumped up from the table [to] go and have fun."

Then Murphy asked what Lacey had told her about Garnett's condition in the week before he was admitted to Nyack Hospital.

"She said that he was having seizures," she replied, "and she [had taken] him to the Good Samaritan Hospital three times . . . and the pediatric health clinic."

The prosecutor then asked about Lacey's urgent call on Friday, January 17, 2014.

As the jury listened with rapt attention, Younger described how Lacey had frantically called her at around 2:00 P.M., saying Lacey had to get Garnett to the hospital because he was having more seizures.

"She was frantic," recalled Younger. "She was screaming. And at the Fellowship we have community cars that coworkers can borrow. There was one car in particular she borrowed . . . and the woman in charge of that car is Judy. So she kept screaming, 'Get Judy's car! Get Judy's car!'"

After Judy gave her the keys, Younger said she had driven straight over to Lacey's apartment, expecting Lacey and Garnett to be waiting outside to save time. But there was no sign of them, so Oona honked the horn and went into Lacey's apartment.

"I saw Lacey standing in the middle of the [living] room," Oona told the jury. "Garnett was on the couch, laying on his stomach, and I could see that he was [being fed from] this very white and creamy bag. I observed the feeding bag and the feeding apparatus attached to the tube which was used to feed him."

Younger said she had then told Lacey that they had to go to the hospital.

"Any reaction from Lacey?" asked Murphy.

"Not really," Oona replied. "She started talking about [how] Garnett's teacher had been there recently that day and was very concerned about him."

"Can you tell the jury the tone of the voice she uses," asked the prosecutor, "when you're speaking to her in the room, and contrast that to what you heard—"

"Objection!" shouted David Sachs, rising to his feet.

"Overruled," said Judge Neary.

"She was very, very calm," answered Younger, "but on the phone she was very frantic."

Oona said that during the ten minutes she was in Lacey's apartment, Oona had tried to comfort Garnett, who was in obvious discomfort.

"I stroked his back," she said, "and [he] kind of squirmed and made some moaning noises. I kept saying, 'Let's go. Let's go. We need to get going.' And then finally [Lacey] said, 'Let me pack some bags.'"

"The whole time that you are there," asked Murphy, "was that feeding bag and feeding machine close to the child?"

"Yes, until she finally unhooked him from it."

"Did anything surprise you about the feeding bag?" asked the prosecutor.

"What really surprised me was the color of the liquid that was inside it," she replied. "Because Lacey had always said she would feed him things through the bag that she made herself. She would add greens and healthy vegetables. But there was nothing green about that bag."

Oona said she had then left to get the car ready, leaving

Lacey to pack some bags and disengage Garnett from the feeding machine.

"And then she came outside and put him in the car," said Younger. "I told her I could get someone to cover for me and I would drive her [to the hospital]. She said no and insisted on driving herself. She's in the front driver's seat and Garnett's in the back, in his car seat."

"And where are you?" asked Murphy.

"In the passenger seat," said Younger. "She dropped me off at Hilltop House."

The prosecutor then asked if she had visited Garnett in Nyack Hospital. Oona said she had gone with her husband, Howard Friedman, the following evening.

"[Garnett] was attached to the [EEG] machine and had bandages around his head," she told the jury, "and he was tethered to the machine with wires. Basically, he was in bed and could walk as far as the bathroom."

"What was his apparent condition?" asked the prosecutor.

"He looked great," she said. "He looked like his old, normal self."

"How long did you spend with him there?"

"Maybe an hour or so," she answered. "I spent time alone with him while Lacey and my husband took a walk in the hospital."

The prosecutor then asked if she had talked to Lacey on Sunday evening.

"Yes, I did," said Oona. "I spoke with Lacey after he took a turn for the worse. She said he was being taken to Westchester Medical Center and I told her I would come right over."

She said she had arrived at the hospital and had seen an intubated Garnett being carried inside on a stretcher. She had then told Lacey how sorry she was about his relapse.

"Did you get any response from her?" asked the prosecutor.

"Not much," replied Oona. "She smiled."

Soon afterwards, their friend Nellie Grossenbacher arrived, and they both accompanied Lacey into the office of Dr. Carey Goltzman, who needed information about Garnett's medical history.

"He asked Lacey some questions," Oona recalled, "and she wasn't really exactly answering. And I started to remind her of things that she had told me."

"Did she say anything to [the doctor], in the week leading up to it," asked Murphy, "about his gastrointestinal condition?"

"Lacey did tell him that Garnett had not had any feeding with the feeding bag for over a week before he got to Nyack Hospital," said Younger. "I was very surprised."

During cross-examination, David Sachs homed in on Younger's damaging testimony that Lacey had lied about the last time she had tube-fed Garnett before coming to Nyack Hospital.

"Miss Younger," said Sachs, "you testified earlier [that] you overheard Lacey tell a neurologist that Garnett had not had any tube feedings in the week before he was admitted to Nyack Hospital, correct?"

"In over a week," Younger reiterated.

The defense attorney then asked about her statement to the Ramapo Police, two days after Garnett's death, saying that Lacey had not given Garnett any gastrostomy feedings in more than a week, since he entered Westchester Medical Center.

"I might have said it," she conceded, "but if I did, I misspoke. I said Westchester, but I was thinking of Nyack."

Then Sachs asked her about her visit to Nyack Hospital with her husband on Saturday evening.

"And at some point in your visit," said Sachs, "Garnett lay down in his hospital bed. And you lay with him?"

"Yes," replied Oona.

"And isn't it true that, while you were doing that, Lacey had gone for a walk with your husband in the hospital corridor?"

"Yes."

"And while Lacey was on the walk with your husband, you recall that Garnett asked you to go to the bathroom?"

"Yes."

"And at that point," said Sachs, "Lacey came in, and she took him to the bathroom, correct?"

"Yes," she replied.

In redirect, Murphy asked whether Lacey had ever told Oona that Garnett had celiac disease.

"She told me he was being tested for it," said Younger, "and that it wasn't determined that he actually had it."

The next witness was Nurse Janelle Kimler, who was on duty in the Nyack Hospital emergency room when Garnett arrived with his mother at around 3:00 P.M. on Friday, January 17, 2014. After weighing him in the pediatric emergency room, the triage nurse asked Lacey Spears why they had come to the emergency room.

"She told me [Garnett] had three episodes of questionable seizures," Nurse Kimler told Assistant District Attorney Doreen Lloyd. "Eyes rolling into the back of his head, convulsions."

The nurse had then taken Garnett's heart rate, pulse, oxygen, and respiration, which were all normal.

"Describe his demeanor there?" asked Lloyd.

"He walked right into the room," she recalled, "and sat on the stretcher. He was very quiet."

"Did he complain of any pain?" asked the prosecutor.

"No."

"How did he appear to you?"

"Physically," she replied, "rosy cheeks, well appearing. No signs of distress. Normal child coming into the emergency room, a little nervous. We come at them with probes and a bunch of other things."

"Was there anything in particular," asked Lloyd, "that struck you?"

"He had a shaking in his hands," she recalled. "His hands were a little trembly—that I did notice."

"Did she mention that he had any diseases?" asked Lloyd.

"That he had celiac disease," said the nurse, "Crohn's disease and a new outset of seizures. So I put a question mark there, because there wasn't an actual doctor's [diagnosis]."

Nurse Kimler had then asked about Garnett's feeding tube, and Lacey said that she used it for supplemental nutrition. Kimler also asked about immunization.

"She did not vaccinize," said the nurse, "due to religious beliefs."

"Finally," asked the prosecutor, "can you describe the demeanor of his mother while you were in the ER department with her?"

"Very calm," she replied, "and very knowledgeable of medical terminology. She was very extensive in that."

The next witness was Dr. Kevin McSherry, the pediatric doctor on duty in the Nyack Hospital emergency room.

"How important is it," asked Doreen Lloyd, "for the treating pediatrician to receive accurate medical history information regarding the patient?"

"It's very important," replied Dr. McSherry.

"And when the patient is a young child, say five years old, where do you normally obtain your type of medical history information?"

"It has to be taken from the parents," he replied. "We generally can't get very reliable information from a child."

"Did you receive a list of previous complaints for her son?" asked the prosecutor.

"Yes I did," he replied. "She actually provided me with a pretty extensive history, including that he needed tympanostomy tubes and special ear tubes that are placed when children have repeated chronic infections to the ears. She told me that he had about eight of those tubes . . . and did not want a ninth set of tubes placed. She also told me that he had been diagnosed early on in infancy with celiac disease and Crohn's disease."

Dr. McSherry testified that Lacey had told him that Garnett had been hospitalized in Alabama as an infant with a high sodium level of around two hundred.

"I thought that was extraordinarily high," he told the jury, "and basically not compatible with life. So I did not believe that."

The prosecutor then asked if Lacey had discussed Garnett's diet, with regard to his G-tube.

"She did tell me he had some food intolerances," said the doctor, "allergies to food . . . He was pretty much on a limited diet [of] fruits, nuts, and some vegetables. But he was not really capable of eating typical solid foods that children of his age generally will eat."

At that point, Judge Neary recessed for the day, telling the jurors to be back at 2:00 P.M. tomorrow to continue Dr. McSherry's testimony.

On Wednesday, February 4, the temperature was above zero for the first time in a week. At 2:15 P.M., Lacey Spears, wearing a black suit and blue shirt, was escorted into the courtroom by two bailiffs. She looked ghostly pale and drawn. Later, her attorneys would explain that she was now being medicated for nausea and motion sickness, often vomiting in the back of the prison van during the drive from the Westchester County jail to the White Plains courthouse.

"Throughout the trial, [she] was a nervous wreck," explained David Sachs. "They were giving her a medication before she would go, just to transport her."

Once again, Lacey's sister, Rebecca, was in the front row of the public gallery, taking notes on a legal pad. But Terry Spears had left the previous night for Kentucky because he could not take time off work.

Continuing her direct questioning, prosecutor Doreen Lloyd asked Dr. McSherry if he had conducted a physical examination of Garnett after talking to his mother.

"Yes, I did," he replied. "He was lying there quietly on the stretcher. I did notice that a few times during the interview with his mom that he would retch. He would arch his back and make a sort of gagging sound . . . like he was going to vomit."

"And how many times did you see him do this, throughout your examination?" she asked.

"About three or four."

The prosecutor asked him to demonstrate for the jury what he had seen Garnett doing. Dr. McSherry then leaned back in his chair, turned his head to the left, and made a gagging sound.

Lloyd asked the doctor for his "overall impression" of Garnett's physical condition after examining him.

"Fairly normal," said Dr. McSherry. "I did not find any evidence of any active seizure activity."

"Did you observe any of the convulsing or eye-rolling-back, as described by his mother?"

"No, I did not."

"And the retching that you described . . . In any way is that consistent of a seizure?"

"Not necessarily, no," the doctor replied.

Dr. McSherry told the jury that after he discussed the best course of treatment with Dr. Kenneth Zatz and a pediatric neurologist, everyone agreed that the possibility of a seizure disorder must be ruled out, given what his mother had reported.

"And the best way to do that," Dr. McSherry explained, "would be to admit the child to the hospital and perform a video EEG."

Then Garnett was placed on an IV, and routine labs were drawn to check his blood count and electrolytes, including sodium and chloride.

"Specifically," asked the prosecutor, "what was the sodium level upon admission to Nyack Hospital?"

"It was 138," replied the doctor. "The normal range is between 135 and 145."

At the end of her direct, Lloyd asked what the defendant's demeanor had been after she was told that Garnett was being admitted and would have a video EEG to determine whether he was having seizures.

"She seemed just very passive about it," Dr. McSherry replied. "It was okay. There was no anxiety about admitting him to the hospital. No fear."

Then Stephen Riebling began his cross-examination, asking whether Lacey had mentioned glucose being found in Garnett's urine a few days earlier at Good Samaritan Hospital—a possible sign of diabetes mellitus, which could elevate sodium levels. Dr. McSherry said that she had told him that, and that Garnett's urine was then tested, with some glucose being found.

"It should be negative," said Dr. McSherry, "but there was some glucose in his urine."

"So this was an abnormal finding," Riebling noted. "Do you agree?"

"That's correct," he replied.

"Now," the defender continued, "while you and Garnett were in the emergency department, did you order a study for diabetes mellitus?"

"No," he replied. "Only that urine test was ordered, as was a complete metabolic panel, which would have included a serum (blood) glucose."

"I understand," said Riebling. "My question was, as a result of his high urine, did you order any testing for diabetes mellitus?"

"No, I didn't," said the doctor.

In her redirect, Doreen Lloyd asked the doctor to describe the difference between glucose in the blood and in the urine. The doctor explained that the blood of a patient suffering from diabetes mellitus would typically have glucose levels of two hundred to three hundred or even higher, but that glucose has to be around 250 to even show up in a urine test.

"And with reference to . . . the complete blood panel that was taken from Garnett Spears," asked Lloyd, "did it indicate what his serum glucose was?"

"Yes," Dr. McSherry replied. "It was ninety-four."

"Is that normal?" asked the prosecutor.

"That's the normal range," he said.

"And based upon that blood result, does it indicate to you as a pediatrician that Garnett Spears had diabetes mellitus?"

"No, it does not."

The next witness was Detective Joseph Callero, who was assigned to the Westchester County Department of Public Safety's Forensic Investigations Unit. Detective Callero testified that he conducted an in-depth analysis of Lacey Spears's iPhone 4, extracting its entire contents using a forensic software tool called Cellebrite. This state-of-the-art program for mobile devices also captures any texts or phone calls that may have been deleted by the owner.

"What did you get?" asked Assistant District Attorney Christine Hatfield.

"Basically, everything the software was able to extract," Callero explained. "GPS locations, call logs, texts, photos, videos, Web searches, and databases. Pretty extensive."

"And how extensive was it?" asked Hatfield.

"It was very large," he replied. "Printed, it was close to eighteen hundred pages."

The detective said that because of the huge volume, he had prepared a condensed version, targeting specific items, time frames, and categories. Then, as the judge was about to admit the detective's four extraction reports into evidence—covering the period from January 11 to January 24, 2014—the defense objected.

At a sidebar, David Sachs complained that the prosecution had failed to tell the jury that Lacey's iPhone had been seized by a search warrant. The prosecution explained that the detective had been called out of order because he was leaving the next day for a monthlong vacation.

"I just want to find out where we're going," a visibly frustrated Judge Neary told the attorneys.

When the jury returned after a short recess, the judge sent them home early.

"Folks, I think we're going to suspend the detective's direct," Judge Neary told the jury. "Tomorrow we'll start with another witness. It's a scheduling conflict. It really shouldn't concern [you]."

On day three of the trial, lead detective Dan Carfi took the stand to get the prosecution's case back on track. Under Patricia Murphy's questioning, he explained how he had obtained a search warrant to seize the defendant's iPhone and laptop computer.

He told the court that on Saturday, January 25, 2014, he had gone to Lacey Spears's room at the Comfort Inn and knocked on the door.

"I got directly from Lacey," he testified, "the iPhone and the laptop computer."

"Anything else obtained?" asked Murphy.

"Yes, from Lacey's sister, Rebecca, I obtained an Apple iPad."

Detective Carfi had then brought all three devices back to his office, giving them to Detective Callero the following day. Then, on Monday, Carfi obtained a second search warrant, allowing Callero to extract everything from the phone.

"How was the phone stored at police HQ?" asked Murphy.

"The moment I received the telephone from Miss Spears," said Carfi, "I didn't touch it. I powered it down. I put it inside a special bag for electronic items so that messages and phone calls cannot go in or out."

Detective Callero was then recalled to the stand to continue his testimony. Sachs immediately objected to the admission of all four reports of evidence found on his client's smartphone, but Judge Neary allowed them all.

Assistant District Attorney Christine Hatfield then asked Detective Callero about a search Lacey had made at 6:16 A.M. on January 13, 2014, three days before she brought Garnett into Nyack Hospital.

"The search terms were 'Normal Sodium Levels for a Child,'" said Detective Callero. "It was a Google search."

Hatfield asked about other searches that night.

"'Dangers of High Sodium Levels in a Child,'" replied Callero. "'The Effects of Excess Sodium on Your Health and Appearance,' 'Signs of Elevated Sodium Levels,' 'hypernatremia,' and 'What Happens to Someone if They Have High Sodium Levels in the Blood.'"

The prosecutor then asked how many photographs, taken between January 11 and January 24, 2014, had been extracted from Lacey Spears's iPhone.

"Approximately 215," replied the detective.

Hatfield then singled out eight photographs to show to the jury. They ranged from Garnett happily eating Chinese food and painting several weeks before his death, to being swathed in head bandages and hooked up to an EEG machine, to being on life support at Westchester Medical Center with his eyes closed and mouth wide open.

The photos were passed among the jury. It was the first time they had seen a picture of Garnett Spears. One of the jurors openly cried as she looked at the photographs, and several others were visibly moved.

Lacey Spears sat at the defense table with her head in her hands, dabbing her eyes with a tissue. Her sister, Rebecca, who was celebrating her thirtieth birthday, teared up in the public gallery.

Then David Sachs began his cross-examination, directing the detective's attention to some of his client's other Google searches, which were not mentioned by the prosecution, trying to portray his client as a loving mother. He had the detective read out some Google searches that Sachs characterized as ones that a concerned mother might make. These included "What Causes High Magnesium," "Renal Glycosurie," and "Could Pin Worms Cause seizures?"

After a lunch break, Sachs continued his cross-examination, concentrating on a flood of texts from Lacey after Garnett's death, that said how deeply she loved Garnett and that she was devastated. He had the detective read out some of Lacey's texts.

He then turned to Lacey's Google searches, made the

day after Garnett's death, about various ways to commit suicide, such as by overdosing on sleeping pills or self-injecting insulin. Sachs had the detective read fifteen of these suicide searches to the jury, which looked unmoved.

In redirect, Christine Hatfield pointed out that, throughout Garnett's hospitalization and subsequent death, Lacey had been posting continuous updates on Facebook. Then she asked Callero if Lacey had received a text message at 7:11 P.M. on Tuesday, January 21.

"Yes," he replied. "[It read] 'I just saw the last post on FB. Stay strong, Sending healing thoughts to G.'"

"Did the defendant receive another text message on January 19 at 10:23 P.M.?" asked Hatfield.

"Yes," the detective said. "'Saw your Facebook love, I'm praying, you know family is here too. Whatever you need, please let me know, and I'm always here to talk and I love you, huge hugs for you two.'"

The final witness of the day was Tedjan Wojohk, whose company had installed and operated the video EEG machine in Garnett Spears's room. Under Christine Hatfield's direct, he told the jury that he analyzed data on a daily basis, texting a patient's doctor if there were any signs of seizures.

He said the video EEG machine had been connected to Garnett from just after midnight on Saturday, January 18, 2014, until Sunday, January 19.

"It was approximately forty-two hours," said Wojohk, "except for a short time when the EEG was turned off."

In mid-February 2014, Wojohk said, the entire EEG video was downloaded from his system's hard drive onto a flash drive, which was then provided to the Westchester County District Attorney's office.

The flash drive was admitted into evidence, to be shown in court on Monday.

"Put your helmet on," one of the female jurors whispered to another.

At 4:25 P.M., Judge Neary dismissed the jury, telling them to be back at 9:30 A.M., Monday morning. There would be no court on Friday because one of the jurors had a previously planned vacation.

39

THE EEG VIDEO

On Monday, February 8, another big snowstorm delayed the courthouse opening until 11:00 A.M. It was almost midday when the fourth day of the trial got underway.

Before the jury came in, Stephen Riebling had an urgent matter to bring to the judge's attention. *Journal News* reporter Lee Higgins had overheard the juror's "helmet" comment, including it in his story that ran Friday.

"It appears that at least some of the jurors," said Riebling, "are making comments about what might be coming. It was written in the paper that one of the jurors said, 'Put on your helmets,' or something along those lines. Now I don't want to make a big deal out of it, but the jury clearly should not be discussing anything amongst themselves, or whispering."

"I didn't hear anything," said Judge Neary, "but I saw the article in the paper."

The judge agreed to remind the jury not to discuss the case, and when they came into the courtroom, he told them to "remain stoic" and not to comment on the case.

The prosecution then called its seventh witness, Keith Mancini, a forensic photographer at the Westchester County Forensic Science Laboratory in Valhalla, New York. Over the next two days, Mancini, who photographs crime scenes and autopsies, would screen forty video extracts from the EEG video for the jury.

Under prosecutor Christine Hatfield's questioning, Mancini said he had received from Tedjan Wojohk the thirty-two-gigabyte flash drive of video taken on January 18 and 19. He had then edited the forty-plus hours of video into forty clips, totaling 130 minutes, to make it "a little user-friendly." He also had exported thirteen still frames from the video and had printed them up so they could be passed among the jury.

Then Mancini began playing the video clips on a TV monitor set up in front of the jury box. The first dozen, from Saturday morning, showed Garnett wearing a large head bandage, happily playing with his toys. His mother talked on her cell phone, tidied up, and occasionally took him the bathroom, which was out of camera range.

At 12:35, Judge Neary broke for lunch, and two hours later, when the jury was back in its seats, the video clips resumed. They showed that, as Saturday progressed, there was no sign of any seizure activity in Garnett. A three-minute clip, starting at 8:47 P.M., Saturday night, showed Oona Younger sitting next to Garnett on his bed, reading him a story. In another clip, a doctor came in to examine Garnett, and the boy appeared alert and responsive.

On Sunday morning, Garnett looked well and very animated as a nurse came in and disconnected his G-tube from his night feeding. The next clip showed him sitting up in bed, eating breakfast. His mother helped him drink from a juice box.

But in the twenty-fifth clip, running from 10:25 A.M. to 10:46 A.M., everything changed. The jury was riveted to the TV screen as the clip began, showing a smiling Garnett sitting on the bed, kicking his legs around. Then his mother picked him up off the bed and took him into the bathroom. A few seconds later, she emerged and walked across the room and out of camera range.

Hatfield asked Mancini to slow down the video as Lacey came back into the shot, about thirty seconds later. In one hand she was holding a large cup, and in the other was a thin feeding tube connector. She then went into the bathroom with Garnett. Thirty seconds later, she came out, walked over to the other bed in the room, collected something, and then returned to the bathroom.

Several minutes later, she brought Garnett out of the bathroom. The boy was looking dazed and lethargic. When she picked him up and put him on the bed, he dropped down, as his legs could no longer support him. For the next few minutes, Garnett lay on the bed with his legs up to his chest, looking terrified. Several times, he wiped his nose with his hand.

About a minute later, his mother came out of the bathroom, holding some clothes. She walked straight past Garnett, who was now squirming on the bed. She examined his G-tube and then placed the nurse call button on the pillow beside her.

She then knelt on the bed with her hands clenched together, watching Garnett writhe in pain. Garnett struggled to stand up, but then he fell forward on the bed, desperately trying to vomit. It was then that Lacey Spears pressed the call button and Nurse Nora Bompensiero rushed in.

Several female jurors wiped away tears as they watched the little boy visibly suffering. Lacey was quietly sobbing at the defense table, dabbing her eyes with tissues.

Now, with Nurse Bompensiero in the room, Lacey started stroking Garnett's back and comforting him. For the next several minutes, Garnett tried to retch, repeatedly falling flat on his face. The nurse took his blood pressure, placing in front of him a large plastic container to be sick in.

Dr. Sarika Sunku then came into the room and checked Garnett's lungs and chest with a stethoscope. He just stared at his mother as she knelt besides him, looking concerned. She then gave Garnett some water, which he drank.

Garnett started trying to retch again, repeatedly falling forward onto his mother. Nurse Nora took his temperature with a rectal thermometer as another nurse came in to help.

After the clip finished, Christine Hatfield passed out to the jury some still shots from the video. They clearly showed Lacey on her way to the bathroom with the cup and connector tube.

The prosecutor then screened more video clips, which showed Garnett's condition worsening over the next hour as he rolled around in agony and had several episodes of explosive diarrhea.

All through the clips, Lacey Spears sobbed at the defense table while the jury looked visibly shocked at seeing Garnett suffer.

By the thirty-fourth clip, taken at 3:51 P.M. on Sunday, Garnett seemed much improved and was sitting up, throwing a balloon around.

Two video clips later, at 4:19 P.M., Lacey dressed Garnett in a medical gown and took him back into the bathroom. Three minutes later, they emerged, and the change in him was obvious. All the life had gone from his eyes, and he looked stupefied as he lay on his back with his legs up to his chest. Then he had several bouts of diarrhea while his mother cleaned him up and changed his diapers.

Lacey curled up beside him, waiting. There was a

blank look on her face as Garnett rolled around the bed and onto his stomach in pain. Then she pulled him up by his wrists and put on his pajama bottoms as he fell back onto the bed, convulsing.

A nurse came into the room, and Lacey's whole demeanor changed. She started stroking Garnett's back as he made violent retching movements. By the thirty-eighth clip, starting at 5:37 P.M., Garnett is having convulsions on the bed, surrounded by doctors and other medical staff. Lacey sat on the other bed, dabbing her eyes with a tissue, while Nellie Grossenbacher, who had just arrived, comforted her.

The thirty-ninth video clip showed a doctor putting Garnett onto a stretcher. The boy was still convulsing, his legs shaking uncontrollably. The final one-minute clip, beginning at 6:18 P.M., showed the little boy lying on the stretcher, flailing his arms.

At the end of the clip, Judge Neary recessed for the day, and the jury filed out of the box, looking shaken. At the defense table, David Sachs comforted his weeping client until she was handcuffed by a court usher and led out of court, watched by her ashen-faced sister in the public gallery.

On Tuesday, February 10—the fifth day of the trial—Christine Hatfield began by displaying a still photograph taken from the EEG video. It showed Nurse Nora Bompensiero closing Garnett's MIC-KEY button, which was still open after Lacey's last visit with him to the bathroom. Then Hatfield showed a second photograph, taken one minute later, after the nurse had called a Code White on the distressed child.

The two photographs were then passed among the jurors, and Hatfield had no further questions.

Stephen Riebling began his cross-examination, which

would last the rest of the day. He immediately zeroed in how the forty-hour video had been edited, asking Keith Mancini about portions of the video that may have been favorable to his client but had not been included in the extracts.

Under questioning, Mancini said he had had several meetings with prosecutors to discuss the required video edits and had received a timeline from which to work.

The defender then screened a series of clips, asking about what the jury had not been shown, using Mancini's own notes to illustrate his point. This extra footage, from the beginning and the end of the prosecution-edited clips, showed Garnett interacting with his mother in the hospital room.

One of the clips Riebling referenced started at 10:25 A.M. on Sunday. It showed his client getting out of bed and walking around the room.

"Now," said Riebling, "what we don't see in the video is what happens right before Miss Spears gets out of bed. Right?"

"It's not included in that clip, no," Mancini conceded.

"We are physically prevented from seeing that, because of the way the video is edited. Is that correct?"

"It's not included in that clip, no."

"But you know what's included before this?" asked the defender.

"I have seen some of it, yes."

"In fact, it's reflected in your notes of your timeline."

"Right," said Mancini. "The timeline was provided to me."

"Now [from your notes], what's not shown in this clip," said Riebling, "is the young boy speaking to a lady before she gets out of bed?"

"Yes," he replied. "I don't believe that it says in the notes that she was speaking to him."

"But that's not shown in your video?"

"I guess not, no."

"So, the part of the video before," Riebling continued, "where Garnett speaks with Lacey, was cut out at the direction of the assistant district attorney, Christine Hatfield. Is that correct?"

"Yes, it was," he replied.

After the lunch break, Riebling continued to show harrowing portions of the video, including extra parts that had not been included by the prosecution.

The final video clip he screened for the jury was chilling. It showed Garnett after he had coded Sunday night, lying motionless on his hospital bed. His mother came over and appeared to try to revive him. She then walked out of the camera shot, returning with several nurses, who tried to help Garnett.

Suddenly, Lacey Spears slumped down on the defense table, shaking and gasping. Then she began sobbing loudly.

After the clip was finished, Riebling had no further questions for the witness, and Judge Neary recessed for the day.

40

The trial resumed for its sixth day at 2:30 P.M. on Wednesday. Lacey Spears was led into court in handcuffs, wearing the same heavy black woolen sweater she had worn at her arraignment.

The prosecution's eighth witness was Dr. Ariel Sherbany, a pediatric neurologist affiliated with both Nyack Hospital and the Westchester Medical Center. He told the jury that he had been called into Nyack Hospital on Saturday, January 18, 2014, to examine Garnett Spears.

"Prior to doing your examination on the child," asked prosecutor Patricia Murphy, "did you speak to his mother?"

Dr. Sherbany said Lacey had told him that Garnett had suffered a series of seizures in the days prior to him being admitted, the longest lasting for four minutes.

"The seizures were preceded by a family of complaints of headaches, stomachaches," he said. "Also, the mother had worked in many nursing facilities in the past, so obviously that raised my concern that if she thought it was a seizure, then it was. So I needed to make sure we're not missing anything."

Dr. Sherbany had then performed a neurological examination of Garnett, checking the boy's cranial nerve, his muscle strength, and his ability to flex his neck.

"I thought his examination was fine," said the doctor, who decided to continue with the video EEG, which until then had not revealed any abnormalities.

Dr. Sherbany said he had next received a call from Dr. Sunku, at 6:00 Sunday night, saying Garnett was having seizures. He had then asked Dr. Neelima Thakur, an epilepsy specialist, to review the EEG remotely through her computer. Dr. Thakur had done so, reporting that something was happening but that she was uncertain it was seizures.

"I headed to the hospital," said Dr. Sherbany, "to try and look at things myself, to see what's really going on from my perspective as a consultant neurologist."

By the time Dr. Sherbany arrived at around 8:30 P.M., Garnett was intubated and paralyzed by sedatives.

"When you got to the hospital," asked Murphy, "did you learn what Garnett Spears's most recent sodium lab test was?"

"Yes, I did," he replied. "It was 182."

"When you heard that number, 182," asked the prosecutor, "what did it mean to you as a specialist in pediatric neurology?"

"Well, I was surprised by it," replied the doctor. "So then I asked the mother, was he drinking and urinating a lot? And she did say yes, that he was. I was actually puzzled that he was supposedly having seizures in the first place, but I was also puzzled by the high sodium. I couldn't understand what it was."

"You were concerned about that number?"

"Absolutely," replied the doctor, "because it's such a high number. It's not compatible with life."

Dr. Sherbany said that when Garnett's mother provided her son's medical history the day before, she had mentioned him having a sodium of two hundred when he was ten weeks old.

"And I was questioning the fact," he said. "I recall telling her, 'Are you sure it was two hundred, because a sodium of two hundred is not compatible with life. Are you sure it wasn't diabetes of high sugar which was two hundred?'"

Dr. Sherbany had next seen Garnett at around midnight on Monday night in the Westchester Medical Center's pediatric intensive care unit. Garnett had now been extubated, but he was groggy from all the paralyzing medication he had received.

"I was told he was waking up throughout the day," he said. "And so, by the time I saw the child, he was still lethargic, but . . . better than he had been earlier in the day."

Dr. Sherbany had then done a neurological examination, finding nothing that concerned him. He left the hospital satisfied that his patient was recovering well.

The next day, he told the jury, he had received a call informing him that Garnett's brain had herniated, and he would not recover.

"He had clearly deteriorated," said Dr. Sherbany, as Lacey began sobbing at the defense table. "It sounded like a catastrophic decline in the child's condition. I remember feeling shocked about it, but at that point it was clear that he wouldn't [recover]. I was told there was no need to be there."

In his cross-examination, Stephen Riebling referenced a medical progress note Dr. Sherbany had written on Sunday, January 19, about how Lacey had reported Garnett had had polydipsia (excessive drinking) and polyuria (excessive urination) that day. He then asked the doctor about Lacey's claim that Garnett had had a sodium of two hundred as an infant.

"And you indicated that that was not compatible with life," said Riebling. "Is that right?"

"Correct," Dr. Sherbany replied.

"It was clear to you that the number must have been a mistake?"

"Objection," said Patricia Murphy.

"Sustained," ruled the judge.

"Doctor," Riebling continued, "you indicated on direct that you questioned the mother and you felt that she'd made a mistake. You asked her could that be . . . from another possible source, such as sugar or something like that?"

"Yes," he agreed.

"Because you realized that the number of two hundred couldn't have been possible, so that it had to have been something else?"

"She insisted that it was sodium," the doctor replied. "She seemed quite certain it was sodium."

On redirect, Murphy asked if the doctor had been expecting a sodium jump from 144 to 182 in his young patient.

"I was honestly very puzzled by seeing this jump," Dr. Sherbany said. "When I was in medical school, [my teacher] used to tell me, 'Always trust the mother.' So I asked [Lacey Spears], 'Was he drinking a lot? Urinating a lot?' [I was] trying to find some reason. I was not really comfortable about how this came about, and I was very puzzled."

When Lacey had told him her son had been drinking and urinating a lot, he had considered the possibility that Garnett might have had diabetes insipidus, which can raise sodium levels.

"I did put it in my notes as a question mark," he explained, "giving the mother the benefit of the doubt."

After a ten-minute recess, the prosecution called Dr. Neelima Thakur to the stand. The board-certified epileptologist had monitored Garnett Spears's EEG and had supervised its setup. Under Patricia Murphy's questioning, Dr. Thakur said that she had reviewed Garnett's EEG on Saturday evening, and there was no sign of seizures.

"Did you discuss what you had reviewed with his mother?" asked Murphy.

"Yes," she replied.

"And was there any reaction when you told her that there was nothing wrong?"

"No," said Dr. Thakur. "I think she took it in the right spirit. I said I'm going to continue the study . . . and get more information."

When the doctor checked in again on Sunday morning, the EEG was normal. But then, at around 6:30 P.M., she received a call from Dr. Sherbany, who reported that Garnett could be having back-to-back seizures.

"I looked at the EEG video [from my computer]," she testified. "I could see a lot of doctors in the room, trying to treat the patient. I did not see any seizure activity . . . but I saw a significant amount of slowing in the wave forms. The brain had a very severe dysfunction."

Dr. Thakur explained that normal Delta brain waves should be between six and eight hertz, but that Garnett's had slowed to just two or three hertz.

"This slowing that you describe," asked Murphy, "is that dangerous to the child's brain?"

"Depending on the severity, yes."

"Can you tell us, Doctor," asked the prosecutor, "in your experience, what could cause such a diffuse slowing of the brain waves in a child?"

"Anything that can injure the brain," Dr. Thakur replied, "can cause that wave to slow. Anywhere from infections, toxins, high glucose, high sodium, or any head injuries."

"Doctor, you mentioned high sodium," Murphy continued. "Would a sodium rate of 182 be what you would consider to be a high rate of sodium?"

"Yes," replied Dr. Thakur.

In cross-examination, Stephen Riebling suggested that Garnett Spears could have had metabolic acidosis, a condition in which the kidneys are not removing enough acid from the body, which can lead to brain damage.

"Do you know how metabolic acidosis is diagnosed?" Riebling asked.

"It's diagnosed by arterial blood gas," replied the doctor.

"Do you know if a blood gas was taken from Garnett Spears on the afternoon or evening of January nineteenth?"

"I was not involved, so I don't know."

Then the attorney showed her Garnett's discharge document from Nyack Hospital, which recorded a blood gas result collected at 6:30 P.M. on Sunday.

"That would have been around the time Dr. Sherbany called you?" he asked.

"Yes."

"Now, if you look at the blood gas result," Riebling continued, "this is the one way that we can determine metabolic acidosis, correct?"

"It is," agreed Dr. Thakur. "But I do not read blood gases and I do not diagnose metabolic acidosis, so this is completely out of my field. My field is neurology and seizures, and I'm not trained for this."

"But you indicated that metabolic acidosis could have an effect on someone's brain?"

"Yes," she said.

"So by looking at the values on this page, you would not be able to tell us whether or not he had metabolic acidosis?"

"I cannot say," she replied.

"I object to it," said Murphy, rising to her feet.

"Yes, I think the answer to that is that she said she's not qualified in that area," said Judge Neary. "So stay away from it. I sustain the objection."

"With regard to pH values alone," said Riebling, "does that help us determine whether someone's blood is acidic or basic?"

"I'm going to object," said Murphy.

"The pH is the acidity of fluid in the blood," said the judge. "The doctor said she's not qualified. Did I hear it correctly, Doctor? You're not qualified to determine that?"

"Yes," she replied.

"Doctor," the defender said, "I want you to assume for a moment that the results that you have in front of you indicate that Garnett Spears had a metabolic acidosis at 6:30 on January 19, 2014. Is that right?"

"Again, I'll object," said Murphy.

"We're moving on at this time," Judge Neary told him.

"I'm going to ask her," Riebling continued, "that she's already indicated, Judge, that metabolic acidosis can effect an insult [of the brain]. If she makes that assumption, that would explain his brain swelling at 6:30 P.M. on January 19?"

"Doctor," asked the judge, "do you feel qualified to answer a question like that?"

"Yes, to the extent that metabolic acidosis is diagnosed."

"Would you know, Doctor," pressed Riebling, "if metabolic acidosis is caused by kidney failure?"

"I'm not qualified," she answered.

"Do you know if metabolic acidosis can be caused by excessive diarrhea?"

"Objection," said Murphy.

"Do you have the next question?" asked the judge, running out of patience.

"Dr. Thakur," said Riebling, "you can't answer it because you don't know, or because you're not qualified?"

"Objection."

"She can answer it," said the judge.

"Because I don't know," she replied.

"Nothing further," said Riebling, walking back to the defense table.

Judge Neary then recessed for the day, telling the jury to be back on Friday at 10:15 A.M. because the court would be closed on Thursday.

41

NURSE NORA

At 10:43 A.M. on Friday, February 13, the prosecution called its tenth witness, Nurse Nora Bompensiero, who had been Garnett Spears's primary pediatric nurse at Nyack Hospital. She told the jury that she had first met Lacey and Garnett Spears when she came on duty at 7:00 A.M., Saturday, January 18, 2014.

"What was the plan of care for that Saturday?" asked Assistant District Attorney Doreen Lloyd.

"Basically to monitor him with the video EEG," she replied.

Nurse Nora said that everything had gone well that day, with no signs of any seizure activity. Just before ending her shift at 7:00 P.M., she had prepared Garnett's feeding tube for the night nurse because he would be having overnight feeds.

"When you said you set him up for the feed," asked Lloyd, "that would be gastrointestinal food?"

"Correct," she replied.

"And is there any specific tubing that's required to hook him up to the feeding machine," asked Lloyd.

"Yes," she said. "There was a tube into the abdomen, with a MIC-KEY button, and there's a connector tube that clips onto it. Our hospital didn't have that tube."

"What happened as a result of you not having that particular connector tube?"

"I asked his mother to provide one," she said. "And she had one and gave it to me."

When Nurse Nora came back on duty at 7:00 A.M. on Sunday, the outgoing nurse said Garnett had had "an uneventful night," and they had looked into his room to see him.

"And how did he appear when you first saw him on Sunday?" Lloyd asked.

"Like the Saturday, healthy and normal."

Nurse Bompensiero had returned to Garnett's room at around 8:30 A.M. and disconnected him from the overnight feeding, closing up his MIC-KEY button port.

"What, if anything, did you do with the connector tube?" Lloyd inquired.

"I gave it back to his mother."

Everything was normal that Sunday morning until around 10:30 A.M., when a warning light in the hallway lit up after Lacey pushed the call button. Nurse Bompensiero rushed into the room and saw Garnett gagging.

"He had all the motions behind throwing up," she explained, "but not the actual vomit coming out."

"And what was your assessment of that?" asked Lloyd.

"I definitely knew there was a change. He was dry heaving, and then afterwards he was complaining of a severe headache and yet [was] extremely agitated. He was rolling around in bed. He was clutching his head. He was screaming. The video EEG fell off because he was so upset. It went on for about ten to fifteen minutes."

She testified that she had immediately notified Dr. Sunku, the pediatric physician on duty.

"She came to his bedside," said Nurse Bompensiero. "We gave him medication [through an IV]. Zofran . . . to decrease the nausea, and the Motrin, to help with the headache."

The nurse said the medication seemed to work, and Garnett stopped dry heaving and his headache improved. But, around midday, he started "shivering and shaking" and having severe diarrhea.

"And would you describe what you saw Garnett doing?" asked the prosecutor.

The nurse then physically demonstrated for the jury.

"He had his hands very close to his body," she said, "and he was really just shaking. His body was shaking."

She had then paged Dr. Sunku, who ordered a glucose test, which found Garnett's glucose to be elevated, at 239. Dr. Sunku then ordered a complete lab test, and blood was drawn from Garnett at 1:20 P.M. About an hour later, Nurse Nora went in to check on Garnett.

"Did you have any conversation with the defendant?" asked Lloyd.

"Yes, she called me into the room," said the nurse, "and was asking about the results of the lab work."

The results had just come in, and the nurse went through them with Lacey Spears, saying everything seemed to be normal.

"And what did she say after you told her it was normal?" Lloyd inquired.

"She asked me about the sodium, [and] if it was normal."

Nurse Bompensiero explained to Lacey that her son's

sodium was 144 and in the normal range, but that his 114 chloride level was elevated.

In the afternoon, Garnett's condition had improved, but at around 4:30 P.M., Lacey pressed the call button again, and the nurse rushed into his room.

"He appeared to be dry heaving again," she told the jury, "and again had all the motions of throwing up without actually doing it."

Dr. Sunku then came in and ordered Garnett to be given an antinausea drug through an IV.

"And what, if anything, did you observe while you were administering it?" asked Lloyd.

"While I was leaning over him," said the nurse, "I noticed that the G-tube port was open. So I just said, 'Mom, the G-tube is open.' And she said okay, and we just closed it up."

"And had Garnett Spears been fed through his gastrointestinal tube at that time?"

"No," she replied.

Then the prosecutor showed the jury a still photograph, taken from the EEG video, that showed Nurse Nora closing up Garnett's MIC-KEY button.

"And what was his physical condition . . . around 4:30?" asked the prosecutor.

"It seemed to me like everything from the morning was starting up again," she said. "He started complaining of a very severe headache again, his eyes were tearing. He was rolling around again."

Nurse Bompensiero said that Garnett was then given more Zofran and Motrin.

"What happened next?" asked the prosecutor.

"I heard a page: 'I need a nurse to 242,' " she said. "So I ran into the room and observed him on the bed. He was totally incontinent of urine and stool. The bed was soaked through. He appeared to be twitching. His eyes were moving around in his head. So, at that point, I called a Code White so I could get additional help in the room."

"And what, if anything, was the defendant doing when you entered the room?"

"She was screaming and pointing to look at him."

Within seconds, Dr. Sunku and half a dozen other medical staff were in the room, working on Garnett.

"So we were trying to control the twitching and the worsening seizures," the nurse explained. "They gave him a dose of Ativan. We were just trying to assess and monitor his vital signs."

After checking his blood pressure and heartbeat, which were normal, they changed Garnett's sheets and diaper. He was then given repeated doses of Ativan to try to stop his body from twitching, but it didn't work.

Then Garnett started having problems breathing, and the decision was made to sedate and intubate him. Garnett was in such a critical condition, Nurse Bompensiero told the jury, that it was decided to transfer him Westchester Medical Center, which has a pediatric intensive care unit.

"And at this point," asked Lloyd, "what was the defendant doing?"

"So, while we were in the room," said Nurse Bompensiero, "she was down the hall with some friends."

"Did you have a conversation with the defendant?"

"While we were in the room," recalled the nurse, "she came in and asked us to check the labs. And she said, 'The last time this happened, his sodium was high. Have you checked on that?'"

The nurse said Garnett's blood was then drawn at 6:30 P.M. Forty-five minutes later, she received a call from the laboratory with the results.

"Is that normal?" Lloyd inquired.

"It's normal when there is a result that is very critical."

The lab told her that Garnett's sodium level was 182 and his chloride was 160, which was dangerously high.

"I immediately called Dr. Sunku," said the nurse. "They wanted to repeat the results because it was so high."

The labs were repeated at 7:37 P.M., and the results came back half an hour later.

"His sodium was still elevated, at 178, and chloride 155," said Nurse Bompensiero.

After the arrangements were made to airlift Garnett to Westchester Medical Center, the nurse told Lacey what would be happening and that Lacey could fly over with him in the helicopter.

"She said she wanted to drive with her friend," said the nurse, "and she wouldn't come with him."

"And did you have any conversations with her with respect to the sodium level?" asked the prosecutor.

"After . . . we had him sedated and basically just waiting to transfer to Westchester, intubated," said Nurse Bompensiero, "Lacey came back into the room. And I just said to her, 'The sodium was elevated.' And she said, 'Yeah, I know it.'"

"And as you were waiting for this helicopter," asked the prosecutor, "where were you?"

"I was at the bed with him."

"And where was the defendant?"

"She was walking in and out of the room."

"And what, if anything, was she doing?"

"She was on the phone . . . just talking to friends in the playroom."

"And what was her demeanor?"

"She was very calm."

In his cross-examination, Riebling asked the nurse about the Saturday night tube feeding she had set up for Garnett before going off shift.

"You needed a connector tube to go from the port on Garnett's stomach in order to connect it?" he asked her. "And it's true the hospital didn't have [the right size] connector tube, correct?"

"Yes," she replied.

"So it was a good thing mom had it there that night."

"Objection," said Doreen Lloyd.

"To say it's a good thing . . . ," said the judge. "Rephrase, please."

"If mom didn't have the connector tube with her that night, the hospital would not have been able to perform the feeding that was ordered. Is that correct?"

"Yes," she answered.

After lunch recess, Nurse Bompensiero returned to the stand. Riebling questioned her about Garnett's incontinence late Sunday morning, because a drastic loss of body fluids can elevate sodium levels.

"In fact," he said, "at 11:30, Garnett Spears had a very large episode of diarrhea and urine, and it went through the diaper onto his clothing?"

"Yes," she agreed.

"And at that time the bed linens had to be changed?"

"That's correct."

"You didn't change the diapers?"

"No, I didn't."

"That was done by his mother, correct?"

"Yes," she said.

Riebling then moved on to Garnett's second episode, on Sunday afternoon, portraying his client as a deeply caring mother.

"Now, during that hour," said the defender, "when he was having the shivering and being uncomfortable after the medications, isn't it true it was mom who kept calling you into the room to say, 'Look, he looks uncomfortable. Can you check on him?' "

"Yes," she agreed.

"She also asked you, when she reported him being uncomfortable and seeing him shivering, 'Is the doctor aware of this?' "

"Yes."

"Isn't it also true that Miss Spears called you into the room and said, 'Look, I believe he's getting worse . . . Can you come and look at him?' "

"I don't remember her saying that," the nurse replied, "although she did call me in frequently."

Riebling then pointed out that people can become dehydrated through urination and diarrhea.

"You actually witnessed Garnett Spears having large, watery bouts of diarrhea throughout the day. Is that correct?"

"That's correct," she replied.

"So would it be fair to say that he was losing water as a result of that diarrhea?"

"That's correct."

"And we also have a report that he was having polyuria throughout that day, and he was losing water through urination. Is that correct?"

"Objection," said Lloyd.

"Okay, go ahead," said the judge.

Riebling then asked the nurse to look at a progress note she had written on the Nyack Hospital chart Sunday at 8:30 P.M., which read, "Earlier mom reports polydipsia and polyuria today."

"So, it's clear," said Riebling, "that mom—Lacey Spears—was reporting that her son had polyuria, is that correct?"

"That's correct."

"So polyuria is excessive urination, which is excessive water loss. Correct?"

"Yes," agreed the nurse.

The defender then made the point that excessive water loss can lead to dehydration and excessive thirst.

"Now, isn't it true," he continued, "that when someone becomes dehydrated through water loss, that can cause hypernatremia?"

"It can," she agreed.

Riebling then defined *hypernatremia* as coming from the Latin words *hyper,* meaning elevated, and *natremia,* meaning salt.

Finally, he asked if any attempts had ever been made at Nyack Hospital to aspirate (or remove) the contents of Garnett's stomach through his G-tube.

"Not that I know about, no," she replied.

"Drawing fluids out of his stomach out of the G-tube, there's no indication in your chart that was ever done?"

"No," she agreed.

On redirect, Doreen Lloyd asked Nurse Bompensiero about the defense attorney's question about aspirating Garnett through his G-tube site.

"Now, did anyone tell you," she asked, "that they put salt in the body of Garnett Spears and that you should aspirate it out?"

"No," said Nurse Bompensiero.

"Did his mother ever tell you that she had put salt in his G-tube and you should aspirate it out?"

"No."

"Nothing further," said Lloyd.

After a five-minute break, Patricia Murphy called her next witness, Dr. Sarika Sunku, to the stand. The Nyack Hospital pediatric physician told the jury that she had first seen Lacey and Garnett Spears in the emergency room, soon after they arrived on the afternoon of Friday, January 17. The defendant informed Dr. Sunku that she had brought Garnett to the emergency room because he was complaining of abdominal pain. He had also had "a large bowel movement" followed by a seizure in the car on the way over.

"She told me that he had had a fever five days prior to admission at Nyack Hospital," said the doctor, "and she took him over to Good Samaritan Hospital. And he's also had episodes of seizures—approximately three, lasting one to two minutes. She described shaking movements of the arms and legs, with the rolling of the eyes."

The doctor said Lacey had told her that Garnett had been diagnosed with Crohn's and celiac diseases.

"And did she tell you who diagnosed the child with Crohn's disease?" asked the prosecutor.

"She told me that it was the GI specialist."

The defendant had also mentioned that her son's sodium level had risen to two hundred when he was an infant, when he had spent more than a month in the PICU.

"Now," asked Murphy, "when you heard Miss Spears talk about a two hundred sodium, what was your opinion of that?"

"Two hundred was way too high," said the doctor, "so maybe she got confused with the number."

"If he had a two hundred sodium, what would it have done?"

"It probably would have caused considerable brain damage," explained Dr. Sunku, "or taken his life."

Dr. Sunku said that, before coming off her shift at 8:00 P.M. on Friday, she had seen Garnett, who had just been admitted to Nyack Hospital.

"And what was his condition at that point?" asked Murphy.

"He was a happy child," replied Dr. Sunku. "He was

very excited because there was a TV in the room, and kept saying he wanted to watch the TV."

Dr. Sunku had Saturday off and started her next shift at 8:00 A.M. on Sunday. Soon after arriving, she asked Lacey how her son was doing.

"She told me he had a mild headache, and that was it," said the doctor. "He was doing well."

When Dr. Sunku examined Garnett, everything seemed fine. She checked his lungs, heart, and abdomen, and they were all normal.

"Did you describe what your treatment plan was to the mother?" asked Murphy.

"Yes, I went over it," said the doctor. "I told her that the EEG recordings until that morning were normal, and that Garnett was scheduled for an MRI the following day. So I told mom that if the MRI shows normal results . . . he would go home, and he doesn't have seizures. He won't have seizures."

"So how did she react to this good news?" asked the prosecutor.

"Well, she was just calm. She didn't really say anything."

An hour later, Dr. Sunku said, she had been paged to go to room 242 immediately.

"And what was going on at that point?" asked Murphy.

"Garnett was holding onto his stomach and trying to throw up and couldn't. He was in a lot of pain. He was turning and tossing, holding his stomach, and asking for water, which I thought was strange. Because if you have so much nausea, you won't be able to drink anything. And he kept asking for water."

Dr. Sunku had then ordered Zofran for Garnett's nausea, which his nurse administered through an IV.

"Now, as Sunday morning goes on, do you continue to check on Garnett Spears?" asked Murphy.

"Yes," replied the doctor. "Actually, when he was having that retching motion, the only way he can get rid of whatever was in his system was to push it out the other way—to have a bowel movement. So we were hoping that he will just pass it out and get rid of whatever it was."

Dr. Sunku said her patient eventually had "one large bowel movement," and she ordered a half amount of saline to prevent dehydration. Over the next few hours, Garnett's condition improved, and he returned to normal.

"As the day went on," asked Murphy, "can you tell us what happened?"

"Well, I was in the office and I heard a shriek," she told the jury, "and then the nurse was paging me. So I went into the room and I saw Garnett's mom on the bed, screaming. Garnett was laying on the bed, and he was having shaking movements of his arms and legs and rolling of his eyes."

Dr. Sunku thought he was having a seizure, and she checked his airway, breathing, and circulation. Then she ordered Ativan to try to stop the seizure activity.

"The first dose didn't do anything," said the doctor, "and we gave him a second dose that kind of stopped the seizure-like activity for a few minutes. And then he went on to have another seizure, so we gave him a third dose . . . and then a fourth."

The seizures subsided for a short while but then started again, so the doctor ordered fosphenytoin, an antiseizure medication.

"After the loading dose, he stopped for some time," said Dr. Sunku, "and then he needed another dose of fosphenytoin to stop the seizures."

Then Garnett's oxygen levels began to drop, and he was not getting enough oxygen.

"It's become a critical situation," said Dr. Sunku, "and he could not even make his oxygen levels, so we had to

intubate him . . . And they put a tube down his throat and
hooked him up to oxygen."

Then Dr. Sunku decided to transfer Garnett to the
Westchester Medical Center's PICU, which was far better equipped to deal with the emergency.

"If he was breathing on his own," explained Dr. Sunku,
"and the seizures were under control with the medications
that we gave him, we could have managed him over here.
But because he was not able to breathe on his own and
we couldn't stop the seizures, it had become a critical situation."

She called Westchester Medical Center to arrange to
fly Garnett there as soon as possible. Then, at 6:30 P.M.,
she ordered a new set of labs to try to find out what was
causing these uncontrollable seizures.

"How about the sodium at 6:30 on Sunday?" asked the
prosecutor.

"That was very high," replied the doctor. "182."

"So [at] 1:20 on Sunday, this kid's sodium was 144?"
said Murphy.

"Yes."

"And by 6:30 it's 182?"

"Yes."

"And his chloride went . . . "

"From 114 to 160."

"Is there any medical explanation for that jump over
such a short period of time?" asked the prosecutor.

"No," replied Dr. Sunku.

The doctor said she had informed Dr. Carey Goltzman,
the director of Maria Fareri Children's Hospital, of the
results. He refused to believe that 182 sodium was possible. He asked her to repeat the test immediately because
there must be a mistake. But when the results came back
an hour later, she said, the sodium was 178 and the chloride was 155.

"Can you give us a sense of how high a number is 182 and 178 for sodium in a child?" asked Murphy.

"It's a very high number," Dr. Sunku told the jury. "The sodium is normally between 135 to 145. As it goes higher, we get worried about the sodium because it shifts the water from the brain and basically shrinks it and can cause damage. So we get worried once it starts reaching 150; 182 was way, way too high."

Then Judge Neary recessed for the day, telling the jury to be back at 9:30 A.M. on Tuesday because Monday was President's Day.

42

"SHE JUST HAD A SMILE ON HER FACE"

Just after 10:00 A.M. on Tuesday, Dr. Sarika Sunku retook the stand for the eighth day of the trial. There had been another snowstorm that morning, and a second alternate juror had been excused after being hospitalized over the weekend.

Patricia Murphy resumed her direct, asking if the doctor had discussed Garnett's increase in sodium with his mother.

"What, if any, reaction did Miss Spears have?" asked the prosecutor.

"She just had a smile on her face," Dr. Sunku said.

The assistant district attorney then asked Dr. Sunku if she was aware that Garnett Spears had a gastrostomy tube in his abdomen. The doctor said she was.

"Can fluids containing salt be introduced into his stomach through that G-tube?" inquired Murphy.

"Yes," replied Dr. Sunku.

"And what would the body normally do if salt is introduced into the stomach?"

"If it is introduced into the stomach," said the doctor, "because the salt has sodium in it, it is frequently absorbed rapidly from the body. But, most of the time, the body tries to get rid of anything that you introduce in excess. The body tries to flush it out, either by urination or by passing of the stools."

"And in a normal child, vomiting would be a possibility?"

"Yes."

"But because of the Nissen that was done on this child, can Garnett Spears just vomit?"

"He was trying to," said the doctor, "because he was retching so badly. But he couldn't because of the Nissen."

"Doctor, if you had learned [quickly] that an amount of salt had been introduced into Garnett Spears's . . . stomach directly, is there anything you could have done at that point?"

"Yes," she replied. "I could have tried to aspirate as much as possible from the stomach, to prevent his sodium from being . . . 182."

Murphy then asked what doctors can do to treat such a high sodium level.

"We just have to bring the sodium level slowly to normal," said Dr. Sunku, "over a period of two to three days. Because if you do it fast, the water from the blood will rapidly go into the brain and swell the brain."

"Thank you, Doctor," said Murphy.

In his cross-examination, Stephen Riebling utilized his wide experience with medical malpractice suits to go on the attack, trying to find fault with Garnett's treatment at Nyack Hospital. He started by going through Dr. Sunku's medical notes, bringing up minor inaccuracies.

"Now, you told us a moment ago," said the defense

attorney, "that the lab was drawn at 1:30 [January 19], is that right?"

"Yes," replied Dr. Sunku.

"And that's the lab result that resulted in the 144 sodium?" he asked.

"Yes."

"So, if I was just to read your transfer note," Riebling continued, "I would have gotten the impression that his lab was drawn at 12:30 P.M.?"

"Objection," said Patricia Murphy.

"Sustained," ruled the judge.

"That number, 12:30, is in fact incorrect, because that's not when the lab was drawn?" he asked.

"I made a mistake," conceded Dr. Sunku.

"Okay. Now, below that, Doctor, we have another entry, that says on 1/19, that's written at 5:12 P.M.?"

"It could be five or six."

"You can't tell, and that's your handwriting," said Riebling.

"Yes, it's probably writing five and probably changed to six. I can't tell."

Riebling then pointed out that, by changing that number, Dr. Sunku was not following hospital protocol, which dictates crossing it out and then writing the number correctly.

"You deviated from protocol," he said.

"Yes," the doctor agreed.

"Now, in either case," said the defender, "it would have been impossible for you to have known the sodium level at 5:12 or 6:12, because his blood wasn't even drawn until 6:30. Is that right?"

"I agree," said Dr. Sunku. "When I was writing my notes, I did not look at the particular times: I made a rough estimate from what I could remember—what time the blood was ordered to be drawn—and that's how I wrote. I did not look at the chart and write exactly the time it was drawn because . . . the value of the labs are important, but the timings will not change anything."

"The timings of when the labs were drawn is not important?" asked the defense attorney, incredulously.

"I mean it can be 5:00 or 6:30 or 7:30," she said. "I mean it doesn't matter because we can always go back and cross-check when the lab was drawn."

On Tuesday afternoon, the prosecution called Nellie Grossenbacher to testify against her former friend Lacey Spears. Under Doreen Lloyd's questioning, Nellie said that she had two sets of twins and that all went to the Green Meadow Waldorf School in Chestnut Ridge, New York.

"When did you first meet the defendant?" asked Lloyd.

"One day after school," said Nellie. "My boys were outside playing in the sandbox [and] her and her son, Garnett, came over. They all started playing together."

She told the jury that she had viewed Lacey as a single mother in need of a friend, and their children all played "beautifully together."

They began socializing several times a week after school, going to IKEA or chatting while their kids played.

"And could you describe Garnett to the jury, and what his demeanor was like?" said Lloyd.

"Well, he was so happy and cheerful, and just a fun-loving, inquisitive child," she said, "and I just loved being around him."

"And did he like to play a lot?"

"Yes, he was an active boy that liked to run around," she said. "And all five kids, my four and Garnett, would play in the backyard, playing ball, wrestling, and having a great time."

Lacey and Garnett often ate at her house, she told the jury, as well as going out to restaurants.

"And can you describe what you observed Garnett eating?" asked Lloyd. "The types of food?"

"When he was at my house, he [ate] whatever I fed my children, from peanut butter and jelly to lentil stews, pizza, or snacks. Whatever I put out he would eat."

She said that Garnett always ate by mouth and never had any difficulty swallowing.

"And what kind of volume of food would he eat?" asked the prosecutor.

"A large volume," replied Nellie. "He was a busy boy, and so whatever food was out, it usually got consumed."

"And did you ever discuss with the defendant Garnett Spears's medical history or his health?"

"Yes," replied Nellie. "She told me that he had a cochlear implant."

"What do you know that to be?"

"It's an implant that is in the ear and comes out. And it's attached to the back of the head. It's a visible tube."

"And did you see that in Garnett Spears at all?"

"No," said Nellie.

Lloyd then asked if Lacey had contacted Nellie about Garnett's health while they were in Clearwater during Christmas 2013.

"She told me that he wound up in the hospital, in the PICU unit in Florida," said Nellie, "because he was having seizures and vomiting."

The prosecutor then asked if she and her friend Doris Sanchez had visited Garnett in Nyack Hospital on Sunday, January 19, 2014.

"I went to the hospital in the afternoon," said Nellie. "When I walked in the room, Garnett was on the bed, with hospital staff around him, having what appeared to be a seizure."

"And was there anybody comforting him?" said Lloyd.

"Doris and me," she replied.

"Where was the defendant?"

"Out in the hallway, on the phone."

Nellie said she had stayed with Lacey during the ninety-minute wait for the helicopter to airlift Garnett to Westchester Medical Center.

"Can you describe the defendant's demeanor?" asked the prosecutor.

"She seemed real withdrawn," said Nellie. "Scared."

"Did you see if the defendant was crying at all?"

"I did not see her cry."

Finally, Lloyd asked if Lacey had posted anything on her Facebook page while her son was in the Westchester Medical Center.

"Yes," replied Nellie, "numerous pictures of him brain dead and on life support."

"And can you describe what those photographs looked like?"

"He looked like a dead child," she replied, as Lacey broke down sobbing at the defense table.

After a five-minute recess to allow Lacey to compose herself, David Sachs stood up to begin his cross-examination. He began by asking Grossenbacher if she was aware that Lacey had been calling her father from the hallway at Nyack Hospital while they were waiting for the helicopter to arrive.

"She was phoning her grandmother," replied Nellie. "She told me she was calling her grandmother."

"Did she make any other calls?"

"Not that I'm aware of," Nellie replied.

* * *

The next witness was Dr. Ivan Darenkov, who had been Garnett Spears's pediatric gastroenterologist. Dr. Darenkov told the jury that Lacey had first brought Garnett to his office for feeding difficulties in April 2013. He had examined the boy, noticing that he had had surgery to tighten his lower esophagus and had a G-tube inserted.

"It was intense," remembered Dr. Darenkov. "And mom said the child had those three major complaints—feeding difficulties; not taking by mouth, maintaining the G-tube; and celiac disease."

The doctor testified that he had seen Garnett on three or four visits. Each time, he had told Garnett's mother that the boy should undergo a thorough nutritional evaluation, to get a clearer picture of his feeding problems.

"And did you recommend this type of evaluation to the mother of Garnett Spears?" asked prosecutor Patricia Murphy.

"Yes," Dr. Darenkov replied. "I did on numerous times, by the way."

"Did she ever follow up on your recommendation?"

"No."

Dr. Darenkov said that in June 2013, he had performed an endoscopy test on Garnett under anesthesia, so he could take tissue biopsies for any diseases.

"Did the biopsy of tissue from Garnett Spears," asked Murphy, "show any evidence of celiac disease?"

"No," replied the doctor.

"Did you speak to the mother, Lacey Spears, about the result of your test?"

"Yes, I did."

The doctor had last seen Garnett in November 2013, when Lacey said he was doing better and was taking more food by mouth. Once again, the necessity for the G-tube was raised, and Dr. Darenkov told Lacey that her son "absolutely needs" to have a feeding evaluation.

"I was always asking," said Dr. Darenkov, " 'Do we really need it? Can we at least stop feeding through the G-tube and see how the child is gaining weight?' That was our conversations."

"Did you get any reaction from Miss Spears?" asked the prosecutor.

"There was some anxiety," he replied. "What if the child is not taking enough food . . . ? But without trial, we cannot know."

During his cross-examination, Stephen Riebling pointed out that a feeding evaluation would have necessitated Garnett being in the hospital for several days. He then read out Dr. Darenkov's notes from his last appointment with Garnett, in November 2013, where it had been agreed to cut down his night feeds and see if his appetite improved.

"So the plan at that point," said Riebling, "was to continue to see [whether] to proceed to that nutritionist's evaluation. Is that right?"

"Yes," replied the doctor.

"In fact, Lacey Spears never said, 'No, I will not have Garnett do that evaluation,' did she?"

"She never said no," agreed Dr. Darenkov.

On redirect, Murphy pointed out that although the defendant had never actually refused to allow Garnett to have a feeding evaluation, she had never gone through with it, either.

Then Dr. Darenkov was dismissed, and Judge Neary recessed for the day.

On Thursday, February 19—the tenth day of the trial—Dr. Carey Goltzman took the witness stand. Under Doreen

Lloyd's questioning, the director of Westchester Medical Center's PICU told the jury about several telephone conversations with Dr. Sunku to arrange an airlift of the intubated Garnett Spears from Nyack Hospital.

Then he received a phone call informing him that the results from a second set of electrolyte tests had just come in and showed that Garnett's sodium level had risen to 182.

"I remember being flabbergasted," said Dr. Goltzman. "I said, 'You just told me an hour and a half ago that he had a normal sodium level. How did his sodium jump from a 144 to 182?'"

"And as an expert in pediatric critical care," asked Lloyd, "what was the significance of his sodium level of 182 when you heard it?"

"It's remarkably aberrant," he replied. "It's way over the normal range . . . and is inconsistent with life in a normal child. His chloride was 160, which is also markedly aberrant."

Dr. Goltzman said it was the first time in his twenty-one years at Westchester Medical Center that a patient had ever been flown in from Nyack Hospital. After arriving, Garnett Spears, accompanied by his mother, had been brought into room 2108.

"After the nurses got Garnett settled into bed," he told the jury, "I went in and examined him . . . And the one remarkable thing he had [was] a gastrostomy tube, which was in the left upper quadrant of his abdomen. I thought immediately, *Could this youngster have been given an exogenous (outside) dose of sodium chloride that could account for both his sodium and chloride level going through the roof?*"

Lloyd then asked whether Dr. Goltzman had discussed Garnett's past medical history with his mother.

"Yes, very basic history," he replied. " 'How long has Garnett had the G-tube?' And she was like, 'Oh, he got it early on.' If I remember correctly, Miss Spears said he got the G-tube at around nine months of age. And I said, 'Gee, that's a little early.' And Miss Spears basically, at that point, said, 'Well, the baby showed that he had projectile vomiting emesis.' I said, 'Excuse me?' I didn't expect that term to come from this mom . . . a very specific medical term."

The doctor said the defendant also had informed him that Garnett had been hospitalized at ten weeks with hypernatremia.

"He had a 190 [sodium]," said Dr. Goltzman. "And that was as per the mother."

"Did she use that word, *hypernatremia*?" asked the prosecutor.

"Yes," he replied. "And he also had bleeding from his ears, and she claimed he had had a tonsillectomy and adenoidectomy. She wasn't sure of the dates."

"And, Doctor," asked the prosecutor, "how much salt—sodium chloride—would be needed for Garnett Spears's sodium level to go from 144 at 1:20 in the afternoon to 182 at 6:30 P.M.?"

The doctor said that he had calculated that the little boy would have had to ingest the equivalent of five 16.9-ounce water bottles full of sodium chloride, containing a 0.9 normal saline.

"Can the body physically take that amount of sodium in by mouth?" asked Lloyd.

"Could they potentially take it? Yes. Would they electively take it? No."

After Garnett had been diagnosed with hypernatremia, Dr. Goltzman said he had carefully calculated how to slowly lower the boy's sodium level with the appropriate fluids over a forty-eight-hour period. He had also issued an NPO order, meaning nothing by mouth, to avoid any complications such as pneumonia.

"So nothing by mouth would allow you to control any kind of liquids that are going in his body?" asked the prosecutor.

"That's correct."

At around 7:30 A.M. on Monday, Dr. Goltzman had finished his shift. Before leaving, he advised Dr. Alan Pinto, who was now taking over, about Garnett Spears's plan of care.

"Garnett did very well," said Dr. Goltzman. "His sodium was coming down nice and slowly, as I'd calculated and expected."

On Monday, which was the Martin Luther King Jr. holiday, Garnett's condition continued to improve.

"He was successfully extubated," said Dr. Goltzman, "despite the mother not being in favor of [it], because she expressed that she was sure he would be in pain."

The doctor had started his next shift at around 7:00 A.M. on Tuesday, and he and Dr. Pinto had looked in on their young patient in room 2108, giving him a brief physical examination.

"Although Garnett was sleeping," he told the jury, "he was behaving normally, and things looked good."

Fifteen minutes later, Dr. Goltzman was in his office, talking to his nurse manager, when an overhead emergency code bell sounded from Garnett's room.

"I shot out of that office like a bat out of hell," Dr. Goltzman recalled, "and I ran straight into the room."

"And what did you see?" asked Lloyd.

"That Garnett was not breathing at all," he said, as Lacey began sobbing at the defense table. "I looked at his eyes very quickly, and both pupils were blown and dilated. They weren't reacting to light."

"When both pupils are blown, as you observed on Garnett," asked the prosecutor, "what does that indicate to you as his physician?"

"It means that he was having a brain stem problem," he replied.

The doctor and his team then checked Garnett's breathing, put a breathing tube down his throat, and re-intubated him.

"And as this was going on," said Lloyd, "what, if anything, did you observe in the room itself?"

"The one thing I noticed, as I was coming into the room," said the doctor, "was that Garnett's mother was on the side of the bed away from the door as you entered the room. And as I looked in the room, I looked at Garnett, looked at the mom, and looked under the bed. I saw an empty bottle of Poland Spring water, and the first thing I said to the nurse was, 'Get that bottle!'"

"What was the significance of you seeing that water bottle on the floor near the bed of Garnett Spears?" asked the prosecutor.

"I already had an increased index of suspicion that there may have been an exogenous amount of sodium given," Dr. Goltzman explained. "So I don't know if there's any additional sodium in that bottle, or there was the ability to give [him] free water, since Garnett had a G-tube."

"And what would be the significance to Garnett, in this correction phase of the hypernatremia, if he was given a significant amount of water into his body?"

"It could have lowered his sodium precipitously," explained Dr. Goltzman, "and once again caused seizures and shifts of water across the blood-brain barrier. So that would have been bad . . . and I wanted that bottle looked at."

Dr. Goltzman had then ordered a CAT scan, which

showed an acute cerebral edema and herniation of Garnett's brain stem.

"And did you view the CAT scan yourself?" asked Lloyd.

"Yes," replied the doctor.

"And, in your expert opinion, would Garnett have recovered from that cerebral edema?"

"No," said the doctor, as Lacey continued to sob at the defense table.

"And did you explain to [the defendant], as you did to the jury, that Garnett would not be recovering?"

"I explained that, with the way that the CAT scan looked, and that he's herniating, it was probably secondary to the fact that he had this high sodium level. And despite the fact that we were appropriately lowering it very slowly, he was succumbing to the insult that had been received. And that we would continue to support him, but there was a good chance that he was going to enter the realm of brain death."

Then the prosecutor asked about the doctor's next conversation with Lacey, on Tuesday at around midday, in a conference room.

"I said to Miss Spears that it was unfortunate the way things had gone," Dr. Goltzman recalled, "and that this was going to be a negative outcome for this youngster. But I did not have a really good explanation as to why his sodium had risen so precipitously."

He told Lacey that he believed Garnett's condition had been caused by hypernatremia and that he was calling in child protective services because he did not think it was accidental.

"And who did you suspect of giving this child salt?" asked the prosecutor.

"I suspected that Miss Spears may have given the salt exogenously to Garnett, via his G-tube."

"And when you told Miss Spears that you were calling in CPS, did she have any reaction?"

"She had a very flat affect," Dr. Goltzman recalled. "She would stare at me, [but] I felt she was looking right through me."

During cross-examination, Stephen Riebling asked if the police had ever tested the empty Poland Spring bottle he'd ordered confiscated. Dr. Goltzman said he did not know.

"Now, the two possibilities in your mind," asked the defender, "was, one, there was sodium in the bottle, which caused him to code at that point, or there was free water in the bottle, and that's what caused him to code?"

"I was concerned, because we were lowering his sodium, that there was free water in that bottle," Dr. Goltzman explained. "Seizures can occur if your sodium goes too high or it goes too low. So I was worried that maybe Garnett, despite being on an IV-fluid-calculated resuscitation from the moment he arrived on my turf on Sunday night—what if now his sodium has precipitously dropped because he maybe got too much free water or [he was given salt] and it is back on the rise again? I did not know."

Then Riebling asked about Lacey's reaction when she was told that her son was not going to recover from his cerebral edema.

"Now, her reaction to that news is that she broke down and started crying," stated the defender. "Is that right?"

"Initially," replied the doctor, "there was a sort of flat affect. I don't think she had the full comprehension of the gravity of the situation. And then, later on at some point, [she became] somewhat upset."

"She fell on her knees, correct?" asked Riebling. "She started crying?"

"Not at that point that I remember," replied Dr. Goltzman.

"When I told her he was brain dead, she fell to her knees and started crying."

The defense attorney then observed that if a patient received fluids too quickly during the delicate process of lowering sodium, it could cause cerebral edema.

"Doctor," said Riebling, "one of the concerns in treating Garnett Spears for the hypernatremia that he came into the hospital with is that he could develop cerebral edema?"

"It could clearly have been a complication of such a severe elevated level of sodium," agreed the doctor.

"And the complication arises through the treatment of hypernatremia by the introduction of fluid," said Riebling. "That's why you have to introduce fluid very slowly?"

"It's not caused by the introduction of fluid," replied Dr. Goltzman. "We followed accepted measures in lowering his sodium very slowly, so you're going to keep him on IV fluids. But the IV fluids themselves do not precipitate the cerebral edema. His serum sodium levels were clearly improving [and] were slowly being lowered. They were headed in the right direction."

Riebling then pointed out that great care had to be taken in calculating the right amount of fluid, because if it is given too quickly, it can cause cerebral edema.

"We weren't introducing water too quickly," snapped the doctor.

"If a patient comes into your hospital," Riebling continued, "and they have hypernatremia, and fluid is introduced too quickly, it can result in cerebral edema. Is that correct?"

"That is not an appropriate statement," replied the doctor angrily.

"Can you put a stop to this?" said Judge Neary, running out of patience. "Ask another question."

"Doctor, the reason you introduce fluids slowly," said

Riebling, "is because if you introduce them too quickly, you can cause cerebral edema. Is that right?"

"Objection," Lloyd interrupted.

"Give it one more try," said the judge. "He can answer."

"You cannot generalize by saying 'fluid,'" said the doctor. "The appropriate fluid that was introduced, that allowed this youngster's serum sodium to go down slowly, was 0.9 of normal saline, in addition to his dextrose that was included, and potassium."

"So is it your testimony, Doctor," asked the defender, "that the cerebral edema was not a complication of the treatment that he received at the Westchester Medical Center?"

"I believe that we provided exceptional care," replied the doctor, "and I do not believe that our therapy caused his development of cerebral edema. The cause and direct development of cerebral edema was the initial insult of sodium that is incompatible with life. A rapid rise of 144 to 182."

"But when he had his insult," said Riebling, "once again his sodium level was normal, correct?"

"I can't say it was an insult at that point," answered the doctor.

"No further questions," said the defense attorney.

On Friday morning, after the coldest night in fifty years, it was zero degrees when the jury arrived at the West-chester County courthouse. Outside the second-floor court-room, several reporters sat on benches talking. Rebecca Spears waited alone, holding a legal pad full of notes from the trial.

Just down the hallway sat the next witness, Dr. Alan Pinto, the associate director of Westchester Medical Cen-ter's pediatric intensive care unit. He was talking to an attorney named Al Figuretto, a portly, middle-aged man with a toupee and a pink tie, who had spent the last several days observing the trial from the back row of the public gallery.

Just after 10:00 A.M., Lacey Spears was led into court, wearing the same dark sweater she had worn for the previous several days. After a bailiff uncuffed her, she sat down at the defense table and pulled her long greasy hair into a ponytail.

Then the prosecution called Dr. Pinto to the stand. Under Assistant District Attorney Doreen Lloyd's direct questioning, Dr. Pinto said he first saw Garnett Spears at around 7:00 A.M. on Monday, January 20, 2014, when he started his shift at Maria Fareri Children's Hospital. Previously, he had been briefed by Dr. Goltzman that Garnett Spears's sodium level had mysteriously risen from 144 to 182 the afternoon before.

"After discussing the plan of care with Dr. Goltzman," asked Lloyd, "how did [Garnett] appear?"

"He was on a mechanical ventilator that was breathing for him," recalled Dr. Pinto, "so he was sedated with fentanyl, which is an opiate kind of morphine. All his vital signs were normal."

Dr. Pinto said that Garnett was making good progress, and by the afternoon, the boy was being weaned from the sedatives so he could be taken off the mechanical ventilator.

"He was awake," said the doctor. "He was nodding his head to questions, he was breathing on his own, and there was no need to keep him further on a mechanical ventilator."

"And did you have a conversation to extubate Garnett with his mother?" asked the prosecutor.

"His mother did not want us to extubate him at that time," said Dr. Pinto.

"And did she say why?"

"She did not want him to be uncomfortable."

Dr. Pinto had then explained to her the dangers of Garnett remaining on a mechanical ventilator. He warned her about the risks of infections, the tube getting dislodged, or a mechanical failure.

"So, if you don't need to be on a ventilator," Dr. Pinto told the jury, "the best thing is to take it out. It's not a nice thing to have a tube stuck down in your throat."

"And despite the mother not wanting to extubate him," asked Lloyd, "did you make a decision?"

"Yes, we went ahead," said the doctor. "There was no need to keep him on a mechanical ventilator."

Dr. Pinto said it was removed at around 3:30, by which time the little boy was talking, although he was still confused as the sedatives wore off. The doctor then told the jury that he had ordered that Garnett should receive nothing by mouth.

"We didn't want him to be having any extra fluids," Dr. Pinto explained, "because we were trying to control his sodium level count."

By the evening, Garnett's condition had stabilized, and he was not having any issues. At midnight, he was examined by pediatric neurologist Dr. Sherbany.

"And were there any concerns about his neurological status at midnight?" asked Lloyd.

"No," Dr. Pinto replied.

"Overnight, from midnight until the end of your shift at 7:00 A.M.," asked the prosecutor, "did you become aware of any complaints by the patient, Garnett Spears?"

"No," replied the doctor.

Dr. Pinto had ended his shift at around 7:00 A.M., when he did a sign-out with Dr. Goltzman, who was now taking over. They discussed how Garnett was now awake and alert, and his sodium levels were coming down nicely.

Then, a few minutes later, as Dr. Pinto was leaving the PICU to go home, a code alert went off in Garnett's room.

"I dropped my bag, took off my coat, and went into the room," said Dr. Pinto. "Garnett was being bagged with a [breathing] bag because he was not breathing. I went ahead and I intubated him again."

Dr. Pinto said he had remained in Garnett's room until around 8:00 A.M. When he left to go home, the boy was on a respirator.

In his cross-examination, Stephen Riebling asked Dr. Pinto about his conversation with Lacey Spears on Monday afternoon, about her son being extubated.

"And she expressed some concerns to you," said the defender, "that she didn't want him to be extubated because she didn't want him to be uncomfortable?"

"Correct," said the doctor.

"Then you explained the risks associated with continued ventilation?"

"Yes."

"And then after that, he was extubated?"

"Correct."

"So the concerns that she had about him being uncomfortable . . . " said Riebling, "[you explained that this] would be balanced by the risks, and she allowed him to be extubated?"

"Objection," said Lloyd.

"Sustained," ruled the judge.

"Now," Riebling continued, "throughout your shift . . . isn't it true you never witnessed any inappropriate interaction between Garnett and his mother?"

"Correct."

"You also witnessed no strange interaction between Garnett and his mother?"

"Correct."

"And no inappropriate or strange interaction was reported to you by any of the residents or the nurses?"

"Correct."

The defense attorney then showed the witness a document entitled "Routine Death Referral to the Organ Donor Network," signed by Dr. Goltzman on January 20, 2014. He pointed out that Dr. Goltzman had written "Undetermined" as the cause of Garnett's death.

"And it says, 'Diagnosis: seizures, hypernatremia of undetermined ideology'?" asked Riebling.

"Yes," the doctor agreed.

Then the defender told Judge Neary that the last page of the document, which he wanted to question Dr. Pinto about, was missing. After a few minutes of fruitless searching by Riebling, Judge Neary called a recess.

"We'll take a short break," he told the jury. "Amateur hour's over."

After a twenty-minute break, the missing page was found, and the jury returned to continue.

"Doctor," Riebling began, "when you came to court today, did you come with anyone?"

"No," said the doctor.

"Did you meet anyone here?"

"I met with the district attorney."

"Okay," said the defender. "Before you walked in here to testify, were you talking to anybody in the hallway?"

"Objection," said Doreen Lloyd.

"Sustained," said Judge Neary.

"I think the point will be revealed in a minute," Riebling told him.

"I'll let you go a little further," said the judge.

"Were you speaking to anyone in the hallway?" asked the defense attorney.

"There was a reporter from CBS," Dr. Pinto answered. "And the detective was here."

"How about the gentleman in the pink tie, sitting in the back row?" asked Riebling, referring to the public gallery. "Who is that gentleman?"

"He's named Al," replied Dr. Pinto.

"What's his last name?"

"Figuretto."

"Let's have a sidebar," said Judge Neary.

Two minutes later, the court resumed.

"Let's move on," said the judge.

"Did you speak with Al?" the defense attorney asked Dr. Pinto.

"Change the subject matter," ordered the judge. "There's nothing else to indicate that sidebar, please. Or you can sit down."

"Dr. Pinto," Riebling continued, "did you meet with the district attorneys to prepare for your testimony before today's date?"

"Yes," Dr. Pinto said.

"Was the gentleman sitting in the back of the room present during these discussions?"

"Objection," said Lloyd.

"Sustained."

"How many times did you meet with the district attorneys?"

"Okay," the judge told Riebling sternly, "you can sit down. Is there any redirect?"

"No," said Lloyd.

"Right," said the judge. "You're excused, Doctor. Thank you."

Then Judge Neary addressed the defense attorney.

"I told you to change the subject, and you didn't. So . . ."

"I didn't ask him about the gentleman in the back row,"

Riebling replied. "I asked him about the district attorneys."

"Have a seat," ordered Judge Neary, as if chastising a naughty schoolboy. "We're moving on."

43

"I WAS ON A MISSION"

The next witness was Dr. Gerald Karnow, the Fellowship Community and Green Meadow Waldorf School physician. The elderly general practitioner, who got his medical degree from the University of Chicago, told the jury he had lived at the community for forty years, starting his practice there in 1978.

"Do you have a special area that you practice in?" asked prosecutor Doreen Lloyd.

"Human beings," he replied, drawing a laugh from the jury.

Dr. Karnow explained that Lacey Spears had first brought Garnett to his office in November 2012, several days after arriving at the Fellowship.

"They were at that point visiting," he said, "to see whether she would reside there."

The doctor said that the defendant had brought Garnett into his office a total of five times while she was at the Fellowship.

"On January 10, 2014," asked Lloyd, "did you see Garnett Spears as a patient in your office?"

"Yes," replied the doctor. "The complaint was that in kindergarten he couldn't focus and couldn't concentrate. That he had night terrors and was hysteric and had to be with his mom all the time. [She said] that his sleep was very poor. That he was struggling with food—had to be mostly tube-fed. That he wanted to go to the bathroom constantly. That he didn't want to go to school . . . and that he was playing with things of death."

"And did the mother indicate if he had any significant diseases, when you saw Garnett on January 10?" asked the prosecutor.

"I actually recall," said the doctor, "because he was essentially leaving the office and she said that he had Crohn's and celiac disease."

When he examined Garnett that day, Dr. Karnow said, there was no fever or stomach flu. Based on what his mother had reported, he had prescribed a plant-based medicine called Digestodoron, to help with his digestion, and calcarea carbonica, a homeopathic remedy, for his constitution.

"And these types of medication," the prosecutor inquired, "are they holistic?"

"Yes," said the doctor, "they're holistic medication and natural."

"And during this visit," asked Lloyd, "did the mother ever tell you that she had taken her son to a hospital in Florida over Christmas, and that he had been admitted to a pediatric intensive care unit for seizures and high fever?"

"Objection," said Riebling. "Leading."

"Sustained," ruled the judge.

"Nothing further," said the prosecutor.

"Doctor," asked Riebling on cross-examination, "do you prescribe medications that are not medically necessary?"

"No," he replied.

"Isn't it true, Doctor," Riebling continued, "that one of the complaints that was given you on January 10 was that Garnett Spears was having diarrhea?"

"Yes."

"That would be one of the reasons why you would prescribe a medication like Digestodoron, to help him with digestion, right?"

"Yes."

"Diarrhea can be a sign of illness, isn't that right?"

"Absolutely," replied the doctor.

"Nothing further," said the defense attorney.

There was much anticipation about Valerie Plauché, who would testify next and was seen as the prosecution's star witness. She had arrived several hours earlier with Nancy Leopold, and the two Fellowship Community coworkers had sat together on a bench, ignoring reporters' questions.

After being sworn in, Valerie identified her one-time friend Lacey Spears at the defense table. Then, Assistant District Attorney Christine Hatfield asked what she did at the Fellowship.

"I am a coworker, and I have many different duties," Valerie replied. "I take care of the elderly [and] I cook and clean. I'm kind of the hostess, party, festival person, and I do a bit of gardening."

She and Lacey had worked together for more than a year, she told the jury, and saw each other every day.

"Would you consider yourself friends?" asked Hatfield.

"I'd say that we were friendly," she replied, as Lacey looked away.

Valerie told the jury that Garnett was a "really special

child," and they were "very good friends" and used to hang out together.

"Garnett used to come to my apartment every morning and yell at the bottom of the stairs, 'Valerie, Valerie. Can I come up?' He was really cute. In the beginning, he used to come up without telling me, so I said, 'Well, if you have to, let me know if you're coming up.'"

Then Hatfield asked her what Garnett was like, physically.

"He was a little boy," she replied. "He was very dynamic and full of energy."

"Can you describe Garnett's personality?" asked the prosecutor.

"Garnett was very outgoing," she replied, "and he was a very adorable child. He had excellent social skills and intimacy skills. Like, he really knew how to connect."

Under Hatfield's questioning, Valerie said that she had become extremely worried about Garnett while he was in Nyack Hospital and Westchester Medical Center.

Then Hatfield asked what she had been doing on the morning of Wednesday, January 22, 2014, the day after Garnett had coded.

"Well, it was a very emotional day," Plauché remembered. "We had gotten some news the night before about Garnett. I slept very, very little, and I woke up very, very early. I was very caught up with what was going on with Garnett. Very emotional. And I checked Facebook first and saw something . . . about Garnett having passed over."

She had then posted something supportive for Lacey, and at about 6:00 A.M., Lacey had texted her to call, which she did.

"We both cried for several minutes," Plauché remembered. "It was very emotional and we were both sobbing."

"And after that," asked Hatfield, "did . . . You spoke to Lacey again over the telephone?"

"Yes," replied Plauché. "She called me at about 10:15 in the morning."

At first, the call reception was so bad that Valerie had to go onto the roof, where it was far clearer. Hatfield asked what Lacey had said.

"She wanted me to do something for her," Valerie replied. "To go to her house and get a feeding bag in the middle of the room, throw it away, and not tell anybody. She said, 'Can you do it now? Can you do it now?'"

"And what was her tone of voice?" asked the prosecutor.

"Very urgent. Serious."

Plauché told Lacey she would do it, and then she went downstairs, enlisting the help of her friend Chloe McKenna.

"Now," asked the prosecutor, "what is your reason for asking Chloe to join you?"

"Somehow, it just didn't seem like I wanted to do it," she explained. "Lacey had emphasized, 'Don't tell anybody! Don't tell anybody! I don't want you to tell anybody!'"

After collecting a black garbage bag to place the feeding bag in, the two women trudged through the thick snow to Tulip House, knocking on the front door. Lacey's upstairs neighbor Shaiya Baer answered, and they told him they were there to get something for Lacey.

Valerie said Shaiya seemed very nervous about her going downstairs into Lacey's apartment. He told her the police had been in there the night before and had taken three bags of Lacey's belongings away.

Nevertheless, Valerie ignored his warnings, going downstairs into Lacey's apartment, followed by Chloe, Shaiya, and Shaiya's six-year-old daughter, Lizzie. And there, right in the middle of the living room, they saw the feeding bag hanging from an IV pole.

"[I was] trying to figure out what part of the thing was the feeding bag," she testified, "and how to remove it."

"And when you said you were trying to remove this bag," asked Hatfield, "can you describe it?"

"It was attached to this whole stand and tube," she replied, "and it was a bag with liquid in it, but it was a little complicated. It wasn't that easy to just take off. It took a few minutes. We disconnected it."

"What was the color of the contents of that bag?" asked the prosecutor.

"It looked like infant formula type of color, gray."

"So, after you disconnected the bag, what did you do?"

"We put it in the black garbage bag that we had brought with us, and went," she said. "We were in a hurry, and it was very quick."

"Was there a reason you didn't throw the bag away?" asked Hatfield.

"Shaiya said the police had been here," Valerie replied, "and that made me think that maybe I shouldn't."

"Did there come a time when you spoke to Lacey about it?" said the prosecutor.

"I called Lacey when I got back to my apartment," she said, "before going back to work. I just very briefly said, 'I got the bag. Chloe came with me. Shaiya was there. The police had been there.' And that was it."

"Did Lacey respond?"

"No, it was a very quick call, and I was late for work. I just know that I said that I had done what she asked."

She had then gone to work at Hilltop House, "feeling uncomfortable," before telling her supervisor, Nancy Leopold, that "something weird had happened."

Then the prosecutor asked if she had spoken to Nancy Leopold later that day. Plauché said Nancy had called at around 8:00 P.M. and asked her to write out in an e-mail exactly what Lacey had wanted done, and then to send it to her.

"And she was sitting there while I typed it up," Plauché said. "I [then] gave her the bag and she took it."

On cross-examination, David Sachs asked why she hadn't asked Lacey why she wanted Valerie to remove the feeding bag.

"When you were on the phone," he asked, "did your mind click, 'Hey, Lacey, why ask me to do this?'"

"It seemed odd," replied Plauché.

"So it seemed odd during a telephone conversation," said Sachs. "Why didn't you simply ask Lacey, 'Why are you asking me to do this?'"

"I was in a state of wanting to help a desperate situation in any way I could," she replied. "It was very emotional. I wasn't as clear as I might be on a normal day."

"Lacey had also asked you not to tell anybody, correct?"

"Correct," she agreed.

"So then, one of the first things you do was to go and grab somebody else?"

"Yes."

"Did you tell Chloe McKenna exactly what Lacey said to you on the phone?"

"I told Chloe that we were going to do something for Lacey. We were going to get that feeding bag and throw it away."

"And did Chloe respond?"

"Only to say, 'Okay, I'm going to help you. We're going to help Lacey.'"

Then Sachs asked why she still had gone ahead, even after learning that the police had searched Lacey's apartment.

"And when [Shaiya] told you that," asked Sachs, "did

something else click in your mind: 'Boy, I could turn around and just go home'?"

"I think things had clicked in my mind," she replied, "but I really wanted to help Lacey at the same time. So it [was] a conflict of really wanting to do something to help the situation. And the whole thing seemed kind of odd."

"Before going in any further to the apartment," asked the defender, "did you call Lacey on her phone and say, 'Hey, Lacey, what's going on here?'"

"No, I didn't," she replied.

At 12:25 P.M., Judge Neary dismissed the jury for lunch. After they had left, he told Stephen Riebling that he would now put on the record his reasons for halting his cross-examination of Dr. Pinto. Neary said he'd warned Riebling at sidebar not to ask Dr. Pinto any further questions about having an attorney present, and Riebling had disobeyed.

"For the record, Judge," began the defense attorney, "we went to the sidebar and it was my attempt to ask the witness . . . whether or not Al Figuretto was his attorney. One of the claims in this case is that treatment at the hospitals was improper."

Riebling pointed out that Dr. Pinto had treated Garnett Spears in the hours prior to his death, and it was "incredibly relevant" if he had consulted his lawyer before taking the stand.

"And I think it was improper for the court to preclude me from entering that line of questioning," Riebling told the judge. "I believe this needs to be placed on the record, and I reserve my rights to seek any further engagement after I fully discuss it with my counsel."

Judge Neary replied that he had ruled at the sidebar that it was "immaterial" whether Dr. Pinto had legal representation.

"[It] could lead to speculation by the jury as to something improper may be going on," said the judge, "which is absolutely not the case."

The judge told him that witnesses are entitled to have counsel if they so choose.

"So I didn't want to give the impression or mislead the jury in any way that it was improper for this witness or any other witness to have counsel present."

He also observed that he had seen Figuretto sitting in the court's public gallery on a daily basis.

"If he's an attorney representing the hospital, as you indicate," said the judge, "then he's sitting in for all these witnesses' testimony."

"In that regards, Your Honor," said Riebling, "I would like to—"

"I'm not finished," said the judge, cutting him off. "I shut you down because you disregarded the court's direction. I asked you several times to be quiet and . . . given the fact you were disregarding the court's direction, I felt I had no option but to sit you down."

After the lunch break, Nancy Leopold took the stand. Under Christine Hatfield's direct examination, the Fellowship Community's head nurse said that she had met Lacey Spears in August 2013 after returning from a sabbatical. From then on, she had seen Lacey daily at Hilltop House.

"Did you ever observe her working?" asked Hatfield.

"Yes," Leopold replied. "She would come and [be] caring for an older person, and I would be checking in and seeing how things were going. Or, if she had a question, perhaps she would ask me something. It wasn't a lot of interchange, but it was an awareness of another person being there throughout the day, day after day."

Leopold said she also had meals with Lacey and Garnett in the main dining room.

"Did you observe Garnett eating?" inquired the prosecutor.

"I did," she replied. "He had small portions of whatever the common meal was. My impression of him is [he ate] a little bit of whatever was being served."

"Did you ever make any other observations of Garnett?" asked the prosecutor.

"As I saw him go through the community, [he was] very friendly, very active. Always looking around. He would always say hello to you."

Leopold then described how Valerie Plauché had first alerted her to Lacey's strange request. A few hours later, Leopold had gone to Plauché's home to collect the feeding bag, which was still inside the black garbage bag.

"At that point," asked Hatfield, "did you open the bag?"

"No," replied Leopold. "I went to Ladies' Libber Lodge, which is where the offices are located."

She had then unlocked the door of the medical office known as "the lab," going into a small storage room at the rear, which also was locked.

"I opened up the combination lock to the storage room," she told the jury. "I took that bag and put it in a brown cardboard carton box and taped it. I wrote something on it like 'Do Not Open.' I put it in the back of the storage room and locked that door. Then I locked the second door and called Bob Scherer to tell him I had done that."

Christine Hatfield then showed Leopold a cardboard box and asked if she recognized it.

"It is the box," she said, "that I put the black plastic bag in that Valerie gave to me. I put the tape across it."

"And the writing on the box?"

"Yes, it's mine," confirmed Leopold. "I wrote, 'LEAVE FOR NANCY. DO NOT MOVE,' assuming that leaving something for me carries a lot of authority."

"When you put the black bag into the box, did you open it?"

"Yes," she replied. "I opened it . . . and looked away immediately. I hardly glanced inside, and then immediately just twist-closed it again and put it in the box."

"In that quick flash," asked Hatfield, "did you see what was inside?"

"I saw that there was some plastic tubing and what appeared to be some kind of plastic bag."

"Any contents in the plastic bag?"

"I really did not see."

"Who had the keys and the combinations for [the locks] you were describing?" asked the prosecutor.

"People that work in the medical office have the access to those rooms," she replied. "It is a limited number of people."

"Was anyone with you when you brought the bag and put it into the box?"

"Dr. Karnow was still in the office after office hours, and so when I brought it to the back, I met him there."

"From the time you received that black plastic bag," asked Hatfield, "until the time when you placed it into the box and sealed it, did you change anything as to what was contained inside?"

"Absolutely not."

"No further questions."

Then David Sachs stood up to cross-examine Nancy Leopold, first asking if she was a member of the Fellowship Community's executive circle.

"I am a member of the executive circle now," she replied, "but I wasn't at the time."

She acknowledged knowing that the executive circle was in the middle of its weekly Wednesday meeting when she had called Bob Scherer, and he said he would call her back.

"And did you have any indication," inquired Sachs, "why he was going to call you back?"

"Because I knew that part of the executive circle agenda that morning," she replied, "was to talk about Lacey [and what] had been happening in the days previous. So I expected he would call me back and tell me if there was any way that I could be helpful to whatever needed to be done."

"And you say 'whatever happened to Lacey,' " said Sachs. "Would that include the police investigation?"

"We only knew that police had visited her apartment the previous night."

"When you say 'We' . . . ?" asked the defender.

"I mean, in the community it was very common knowledge," explained Leopold.

"And when did you first become aware of this?"

"I think that the morning I heard, the police had come to her apartment the previous night. I certainly knew that the police were involved over in the hospital in Westchester before that."

"Where did you get that information from?" asked Sachs.

"From being told it by someone," said Leopold. "Again, this was from coworkers who had been visiting Garnett in the hospital and had been spoken to by the police. So it [was] the kind of information, of course, that came into the administration of the community."

She said that right after she told Bob Scherer that she had secured Lacey's feeding bag, he had called the Ramapo Police.

"When did you happen to glance in it?" asked the defense attorney.

"Right before it was put into that box," she said.

"Did you take a quick glance?"

"Yes," she replied. "It was very quick. I was reluctant

to do it. To my mind, with a quick glance, it looked like tubing and a plastic bag that, from my medical experience, looked very much like a feeding apparatus."

"Nothing further," said Sachs.

The twenty-first witness for the prosecution was Garnett Spears's nursery school teacher, Carol Grieder. She testified that besides being a kindergarten teacher at the Green Meadow Waldorf School, she was also a registered nurse.

"Now, in your observation of Garnett, as a teacher in your class," asked Christine Hatfield, "how was he?"

"He was great," she replied. "He was sharp, attentive, very happy to be in school. Very happy to be with his friends, and there were no problems at all in school."

Grieder described Garnett as an energetic child who liked arriving early in the morning so he could greet his friends.

"He knew all their names," she told the jury, "and he would greet all the adults as well. He was a real big part of the class."

She explained how the school provided pupils with home-cooked lunches, but if there were any foods that Lacey Spears disapproved of, she would send in hot containers for Garnett.

"So he would eat that," she said, "instead of whatever the class was eating on that day."

"How did you know what he could eat?" asked Hatfield. "Did that come from the mother?"

"That came from the mother," said the teacher. "In the initial interview that was related to us, which foods he wasn't able to eat."

"And what was it that he wasn't allowed to eat?"

"He seemed to have a problem with glutens," she replied. "He was not allowed to have anything that was wheat and which contained gluten. But then there were lists of other foods [that] we didn't serve at school."

"Did you ever observe Garnett having trouble eating?" asked the prosecutor.

"No," Grieder replied. "He always ate well. He had seconds, oftentimes thirds. In the beginning, I had to ask Lacey to send more because he was eating so well. Actually, he was one of the children who really ate best [and] was very happy to sit down and eat."

"Miss Grieder," chided Judge Neary, "just try and confine the answers to the questions because we have to move it along."

At the beginning, Grieder told the jury, she had little interaction with Garnett's mother besides seeing her dropping him off in the morning and picking him up at night. But that changed during Christmas 2013, when Lacey began sending her e-mails from Florida, where she and Garnett were spending the holidays.

"I think it was on the twenty-seventh of December," Grieder recalled. "[She] said he had a fever of 104, and he was very sick and not eating. He had to have his port accessed for fluids and was receiving different Chinese herbs and remedies for that."

"Now, you referred to a port," said the prosecutor. "Did that have any meaning to you?"

"I was surprised," she replied, "because I had never heard that [Garnett] had a port. I knew he had a G-tube, but I was not aware that he had a port. The port is basically an intravenous access device . . . in the chest. It's an implanted device that had to go in there with an operation. I was not aware that he had one."

"Now, did you receive another e-mail from the defendant in that holiday break?" asked the prosecutor.

"It was December thirty-first," Grieder told the jury. "She said he had been hospitalized in the PICU. He was apparently very sick, and his fever had spiked to 105. He had been diagnosed with Crohn's and a casein allergy—which is a milk allergy. She said she was giving him breast milk [and] that's the primary way he was being fed."

"Did she describe any other symptoms that he had at that time?"

"He was vomiting," she said. "He had an intestinal virus."

Grieder said Garnett had returned to school the first week of January, looking fully recovered.

"He was the usual Garnett," she explained. "He was very happy to be back. Very happy to play. Happy to do what everyone was doing, and eating well."

"Drawing your attention to Friday, January 10, 2014," said the prosecutor, "did Garnett attend that day?"

"He did not come to school," replied Grieder. "On Saturday I got an e-mail that he had a fever of 104."

The next day, she received another e-mail from Lacey, saying Garnett was still running a high fever.

"She said in the e-mail that she was bringing him to the pediatrician the next day to have his sodium levels checked," said Grieder, "because the slightest rise in sodium levels causes him to have seizures."

The following week, Garnett did not come to school, and Lacey said she had taken him to the emergency room twice.

"Did there come a time when you saw Garnett that week?" asked Hatfield.

"I saw him on Friday, January 17," Grieder replied. "Well, I knew he was sick all week, and I told Lacey I would be happy to go on my lunch break to see him."

"When you went to the apartment, did you go inside?"

"I did," said Grieder. "[I went into] the living room. Lacey was there and she was holding Garnett on her lap. They were sitting on the couch."

"What were your observations of Garnett?"

"He definitely wasn't the Garnett I was used to. He was lying there, holding his head. He seemed like a child who was having a headache. He was kind of whimpering and he was sucking that pacifier a lot . . . and his head was arched back."

"What was Lacey doing?"

"She was just holding him and really not doing much. And so I asked, 'What happened?' She said in the morning he had been perfectly fine and happy and joking around, and then all of a sudden, this happened."

"Being a nurse," asked the prosecutor, "what were your observations of Garnett?"

"Clearly, these symptoms that he was having didn't make any sense," she replied. "It was not a seizure, but it was not the symptoms that I really knew from my practice. I [did not] understand what was happening."

"Did you communicate your concern to Lacey?"

"I did," she replied. "I said, 'You should bring him to the doctor or the emergency room.' I asked if she had a ride, and she said . . . she would call someone to get a car."

"When you entered the living room," asked the prosecutor, "were there any other observations that you made?"

"Well, in the center of the living room there was a pole with a feeding bag and a feeding machine—just two yards away from the couch. Tubing was running through the machine, so it was either ready, had just been used, or was ready to be used."

"Were they connected in any way?"

"No, he was not connected, but there was a light-brown liquid . . . in the feeding bag."

Grieder then left to go and ask Dr. Karnow to come and look at Garnett, but his office was closed. Soon afterwards, Lacey phoned to say she was on the way to Nyack Hospital with Garnett.

"Did you have an opportunity to see Garnett and his mother again?" asked Hatfield.

"Yes," Grieder replied. "I did see Garnett again, on Sunday, in the late afternoon, when I received a frantic phone call saying they had put him on life support at Nyack Hospital. And I said to her, 'Are you alone? Would you like me to come?' She said yes, and so I went over."

"What time did you arrive at Nyack Hospital?"

"It was about six o'clock."

"And did you see Garnett?"

"Yes, he was in a hospital room with a lot of doctors and nurses tending to him."

"And where was his mother?"

"His mother was out in the corridor [with] some friends."

Grieder had remained with Garnett at Nyack Hospital until he was airlifted over to Westchester Medical Center.

"His mother went with him," she said. "She was not going to fly with him, but then she did."

"Now, Miss Grieder," asked the assistant district attorney, "did you ever communicate [with Lacey] over Facebook?"

"I did not," she replied, "because I wouldn't befriend a parent in my class. But I did get a friend request from her when [Garnett] was in Westchester hospital, either the first or second night."

"No further questions," said Hatfield.

During cross-examination, David Sachs asked Garnett's teacher about a voice mail she had received from his client on Sunday, January 19, after the child had coded at Nyack Hospital.

"And she was crying," said Sachs, "and telling you that

Garnett had a seizure and they were putting him on life support?"

"Yes," Grieder replied.

"And after the voice mail, you called back, correct?"

"Yes."

"And Lacey told you that Garnett had a seizure, he's not breathing, he's on life support?"

"Yes."

"And during that conversation, she was crying, correct?"

"She was upset," replied the teacher.

"She was crying?" repeated Sachs.

"I wasn't there to say whether she was crying or not. But she was upset."

After dismissing the witness, Judge Neary recessed for the day, telling the jury to be back on Monday morning to begin the fourth week of the trial.

44

"182 IS JUST TELLING THE WHOLE STORY"

On Monday morning, February 23, the People called Dr. Robert Pass after flying him in from Birmingham, Alabama, the night before. The Children's of Alabama pediatric physician, who had treated Garnett Spears for hypernatremia when the boy was nine weeks old, was potentially one of the most damaging witnesses to the defense.

Stephen Riebling immediately objected to the doctor's testimony, and Judge Neary asked the jury to leave while he heard Riebling's argument.

Riebling told the judge that Dr. Pass had not seen Garnett until February 15, 2009, four days after he first entered the hospital with elevated sodium levels.

"By that time, the hypernatremia had already been treated and was normal," said Riebling. "What Dr. Pass did treat him for, Your Honor, was for a failure-to-thrive condition. I don't see the relevance of Dr. Pass's testimony in this case."

Then Doreen Lloyd pointed out that Garnett had been

admitted to Children's hospital with an elevated sodium level of 165.

"Upon admission, he had a spinal tap," she told the judge, "which revealed the cerebral spinal fluid with elevated protein levels."

She said this was very concerning because it could damage brain cells.

"So, when Dr. Pass took over Garnett's [treatment]," said Lloyd, "part and parcel of what he was doing was to try and determine the cause of this hypernatremia. And he will testify that there was no medical explanation for this rise in sodium levels, and Garnett did not have any gastrointestinal issues that would indicate him not thriving. He was able to eat."

Responding, Stephen Riebling argued that any mention of Garnett having a spinal tap "flies in the face of the limiting instruction." He maintained that the judge had only ruled the Alabama hospital records admissible to explain how his client had known about the condition hypernatremia.

"Now we're talking about spinal taps and brain injury and loss of brain cells," Riebling told the judge. "And it's well outside of the scope for which the prosecution established these records would be admitted."

Judge Neary disagreed.

"I think the doctor's testimony is highly relevant to the issues that have been raised in this case," he told the defense attorney.

Judge Neary ruled that Dr. Pass could take the stand, subject to the jury being told that his evidence was not being offered to prove that the defendant had caused her son's 2009 episode of hypernatremia. They could only consider it in the context of her awareness that Garnett had suffered hypernatremia as a baby, at which point she had learned about elevated sodium levels.

After the judge had charged the jury, Dr. Pass came into court and was sworn in. He testified that an intubated Garnett Spears had been airlifted to Birmingham from Decatur General Hospital, suffering from hypernatremia and a possible seizure. He had a sodium level of 165 and was placed in the hospital's intensive care unit. He said the young patient, who had arrived with his mother, had been treated with IV fluids to carefully lower his sodium levels.

"And the diagnosis of hypernatremia was discussed with his mother?" asked Doreen Lloyd.

"I would expect that to happen," replied the doctor. "[She was] the caretaker."

"And the plan of treatment, of lowering his sodium levels, would also be something that would be discussed with his parents, correct?"

"Generally, that would be the case."

After Garnett's sodium levels had fallen back to normal, he was transferred to the general ward, where Dr. Pass supervised the next stage of his treatment. Over the next few days, Garnett had undergone a barrage of tests, including an MRI, a brain CAT scan, a chest X-ray, and a Modified Barium Swallow test, all of which were normal. He was even tested to see whether his mysterious rise in sodium was due to any unseen genetic or metabolic problems, but everything was fine.

"And based upon your treatment and all of the testing," asked the prosecutor, "did you come to any medical explanation for Garnett Spears's rise in sodium level prior to his admission to your facility?"

"No," replied Dr. Pass. "We never did understand why he had an elevated serum sodium."

"So there was no medical explanation for this hypernatremia?"

"None that we found."

"Nothing further."

In his cross-examination, Stephen Riebling pointed out that by the time Dr. Pass had begun treating Garnett, the boy's sodium level was normal.

"So, at the time his hypernatremia was treated at your hospital," asked Riebling, "you were not his attending physician?"

"That's correct," the doctor replied.

"No further questions."

"Again, that evidence was offered by the People," Judge Neary reminded the jury, "just to show that the defendant became aware of the situation of hypernatremia, and can't be used for [anything else]."

The last witness of the day was Christopher Cording, the senior toxicologist with the Westchester County Department of Laboratories and Research, who had analyzed the two feeding bags found in Lacey's apartment. He told the court that he had received the feeding bags—one packaged in a cardboard box and the other in a paper evidence bag—from Detective Dan Carfi on January 24, 2014, one day after Garnett Spears had been officially declared dead.

"What was the condition of the box?" asked Assistant District Attorney Christine Hatfield.

"It was sealed," Cording replied, "and opened at the time of submission, in my presence."

"When you opened the box, what did you see?"

"It contained a plastic bag that was labeled Kendall Kangaroo ePump," he testified. "The plastic bag contained about 275 milliliters of a whitish fluid that looked like milk."

Hatfield then handed the forensic toxicologist the box,

asking him to open it in front of the jury, which he did. She then asked him about the second feeding bag, found in Lacey's garbage in her kitchen.

"It was the same kind of Kendall Kangaroo ePump bag," he said. "It contained approximately three hundred milliliters of the same kind of milky liquid."

"Now, Mr. Cording," she asked, "did you know what substance you were testing for when you received these items of evidence?"

"I was asked to test for the presence of salt," he replied. "Sodium chloride."

The forensic toxicologist said he had taken the bags into the laboratory and used an AutoAnalyzer machine to test for salt. He said the first feeding bag, which Lacey had asked Valerie Plauché to get rid of, contained thirteen thousand milligrams of sodium. The second one, found in her garbage, had seventeen thousand milligrams of sodium in it.

"To understand that more clearly," asked Hatfield, "what is the recommended sodium in a diet?"

"The recommended amount of sodium daily intake by the FDA is, I believe, twenty-three hundred."

He then produced a graphic he had prepared for the jury, which showed that the first feeding bag contained twenty-two servings of sodium—the equivalent of 5.5 teaspoons. The second had twenty-nine servings of salt, equaling 7.25 teaspoons.

Cording told the jury that the first feeding bag contained the same amount of salt as sixty-nine McDonald's salt packets, eight salt bagels, or twenty hot dogs. The second had the equivalent of ninety McDonald's salt packets, eleven salt bagels, or twenty-six hot dogs.

"Is it your opinion," asked the prosecutor, "that those quantities were consistent with salt being the source of that high sodium in each of the feeding bags, to a reasonable degree of scientific certainty?"

"Yes," answered the forensic toxicologist.

On Tuesday, February 24, the prosecution called its medical expert, Dr. Steven Kernie, to the stand. Once again, the defense argued against the jury hearing the doctor's testimony, saying he had not reviewed all of Garnett Spears's hospital records.

Stephen Riebling told Judge Neary that Dr. Kernie's testimony would be "bolstering" and "accumulative."

"He's going to be testifying exactly the previous testimony of Dr. Goltzman," argued Riebling, "and he will give the same answers to similar questions regarding the cause, with regard to hypernatremia."

Assistant District Attorney Patricia Murphy said that Dr. Kernie, who was associate professor of pediatrics at Columbia University and the chief of pediatric critical care medicine at NewYork-Presbyterian Hospital, should be allowed to testify.

"We have engaged an outside expert who has no dog in this fight," she explained, "who can review the medical records and, based on his expert opinion, describe what was done and what the cause is, and treatments for hypernatremia. It's perfectly appropriate for us to pursue."

Judge Neary agreed, allowing Dr. Kernie to take the stand.

Under Murphy's direct questioning, the doctor told the jury that he had reviewed all of Garnett Spears's medical charts from Nyack Hospital and Westchester Medical Center. Murphy then asked for Dr. Kernie's expert opinion about the steep rise in Garnett's sodium from 144 to 182.

"It's extremely worrisome," answered the doctor. "And my first reaction [is] that can't be right."

"And in fact this number was repeated about an hour later, correct?"

"That's correct, and it was 178, which is equivalent to 182. It's still extremely elevated. Hard to explain."

"And the jump in chloride, separately, from 114 to 160. What do you make of that?"

"Chloride goes with sodium, typically," he replied. "You can't have a jump in [one] without a jump in the [other]."

"And they are the two components of table salt?"

"That's correct."

Then the prosecutor asked whether this jump could be the result of any IV fluids or other seizure medications that Garnett had received. Dr. Kernie said it could not.

"What is hypernatremia," asked Murphy, "and how could you achieve it?"

"It's not a common problem," he replied. "It's seen in the ICU, honestly, just occasionally."

The prosecution expert said the only two known causes of hypernatremia were free water loss or "ingesting large amounts of sodium."

Murphy then asked whether Garnett's hypernatremia could have been caused by his three episodes of diarrhea that day.

"No," said the doctor. "I certainly have never seen a sodium level that high from water loss."

"Now, if you take your average child," asked Murphy, "and you gave him a teaspoon of salt by mouth, what would you expect to happen?"

"Well, you couldn't do it," he replied. "If you gave a child a teaspoon of salt and said, 'Eat this,' they would start tasting it and immediately spit it out."

"If you somehow managed to get it into his stomach, what would you expect to happen?"

"They would throw up," he answered. "The most

powerful thing that makes you throw up, that we know about, is sodium chloride, salt."

"Now, if salt was introduced into Garnett Spears," asked Murphy, "would he be able to vomit?"

"No," replied Dr. Kernie.

"And would the retching and abdominal pain, as described and exhibited by Garnett Spears in the hospital on Sunday, be consistent with an attempt to vomit?"

"Yes."

"And are you aware," asked the prosecutor, "that Garnett Spears had a G-tube, and could an amount of salt, or something containing salt, be introduced through that tube?"

"Objection," said Riebling. "Leading."

"Overruled," said the judge.

"Yes," said Dr. Kernie. "The only way you could really get salt into a five-year-old is by forcing it through some kind of G-tube."

"Based on your review of the Nyack records, Doctor, do you have an expert opinion, as to a reasonable degree of medical certainty, whether there is any medical or disease explanation for that jump in sodium and chloride on January nineteen of 2014?"

"Objection," said Riebling.

"Overruled."

"No," answered Dr. Kernie.

Under cross-examination, Dr. Kernie admitted that he had only reviewed Garnett Spears's medical records from Nyack Hospital and Westchester Medical Center, and nothing else. Out of the jurors' presence, he also acknowledged handing over to prosecutors several pages of his notes and calculations that had not been given to the defense during discovery.

"It's incredibly prejudicial," Stephen Riebling complained to Judge Neary. "We're now in court, on the eve of the close of the trial, and finally we are going to be allowed to see the notes."

He then demanded that the doctor's testimony be stricken from the record, complaining that, when Riebling had asked prosecutors before the trial whether Dr. Kernie had made any notes, they said they were uncertain but would ask.

Judge Neary then took an extended lunch break, giving the defense attorney time to review the doctor's notes before the afternoon session.

When court resumed at 2:20 P.M., Stephen Riebling began by asking Dr. Kernie how he was being compensated by the D.A.'s office.

"By the hour," he replied.

"How much are you being paid by the hour?"

"Four hundred dollars."

So far, the doctor said, he had spent around five hours working on the case outside the courtroom, but he was being paid for his time in court.

"Dr. Kernie," asked Riebling, "as far as the work on this case, there was a letter. Who was it addressed to?"

"I believe it was Miss Murphy," he replied.

"On your direct testimony," Riebling continued, "you indicated that IV fluid did not have anything to do with Garnett's [rise] in sodium. Do you recall that?"

"I do recall that."

"Now, don't you indicate in a letter to Miss Murphy . . . that the IV fluid through an intravenous catheter could have been a possibility for the ingestion of a large amount of salt?"

"I'm looking at the letter now," said the doctor, "and I don't see where I say that. I do talk about there's two ways for serum sodium to [happen], from a very large intake of salt or from free water loss."

"Turn to page two of your letter," said Riebling. "The top paragraph, right?"

"Yeah, the top paragraph," said the doctor, looking at the letter. "Oh, 'This could have occurred through his feeding tube or his intravenous catheter.' Yes, I had said that. I said, 'This could have occurred through his feeding tube or his intravenous catheter, though his feeding tube is far more likely, because it's difficult to get such large amounts of salt quickly through an IV.' "

At 2:25 P.M., the prosecution called its final witness, Dr. Aleksandar Milovanovic. The Westchester County deputy medical examiner told the jury that, during his seven years at the medical examiner's office, he had performed approximately three thousand autopsies and had assisted in a further six thousand.

He testified that he had received Garnett Spears's body on Saturday, January 25, after several organs had been removed for transplant donation. He had conducted a full autopsy, starting with a preliminary external examination, and had taken photographs and X-rays.

"Can you go step by step," asked Patricia Murphy, "[with] what you examined and exactly what you observed? Let's start with the head and brain."

"The scalp was pale and there were no bruises," said Dr. Milovanovic. "There was no appearance of injury."

The pathologist said Garnett's skull was intact, with no evidence of any trauma to the brain.

"And the brain was swollen," he told the jury, "so that expansion swelling resulted in flattening of this convolution of gyri, and it's filling [the skull]. That was pretty much the appearance."

"Can you describe flattening?" asked the prosecutor. "What are you talking about?"

"Well, normally there is a kind of arching convolution

of the appearance of the brain," Dr. Milovanovic explained. "So, when there is expansion, the skull itself is resistant and firm. And because of that, there is literally compression—pressure on the skull surface—very smooth surface to the brain. And these peaks and valleys of the brain become more flattened because of that."

Then Murphy asked if he had examined Garnett's entire digestive tract, including his stomach, intestines, and bowels, to see whether there were any abnormalities.

"Everything was normal," said the doctor.

"Doctor," asked Murphy, "did you see anything . . . that would indicate the presence of celiac disease?"

"No," he replied.

"How about . . . any evidence of Crohn's disease in this child?"

"There was none."

Dr. Milovanovic said he had sent a number of cultures from Garnett's body to the Westchester County laboratory, to check for any infectious diseases.

"All results came back as negative," he said, "so there were no infections."

Then Murphy asked if hypernatremia can result in brain damage, and Dr. Milovanovic agreed it could.

"And were you aware of the jump in sodium from 144 to 182," she asked, "on Sunday, the nineteenth of January 2014?"

"Objection," said Riebling. "Leading."

"Overruled," said Judge Neary.

"I was aware, and I was impressed," answered the medical examiner. "182 is just telling the whole story. This is way up. So, that was the realization that there was hypernatremia at one point."

"And, Doctor, did you see anything in all your testing and examinations of the body, and in all the records you were able to review, that would provide an explanation for the hypernatremia that caused the death of Garnett Spears?"

"Objection," said Riebling.

"Overruled."

At this point, the experienced pathologist choked up with emotion and did not answer.

"How did Garnett get to the hypernatremia that killed him?" repeated the prosecutor.

"Objection."

"Sustained."

"You told the jury about his lack of disease and also his lack of infection, correct?"

"Yes."

"Did you come to a conclusion as to what caused the brain death in Garnett Spears?"

"Objection."

"Overruled."

"It's a child getting sodium from the outside," replied Dr. Milovanovic. "Just being injected with sodium."

"Based on everything you saw in this case, did you form an expert opinion, to a reasonable degree of certainty, as to the cause of death to Garnett Spears?"

"Yes, I did."

"And can you tell the jury what your opinion is?"

"He died of hypernatremia due to an exogenous source, which resulted also in brain swelling."

"And did you come to a conclusion as to the manner of death?"

"Yes," replied the doctor. "It's homicide."

In cross-examination, Stephen Riebling asked Dr. Milovanovic if he had spoken to Assistant District Attorney Christine Hatfield before starting the autopsy. Dr. Milovanovic said he had, for about an hour.

"Did she indicate to you," asked the defender, "that the district attorney was pursuing a murder investigation with regard to this case?"

"No," replied Dr. Milovanovic. "It was an informative conversation about what was found so far in this matter, but I would assume that they were. So nobody specifically marked that as a murder investigation."

"But the presence of the assistant district attorney before the autopsy was an indication that they were pursuing a murder investigation?"

"Yes."

Then the defense attorney asked whether any of the lab reports that he had ordered showed the presence of any sodium or hypernatremia.

"Yes," he replied. "There was in fact minimal hypernatremia, but that's postmortem and cannot be fully reliable and has to be put in context."

"But the determination that there's hypernatremia in the blood of Garnett Spears, and there's a lot, is not from the autopsy?"

"No."

"So, it's from the medical records that you read?"

"As I said, the 182 results were just unbelievable."

"Well, my question was, Doctor," said Riebling, "not that the results were unbelievable, [but] that your understanding [of] the hypernatremia didn't come from your autopsy . . . but it came from your review of Nyack Hospital?"

"Because it cannot possibly be coming from my office," he explained. "I'm performing all this as a medical doctor. I cannot do just plucking organs."

"You didn't answer my question yes or no."

"Objection," said Murphy.

"Strike it," ordered the judge.

"Doctor," said Riebling, "is it your understanding that hypernatremia causes brain shrinkage or brain swelling?"

"My understanding is that hypernatremia causes brain shrinkage," he replied.

"I have no further questions," said Riebling.

Then, Patricia Murphy formally rested the prosecution's case, and the judge sent the jury out for a short recess.

Judge Neary met in his chambers with both sides to discuss scheduling now that the People had rested its case. The defense said they still had not decided whether Lacey Spears would take the stand but would have an answer by 9:00 A.M. the next day.

45

"IT'S ALL ABOUT LACEY—MOTHER OF THE YEAR"

On Wednesday morning, the *Journal News* carried the banner headline "Lacey Spears Trial: Accused Mom May Testify."

"Will she or won't she?" it began. "Whether Lacey Spears testifies in her murder trial is the big question."

If Lacey Spears did decide to testify, court would resume at 2:30 P.M. for the defense case to begin. And there was much speculation among reporters that Lacey wanted to take the stand and tell the jury her version of what had happened to Garnett. As one of the stars of her high school forensics team, she had already proved herself an articulate public speaker.

Just before 9:00 A.M., David Sachs and Stephen Riebling arrived, going straight into Judge Neary's chambers. A few minutes later, word filtered out that, on the advice of her lawyers, the defendant would not be taking the stand.

Later, David Sachs would explain that they decided against putting their client on the stand because it was unnecessary. The prosecution's evidence was weak and entirely circumstantial.

"She's always wanted to defend herself," he maintained, "and we did that. And so, when you have a case with no evidence, why put your client through the pain of reliving the death of her son and being asked questions about his death?"

Early Thursday morning, a crowd of reporters and TV crews from all the New York network affiliates began gathering outside courtroom 302 of the Westchester County courthouse for the summations. Sitting by herself on a bench outside, Rebecca Spears looked visibly upset as she chatted with a *48 Hours* producer.

Because the judge had allowed cameras into court for the closing arguments, TV camera crews from the *Journal News* and *48 Hours* were already inside the courtroom, setting up their equipment.

At 9:30 A.M., the courtroom doors opened. The detectives who had worked on the case went in, taking their seats in the front row of the public gallery. Dr. Jennifer Canter, the Westchester Medical Center child abuse expert, who had not been called as a witness, was in the courtroom for the first time. The public gallery was packed with reporters and several members of the public who had been following the case.

At around 9:45 A.M., an ashen-faced Lacey Spears was led into court, sobbing profusely. Wearing a black suit and a blue shirt, she dabbed her eyes with a tissue.

Then, before the jury entered, Stephen Riebling asked Judge Neary to dismiss the case on the grounds that the People had failed to make a legally sufficient case on either of the indictment's two counts.

"The request for a trial order of dismissal is denied," said the judge. "I believe they have made a prima facie case as to the two counts that will be submitted to the jury."

The jury then came in and took its seats in the jury box to hear the closing arguments.

"Right, Ladies and Gentlemen," Judge Neary told them. "When we left [Tuesday] night, the People had rested. I'll now turn to the defense to ask if they have any evidence or witnesses they care to offer at this juncture."

"The defense rests," said David Sachs.

Judge Neary told the jury that, since they had now heard all the evidence in the case, both sides would now give their closing arguments.

"Following summations," he told the jury, "I'll instruct you on the law, and then you can begin deliberating."

Stephen Riebling stood up and walked over to the jury box to begin. He told them that the presumption of innocence is the cornerstone of the American justice system.

"It is a fundamental protection that each of us share with Lacey Spears," he declared. "The burden of proof is borne by the prosecution . . . If they do not prove each and every . . . element of the crime that they have charged beyond a reasonable doubt, then the law obligates you to return a verdict in favor of Lacey Spears and find her not guilty."

He described the People's case as being "riddled with reasonable doubt," and because the prosecution had failed to prove each and every element of the indictment, the jury must return a not guilty verdict.

"You might recall the deafening silence that I referenced in my opening statement," he said. "And I stand here now and submit to you that deafening silence remains. The fact in the matter is that the People have failed to present any direct evidence to you against Lacey Spears."

The defense attorney then asked why Lacey would

"suddenly and inexplicably" poison her son at Nyack Hospital while she was under twenty-four-hour EEG video surveillance.

"And the People," he said, "have presented absolutely no evidence that would explain why."

Riebling said the "essential issue" was how Garnett Spears had become hypernatremic, and he labeled the prosecution's frequent mentions of celiac disease, Crohn's disease, liver disease, kidney disease, and cochlear implants as "red herrings."

"They're meaningless," he told the jury, "and they're meant to draw you off the real focus of the case, which is that Nyack Hospital was negligent. And it was Nyack Hospital's negligence that resulted in Garnett Spears's . . . hypernatremia."

He told the jury that, despite the prosecutors' contention, Garnett Spears was never a healthy child.

"If you look at the medical records, which we did," said Riebling, "we find that Garnett Spears was not a healthy child. He had long-standing and persistent gastrointestinal problems, and those gastrointestinal problems would come back at Nyack Hospital."

He described his client as a mother who "cared deeply about her child," doing everything she could for him in Nyack Hospital. He claimed that the EEG video fully backed this up.

"She was never more than five feet from his side," he told the jury, "which is what you would expect and want a parent to do when they have a sick child in the hospital. Whatever Garnett needed, Lacey did for him. If he needed a drink of water, she got it. He needed his clothes changed after he soiled [them], she did it. He needed something to eat, she got it. She played with him. She got him coloring books. She dressed him. She put two pairs of socks on his feet, so he could play on the floor, so he wouldn't

be cold. If she's planning on killing him, why does sh
care about how cold his feet are?"

Riebling then accused the prosecutors of creatin
many illusions in the case, citing the example of Dr. Care
Goltzman ordering the Poland Spring bottle to be seize
after Garnett had coded at Westchester Medical Center

"The story ended right there," he told the jury. "Th
implication is clear. That water bottle is involved. Th
only one who had access to that water bottle in the mir
utes before Garnett Spears coded was Lacey Spears. An
the implication is . . . she did something with that wate
bottle."

He accused prosecutor Doreen Lloyd of furtherin
"the illusion" by having Dr. Goltzman identify exhib
186, the Poland Spring bottle, for the jury.

"And then the examination stops," he said. "The illu
sion's been furthered. That water bottle was suspiciou
I'm already suspicious. Garnett is suddenly dead. Onl
mom could have done it."

Riebling said he had "quickly dispelled the illu
sion" during his cross-examination of Dr. Goltzma
He then read out an extract to the jury, in which D
Goltzman agreed that the water bottle "is of no conse
quence with regard to his sodium level" because th
doctor's calculations were proving to be correct.

"The illusion is exposed," Riebling announced. "In ju
a few short questions we get the ultimate answer, the u
timate truth. That water bottle was of no consequence a
to what was happening to Garnett Spears."

The defender also pointed out that, in his discharg
summary, Dr. Goltzman had originally written that th
cause of Garnett Spears's death was "undetermined."

"Which means we don't know the cause," he told th
jury. "And if we don't know the cause beyond a reasor

ble doubt, how can we blame Lacey Spears? How can we convict her of the most severe of crimes? We can't."

He then asked the jury to hold the prosecutors to their promises during their summation.

"Ask Doreen Lloyd," he said, "why did she create those llusions with regard to the water bottle? Have her stand up in front of you and explain for herself."

"Objection, Your Honor," said Patricia Murphy.

"Sustained," said the judge. "Let's move on. That's an nappropriate comment."

"This is an emotional case," said Riebling. "There's no denying it. But we need to put aside our feelings and our emotions and look squarely at the facts and what those acts tell us."

He reproached the prosecutors for deliberately playing to the jury's emotions by screening heartbreaking video of Garnett lying in his Nyack Hospital bed.

"This case got particularly emotional," he said, while Lacey Spears cradled her head in her hands at the defense able. "They showed us clips of Garnett Spears . . . with ubes coming out of him, motionless on the bed, doctors unning in and out. And it was emotional. It brought tears to eyes. And that is intentional."

"Objection, Your Honor," said Murphy.

"Sustained."

"What I submit to you," he continued, "is that the prosecution plays on your emotions."

"Objection, Your Honor."

"Sustained."

"Put aside your emotions," he told the jury. "Put aside your sympathy . . . and hold them to their burden of proof. Make them answer all the questions that I asked them."

Finally, he reminded the jury that the People must prove each and every element of the crime beyond a reasonable doubt and that his client had the presumption of innocence.

"Lacey Spears is presumed innocent in the eyes of the law," he declared. "You are required to also presume her innocence until *they* meet their burden, and if *they* fail to, then you must find a verdict in favor of Lacey Spears.

"And based on the credible evidence of the case . . . there is more than significant doubt. And I'm going to ask you, Ladies and Gentlemen, when you have your chance to deliberate, think about these questions of what I presented to you . . . and return a verdict in favor of Lacey Spears."

The defense attorney then sat down after speaking for 140 minutes, and Judge Neary dismissed the jury for the lunch break.

At 2:05 P.M., Lacey Spears was led into the courtroom for the People's summation. In front of her was a large monitor with a blown-up calendar of January 2014. Crucial days in the case were underlined in red. Looking tired and worn, Lacey yawned at the defense table while David Sachs whispered into her ear.

After the jury was seated, Judge Neary asked lead prosecutor Patricia Murphy to begin.

"Good afternoon, Ladies and Gentleman," said Murphy. "I know it hasn't been the easiest case to be a juror on, even putting aside the weather. The subject matter is very difficult. We're talking about the murder of a five year-old boy."

The thickset white-haired prosecutor began by describing Garnett Spears to the jury. By all accounts, she said, he was "a wonderful kid" and "full of life," with a natural gift of making friends with everyone, young and old.

"He loved his school," she told the jurors, "but now

he's never going to get to go back. He's never going to play Little League. He's never going to grow up. And the question is, Why? Because this defendant, for some bizarre reason, chose to ignore the risk of harm of what she did. She completely ignored that giving this kid sodium could result in his sickness and his death."

Murphy said that even after poisoning Garnett, Lacey could have saved his life by telling doctors that she had fed him salt, so they could have changed their treatment.

"But she stayed silent," said Murphy, "and that's where we get the evidence that she clearly didn't care if he lived or died."

Stepping down from the lectern to stand in front of the jury box, Murphy said it was only natural to ask how a mother could do this to her child. But the evidence would allow them to "draw logical conclusions."

"The motive is bizarre, the motive is scary, but it exists," she told the jury. "For some reason known only to her, creating this false persona, this caring mother doing everything she can for this sick child, struggling along to take care of the child—creating that persona was important.

"She apparently craved the attention of family, of her friends, of her coworkers, and most particularly, of the medical professionals. She wanted to be seen as *this* mother. Is this a normal mother? Well, of course not. It's not a normal crime.

"The problem for this fantasy world of 'Look at this burden. I'm carrying this child. If only he would get better, but he doesn't' is the most basic one. And that is that Garnett was not a sickly little boy."

Murphy said that he had difficulties at birth, with the Nissen fundoplication surgery and the G-tube operation.

"But not now," she said. "Not at age four. Not at age five. He's not a sickly little boy."

She told the jury that Garnett had become very inde
pendent, freely wandering around the Fellowship Com
munity and chatting with adults.

"Keep that in mind," she said, "because now he's
five-year-old. And how long will it be before he's able t
figure out what's happening to him and tell people wha
his mother is doing?"

Murphy asked the jury to focus on some of the defer
dant's claims to doctors about Garnett's "supposed ill
nesses." She reminded them that every medical professiona
had based his or her treatment decisions on what Ga
nett's mother told them.

"There is no medical record," Murphy said, "[in which
a doctor said, 'I saw this and I knew that this is the ill
ness.' No, it's the mother that reports the illness, so I trea
it because the mother tells me it exists, and he's a child.

She told the jury that it was only the defendant wh
had said that Garnett needed a G-tube because he coul
not eat normally by mouth and had numerous food aller
gies. But these claims were repeatedly refuted by numer
ous witnesses who saw Garnett eating everything, an
often asking for seconds.

"So who says he needs the G-tube?" she asked. "Th
defendant."

Murphy reminded the jury of Lacey's false claims tha
her son suffered from the serious gastrointestinal disor
ders of celiac disease and Crohn's disease.

"Who would wish that on a five-year-old?" she asked
"Who would want him to have that kind of systemic ill
ness? Nobody normal. But this defendant did. For som
reason, she liked the attention of being the mother of
sick child. It fit her whole fantasy of 'This is me takin
care of my sick child.' And the facts aren't going to ge
in the way."

The prosecutor observed that, from Florida, ove

Christmas in 2013, the defendant had told Garnett's teacher and others that Garnett had been in the pediatric critical care unit, when he had not.

It was on their return to New York after the holidays, said Murphy, that the defendant took things to a "new and very dangerous level."

"[By] January her son is growing older and even more verbal," said Murphy, "and her approach changes."

Lacey, she told the jury, was no longer content just to make up Garnett's illnesses because too many people were becoming suspicious of her.

"Now she's going to make him sick," said the prosecutor, "because people are starting to maybe not believe her when she claims these things. Now she's going to take steps to make sure he's sick."

Then, using a PowerPoint presentation on a monitor in the courtroom, the prosecutor methodically led the jury through a day-by-day account of what had happened to Garnett Spears in January 2014.

It started on Friday, January 10, with the visit to Dr. Karnow's office and Lacey's claims that Garnett was having "night terrors" and "plays about themes of death." It led to Garnett lying brain dead in Westchester Medical Center twelve days later, and Lacey's subsequent call to Valerie Plauché to get rid of the salt-laced feeding bag.

At the end of her presentation, Murphy told the jury that Nyack Hospital and Westchester Medical Center, which had been unfairly attacked by the defense, had provided excellent treatment.

"It wasn't Nyack [Hospital] that killed this child; it's this defendant," said the prosecutor. "The person with means: the G-tube. The motive: this bizarre need to be the mother of a sick child. And the opportunity: a quiet time in the bathroom to kill Garnett by salt poisoning.

There's only one person that has all three of those thing
and that's the defendant."

Murphy told the jurors that Lacey knew all about hy
pernatremia and the damage it could cause, informatio
gleaned during the excess-salt condition that had put Gar
nett in the PICU in Alabama when he was a little baby.

"She also researched hypernatremia," she reminde
the jury. "She knows that it can cause seizure. It can caus
edema. It can cause death. And yet she's deliberately ig
nored this risk. It just got in the way."

The prosecutor said the defendant didn't care whethe
her son lived or died, as long as she could bask in sym
pathy and attention. Then, as Lacey stared dispassionatel
from the defense table, the prosecutor described Lacey'
poisoning of her son with salt as "nothing short of tor
ture."

The prosecutor then asked the jury to consider Lace
Spears's behavior after she learned that Garnett was brai
dead and would not recover.

"She throws herself dramatically on the floor of th
hospital hallway," said Murphy. "She's kicking and flai
ing her arms, and . . . [she] kept up this whole display un
til her own mother came out and said, 'No, no, you'v
got to go inside and be with your son.'

"If you're a charitable person, you could look at tha
and say, 'It's hit her. She realizes what she's done, and thi
is the reaction.' If you want to take a harsher view, yo
could say that this is just another performance. The dis
traught mother, rolling on the floor because of what's hap
pened to her child.

"Because . . . it has always been about Lacey. Thi
case has never been about Garnett. It's all about Lacey—
mother of the year."

"Objection," said Stephen Riebling, rising to his feet

"Overruled," answered the judge.

"Well, Ladies and Gentlemen, that charade should end oday," said the prosecutor. "I'd ask you to use your com- non sense. I'd ask you to put the pieces together—not just ne thing at a time; you've got to look at the context. Put all together to follow the evidence where it takes you. he can't get past those bags in her house.

"And, based on the evidence and based on the law, I'm oing to ask you to do justice . . . for a five-year-old boy vho should not be dead. I'm going to ask you to do jus- ice for Garnett. Thank you."

At 3:02 P.M., Judge Neary took a five-minute break be- ore charging the jurors on the law and then sending hem off to the jury room to begin their deliberations.

he six-man, six-woman jury began deciding Lacey pears's fate at 3:56 P.M. on Thursday. Ten minutes later, he foreman sent out a note. The jury was asking to see he Nyack Hospital lab results on Garnett's spike in so- ium; a portion of the video EEG, showing Lacey going nto the bathroom with a feeding tube; the chart of salt evels found in the two feeding bags; and an excerpt from)ona Younger's testimony. Jurors also asked for a writ- en explanation of second-degree murder and first-degree nanslaughter.

After the jury had deliberated for another twenty min- tes, Judge Neary sent them home, telling them to come ack at 10:00 A.M. on Friday to resume.

At 10:25 A.M. on Friday morning, the jury was back n the courtroom for a read-back of Oona Younger's tes- mony. They particularly wanted to hear the section bout Lacey's claim that she had not tube-fed Garnett in he week prior to his admittance to Nyack Hospital.

After this was read out by the court reporter, the two amning EEG videos were screened on a monitor in front f the jury box. The first one, covering the period from

10:25 A.M. to 10:46 A.M. on Sunday, January 19, 2014 clearly showed Lacey Spears walking into the bathroom holding a connector tube. The jurors watched the defendant then bring Garnett out, and his ensuing suffering.

While the jury watched with rapt attention, the defendant sat slumped at the defense table with her head down.

The next video, from that same day, covered the period from 3:46 P.M. to 4:01 P.M. It showed the defendant taking Garnett into the bathroom a second time. After she brought him out, Garnett looked dazed. His condition deteriorated until he finally coded and had to be intubated and airlifted to Westchester Medical Center.

After viewing both videos, the visibly moved and shaken jurors filed out of the courtroom to resume deliberations.

At 2:50 P.M., the jury requested a written definition of depraved indifference and reckless engagement, two of the key elements of the second-degree murder charge.

When the jury returned to the courtroom, Judge Neary explained that although he could not give them a written definition, he would read aloud the definition provided by the New York Penal Law resources that judges use to instruct juries.

A person has a depraved indifference to human life when that person has an utter disregard for the value of human life—a willingness to act, not because she means to cause grievous harm to the person who is killed, but because she simply does not care whether or not grievous harm will result. In other words, a person who is depravedly indifferent is not just willing to take a grossly unreasonable risk to human life—that person does not care how the risk turns out. Depraved indifference to human life reflects a wicked or inhuman state of mind by brutal, heinous, and despicable acts.

A person acts with a depraved indifference to human life when, having a conscious objective not to kill but to harm, she engages in torture or a brutal, prolonged, and ultimately fatal course of conduct against a particularly vulnerable victim.

Judge Neary then sent the jurors back to resume deliberations. But at 3:30 P.M., they sent out another note, asking the judge to reread the definition of depraved indifference. After he did so, deliberately slower than before, they returned to the jury room to continue.

Finally, at 4:30 P.M., Judge Neary sent the jury home for the weekend, reminding them not to expose themselves to any coverage of the case.

46

THE VERDICT

At 9:00 A.M. on Monday, March 2, Terry Spears and his daughter, Rebecca, arrived at the Westchester County courthouse, anticipating an imminent verdict. Lacey' father had arrived in New York on Saturday, driving all the way from Kentucky in treacherous conditions.

There had been another heavy snowstorm on Sunday night, and a juror had gotten stuck in the snow, delaying deliberations for almost an hour and a half. Outside court room 302, there was great anticipation among the re porters and news crews, who were now betting on when the verdict would come in.

At 11:05 A.M., just fifteen minutes after the jury had resumed deliberations, the jury foreman sent out a note asking the judge to reread the definition of depraved in difference for the fourth time. But there was also another question. The jury asked whether the assessment of the defendant's state of mind included mental illness.

"There's no evidence in this case of mental illness,"

Judge Neary told them, "so it's not being considered at this point."

Then they filed out of the courtroom to continue.

At 12:25 P.M., the court sergeant came out of the courtroom and announced that the jury had reached a verdict. Immediately, all the TV news crews, who had been waiting outside in the hallway for almost two days, rushed in to start setting up equipment to broadcast the verdict live.

Five minutes later, the courtroom doors were opened, and detectives Dan Carfi, Kirk Budnick, and Gregory Dunn took their places in the front row of the public gallery, alongside the jury box. Across the courtroom, behind the defense table, sat Terry and Rebecca Spears, looking apprehensive.

Then Lacey Spears was brought into court in handcuffs, yawning and looking terrified as her attorneys whispered in her ear. Just a few feet away, Rebecca Spears put an arm around her father. Lacey turned around and gave them a weak smile. Then she clasped her hands tightly together and started shaking.

A few minutes later, the jurors came into the court with a solemn look on their faces.

"We received a note about ten minutes ago," said Judge Neary. It says, 'We have reached a verdict,' signed by the foreman. Do you have the verdict sheet? Can I take a look at it briefly?"

After glancing at the verdict sheet, the judge continued.

"Mr. Foreman," he said, "if you stand, our clerk will receive the verdict on behalf of the jury."

"Members of the jury," asked the court clerk, Ellen Uhl, "answering through your floor person, have you agreed upon a verdict?"

"Yes," replied the foreman.

"Members of the jury," said Uhl, "answering through your floor person, how say you to count one: murder in the second degree? Not guilty or guilty?"

"Guilty," said the foreman.

"Is this verdict unanimous?"

"Yes."

"Members of the jury," the clerk continued, "answering collectively, is this your verdict?"

"Yes," said all twelve jurors as Lacey lowered her head and her father closed his eyes in shock. Rebecca put her arm around him.

Judge Neary then thanked the jury for their diligence and conscientiousness during the trial and dismissed them.

After they left, the judge addressed all the attorneys.

"I'd like to commend both sets of attorneys in the way they tried this obviously emotional case," he told them. "They wielded great passion for their respective sides, but they remained courteous to each other and the court. And that's duly noted.

"We'll set a sentencing date of April eighth. Court stands adjourned."

Lacey Spears was handcuffed and led out of the court to return to the Westchester County jail.

Outside the court, the two defense attorneys told reporters that their client would be appealing the verdict.

"We're disappointed," admitted Stephen Riebling. "It's still a mystery as to what caused Garnett's death."

"What's your immediate reaction to the verdict?" asked a TV reporter.

"We feel it's against the weight of credible evidence in the case," said David Sachs. "We intend to appeal and take this case where it needs to go."

"How was Lacey, right after the verdict?" asked another reporter. "Did you speak with her?"

"I did not discuss how she was feeling," Sachs replied. "I think you could see that the verdict was somewhat of a shock to her. I'm not going to speculate beyond that what she was feeling or thinking, because I didn't discuss it with her."

The defense attorneys were then asked if they regretted not bringing up the issue of mental illness at trial.

"Absolutely not," Sachs replied. "As the judge said, there's no evidence of mental illness in this case."

Leaving the court, most of the jurors ducked reporters' questions about how they reached their verdict. But alternate juror Andrew DiGiacomo told CBS News that the disturbing EEG video, showing Lacey Spears going into the bathroom with the connector tube and Garnett's subsequent suffering, had convinced him of her guilt.

"The way she came out of the bathroom," he explained, "sat on the bed with him, and just watched him. Kind of like if you put something in the microwave, put it on two minutes, and then just sit there waiting for something to happen, that you know is going to happen eventually."

Another juror, Michael Brown, told the *Journal News* that he would have liked Lacey Spears to take the stand.

"It helps when somebody stands up and says, 'I didn't do that,'" he said. "I wouldn't leave it to someone else."

Brown said he and the other jurors did not buy the defense assertion that Garnett Spears had died through hospital error.

"The defense was trying to cast innuendo," he said. "It was easy to see though where they were coming from. If you're naive, you can believe that."

Garnett's father, Chris Hill, who watched the verdict live in Alabama, called Lacey "heartless and emotionless."

"She's sick," he told Shawn Cohen, who was now working for the *New York Post*, "and needs to stay locked up for the rest of her short life. I hope they don't give her special treatment and don't put her in solitary. She needs to be put in the general population so she has to fear for her miserable life every day."

That afternoon, Westchester County District Attorney Janet DiFiore held a press conference in her office, publicly thanking all the detectives and assistant district attorneys for getting justice for Garnett.

"Today, as the jury convicted Lacey Spears of the depraved-mind murder of her five-year-old son, Garnett-Paul Spears," said DiFiore, "Miss Spears was remanded back to the Westchester County jail, where she will be housed until sentence, which is scheduled for April eighth. At sentencing, my office will be asking the court to sentence Miss Spears to the maximum sentence allowed under the law, which is a life sentence."

The district attorney singled out the "incredible team" of lead detective Dan Carfi, from the Westchester County Police, and Ramapo Police detectives Kirk Budnick and Gregory Dunn, for their "extraordinary effort."

"This was not a close case," she said. "This team worked, over the course of this past year, to put together a very strong body of evidence that put us in the position to argue to the jury that there was one conclusion to draw, and that was that Lacey Spears murdered her child."

Then a reporter asked about her reaction to the defense's intention to appeal the verdict.

"We will be prepared to meet any and all issues that are raised on appeal," said DiFiore, "and we are very confident that this conviction will be upheld."

Another TV reporter questioned why the subject of mental illness had never entered the case.

"You would have to speak to Miss Spears or her counsel," replied the district attorney.

Later that day, Matt Uppenbrink released a statement on behalf of the Fellowship Community, saying the healing could now begin.

"[We are] looking ahead to a time when young Garnett Spears can be remembered for his life and the joys in it," read his statement, "rather than through the sad events that led to his passing and, ultimately, to the verdict of today."

After the verdict, Lacey Spears continued to proclaim her innocence, saying she was shocked that the jury had found her guilty after all the evidence they had heard at trial.

"I always thought that I would be going home," she said in late June 2015. "I'm innocent, and I never did anything to harm my son."

In her interview for a presentencing report, she blamed negligent medical staff for Garnett's death. She also maintained that Valerie Plauché had lied about the phone call to get rid of the feeding bag.

In the wake of the verdict, Lacey's family stood squarely behind her, expressing astonishment at the jury's verdict.

"We were expecting her to come home with us," said Rebecca Spears, who attended every day of the trial. "We weren't expecting to hear 'guilty.' The prosecution had a lot of things to say, but I felt like David and Stephen also had a lot of good things that supported her innocence. We thought the jury heard a lot of things, and they were going to say she was innocent."

47

"YOU SUFFER FROM MUNCHAUSEN BY PROXY"

At 9:45 A.M. on Wednesday, April 8, Lacey Spears was back in Judge Robert Neary's courtroom for sentencing. Wearing a gray suit and black blouse, she faced a maximum of twenty-five years to life for the murder of her son. There was no trace of emotion on her face.

The courtroom was packed with news reporters and a crew from CBS's *48 Hours,* which was planning an hourlong prime-time show on the case. All the detectives who worked the case were back in the front row of the public gallery, with the exception of Detective Kirk Budnick, who was vacationing in Florida. And Nellie Grossenbacher was in the courtroom for the first time since testifying against her former friend. She clutched a laminated memorial card from the Green Meadow Waldorf School service with Garnett's photograph on it.

"What would the People like to say prior to sentencing?" asked Judge Neary.

"Your Honor," began Assistant District Attorney Doreen Lloyd, "Garnett Spears should be in school today, and he's not, because his mother murdered him."

Lloyd said that she would talk about Garnett Spears because a record of this sentencing would be read by future parole boards.

"He was beautiful on the inside and out," she said. "He had blond hair blue eyes. He was full of energy. He was vibrant. He was inquisitive. Always asking questions."

She described him as "a leader" in his class at school, saying he loved doing the normal things that every little boy did.

"He had a right to grow up," said Lloyd, "a right to grow old, and she stole that from him. She committed the ultimate betrayal that a mother can do. She was supposed to love him, nurture him, care for him, and protect him. And she did the complete opposite, and she killed him."

On hearing this, Lacey, who was standing in handcuffs, flanked by her lawyers, turned away from the cameras filming the proceedings.

"It is unspeakable what this woman has done," the prosecutor continued. "Everything about this case has always been about Lacey. We will never know what Garnett could have become. He will never play in a baseball team. He will never graduate from high school. He will never get married and have children of his own. All because his mother killed him."

Lloyd told the judge that this case had always been about Lacey Spears because she never thinks of anybody else.

"And it's clear," said Lloyd, "because she always characterized herself as a single mother of a special needs, sick child. And that was a facade. It was not true."

Lloyd told the judge that, despite Dr. Ivan Darenkov's repeated requests that Garnett undergo a feeding evaluation to see whether the boy really needed his G-tube, Lacey had refused.

"And she did that for two reasons," said Lloyd. "One because she wanted to continue to portray her son as a sick little boy, for her own bizarre need for attention. And the second reason was because, with that gastrointestinal tube, she can single-handedly control what she put into the body of her son. And she ended up using that G-tube as a weapon to kill him."

Lloyd said the presentencing report had made it clear that the defendant refused to take responsibility for her actions.

"She continues to blame the very medical staff," said Lloyd, "that tried desperately to save the life of her son. She projects blame onto others."

The prosecutor said it was important for any future parole board to know the "amount of pain and suffering" she had put her son through, and how, after poisoning him with salt in Nyack Hospital, she "watches him like a scientific experiment" as she sits there, waiting for the result that she knows will soon happen.

"As sick as that sounds," said Lloyd, "that's what she does."

The most critical evidence, said the prosecutor, was the harrowing video EEG extracts, which spoke "volumes of the mind-set" of Lacey Spears and her actions. One extract, showing Garnett in convulsions after the second time Lacey took him into the bathroom, was particularly disturbing.

"You could hear a pin drop in this trial when that happened," Lloyd told the judge. "But she watched it that day. She watched and she did nothing. As the medical professionals had to intubate and sedate her child . . . she stood there and said nothing to save the life of her son."

The prosecutor said that perhaps the most disturbing aspect of the video was that the viewer knew exactly how it would end.

"The medical staff didn't know how it was going to end," she said, "when they were desperately treating him and trying to save his life. But we knew, and you watched a child die. You know you are watching a child dying. It is horrible, but she watched him.

"Your Honor, her actions were beyond depraved, despicable, and evil. She showed her victim no mercy in that hospital room, the day she poisoned him to his eventual death. And the People respectfully request Your Honor show her no mercy in this courtroom today, and that you sentence her to the maximum sentence allowed under the law, of twenty-five years to life in prison for the death of her very own son, Garnett Spears."

Then Judge Neary asked David Sachs to address the court on behalf of his client.

" 'Thou shalt not kill,' " began the defense attorney. "One of the most fundamental and intuitive maxims of human law and morality is the prohibition of murder. Since the founding of our country, and prior to that, for thousands of years, laws prohibiting murder have existed."

Sachs told the judge that, over the years, these laws have evolved, leading to the New York legislature's drafting of the depraved indifference murder statute, which states that the appropriate minimum sentence for any person convicted of this crime should be fifteen years to life.

"Indeed," he told the judge, "I respectfully submit to this court that the only appropriate sentence in this matter is the minimum sentence of fifteen years to life."

Sachs said that the People's only basis for asking for

the maximum sentence of twenty-five years to life was the repetition of the evidence already heard by the jury.

"The People's description of my client," said Sachs, "is nothing more than a prosecutor's one-size-fits-all description of anyone convicted of depraved indifference murder. However, it is common knowledge that sentencing never rests upon semantics."

He observed that Lacey had no prior criminal convictions and had fully cooperated with the authorities from the very beginning.

"She does maintain her innocence," he declared. "Prior to the passing of her son, Lacey was a hardworking single mother who gave her son unconditional love, provided for all his needs and beyond, and worked tirelessly to improve and better his life."

He claimed that the prosecution's glowing description of Garnett Spears was a direct reflection of his client's parenting.

"The very reason for her move to New York," he said, "was to better the life of her son. And throughout her life she's been a devoutly religious person. She's even done volunteer work for a church, by collecting food for a backpack program to help feed elementary school children."

Sachs also asked the judge to read the positive descriptions of his client in the letters sent to the court by Garnett's family and friends, including one from the chaplain at Westchester County jail.

"They each asked for the court to bestow leniency upon Lacey at sentencing," he said. "The People have elected not to have any of Garnett's family members or relatives speak . . . here this morning on Garnett's behalf. And the reason they have not is clear and simple: [because] they are all seeking leniency.

"A sentence of twenty-five years to life in this would

be unduly severe. Accordingly, Your Honor, I'm requesting that this court sentence my client to the minimum
sentence of fifteen years to life."

Judge Neary then asked Lacey Spears if she had anything to say to the court before he passed sentence.

"No, sir," she replied.

"Miss Spears," he told her, "in many respects your
crime is unfathomable in its cruelty. You give rise to many
questions that I, frankly, don't have answers for. How can
a mother ever treat her innocent child in such a callous,
inhumane, and calculating manner? Do you even realize
the magnitude of your crime? Why didn't you seek help
at some point?"

The judge told her that this was not a spontaneous or
single, ill-conceived, solitary act.

"It was a series of planned and orchestrated actions
that really shock the conscience," he said. "Instead of nur-
turing and protecting a beautiful child, you subjected
him to five years of torment and pain. Anyone that saw
the video trail of evidence of Garnett in the hospital,
writhing in pain, unable to vomit, may never be able to
erase those images from their mind."

He noted that, after her arrest, she had refused to admit
her guilt, accusing the "dedicated doctors and nurses"
who tried to save her son's life of being "negligent, de-
ceitful, and uncaring."

"Nothing could be farther from the truth," he told her.
"You attempted to portray the police and prosecutors as
unethical and willing participants in an elaborate conspir-
acy to deny you justice."

She had brought "shame and heartbreak" to her family and friends, he said, many of whom had written letters
to the court in support of her.

"One does not have to be a psychiatrist to realize

that you suffer from a mental illness known as Munchausen by proxy," he told her. "I hope you, over the next few years, come to terms with your condition and are receptive to any treatment that may be available to you."

Then the judge asked whether something "even remotely positive" could emerge from this tragedy.

"My hope," he told her, "is that the publicity that Garnett's case has and will receive serves to put a spotlight on Munchausen by proxy syndrome and that the public becomes more aware of that condition, and people do not shy away from reporting suspected abusers who exhibit symptoms of this illness."

He told her that the sentence he was about to impose was designed not only to punish her for her crime but also to act as a deterrent to others.

"I am aware that you suffer from a mental illness," he said. "It's not one that affects your competency or ability to stand trial or your ability to know right from wrong and to appreciate the nature and consequences of your act. But it is a mental illness, all the same."

Then the judge told her that, unlike the way she had treated Garnett, he would show her "mercy" by not imposing the maximum sentence.

"I took the bench this morning," he said, "hoping you might say something that would enable me to show you some mercy. I haven't heard it from you. I'm sad that you have not taken responsibility yet for your actions, and I haven't seen any genuine sign of remorse.

"Nonetheless, I'm going to sentence you to something less than the maximum. Based upon you having been found guilty after trial by a jury of your peers for the crime of murder in the second degree, I sentence you to an indeterminate term in state prison, with a minimum of twenty years and a maximum of life."

Stephen Riebling then stood up and informed Judge

Neary that he would be filing a notice of appeal that morning with the clerk of the court.

"Very well," replied the judge, before remanding Lacey Spears into the care and custody of the New York State Department of Corrections to begin serving her sentence.

EPILOGUE

On Monday, April 13, 2015, Lacey Spears walked through the doors of the maximum-security Bedford Hills Correctional Facility in upstate New York. The twenty-seven-year-old inmate, number 15G0289, will be eligible for parole in June 2034.

She joined a list of notorious convicted female killers, including former teacher Pamela Smart, forty-seven, serving life without parole for conspiring with three others to murder her husband; Carolyn Warmus, now fifty-one, serving twenty-five years to life for shooting her lover's wife, Betty Jeanne Solomon, dead in 1989; and Marybeth Tinning, seventy-two, who is serving twenty years to life for killing her daughter.

Many Bedford Hill inmates knew all about the Mommy Blogger, and as soon as Lacey Spears arrived she complained that she was taunted by the other prisoners. She said that one of the kitchen staff even began putting packets of salt in her meals while she was waiting on line in the dining room.

Her sister, Rebecca, who visited from Florida with their grandmother soon after Lacey arrived, said, "Lacey would see [the person] do it. When she walked through the line and it would be her turn to pick up the tray [someone] would put salt packets over her meal and then hand the tray to her."

Eventually, she said, Lacey complained to prison administrators, and it stopped.

On a sunny Friday morning in June 2015, two months after she arrived, Lacey sat down in the visiting room at Bedford Hills for an exclusive interview for this book. Wearing a light-pink short-sleeve shirt and slacks instead of the usual green regulation prison uniform, Lacey and her attorney Stephen Riebling sat across a table from me for the ninety-minute interview.

Throughout the interview, Lacey Spears expressed confidence that she would soon be free again after her upcoming appeal was heard.

"It's been brutal in here," she said. "Crimes involving children are considered the worst here. I hear them talking behind my back, calling me 'baby killer,' 'child killer,' and 'mother of the year.' But I know it's not who I am."

She explained her decision not to go into protective custody, saying it would have meant being locked in her cell twenty-three hours a day.

"It's been very hard, adjusting to being here," she said. "You always have to look behind your back, and I don't trust anyone. I don't have any friends, but I have people to talk to."

She spends her days practicing yoga and working out in the gym. She also takes a creative writing class and reads true crime books, which she orders through the prison.

"I'm starting college in the fall," Lacey said proudly, "to study psychology, sociology, and American literature.

We can't use the Internet here, although I will be able to use the computer to go online when I start college."

She goes to church every Sunday, attending the Catholic service "because I don't like the Protestant one."

She tries to avoid eating prison food, complaining that "it's horrible and all carbohydrates." Instead, she relies on the food boxes her family regularly sends.

She has little privacy in the prison and sleeps with seventy other inmates in a giant bedroom known as the "fishbowl."

"You can work your way up through different levels until you can have your own bedroom," she told me, "but I don't expect to be here that long."

Lacey feels betrayed by many of her friends, especially the ones who testified against her.

"I couldn't believe it when Oona [Younger] took the stand against me," she said. "I always felt very close to her and let her look after Garnett."

She vehemently proclaims her innocence, vowing to fight for justice so she can go back home to Florida.

"Why would I have done it in the hospital?" she asked. "It doesn't make any sense. I didn't give him any salt, and there's no evidence that I did. The hospital made a mistake, and now I'm paying for it."

She said she desperately misses her son, who she knows is now with her mother in heaven.

"I think about Garnett all the time," she said, "and I'll always love him. I had a terrible year, losing my son and then my mother, and now I'm incarcerated. This is all about Garnett. He should be starting first grade."

When asked about Garnett's father, Chris Hill, Lacey claimed that he never made a single attempt to see his son.

"Chris knew that Garnett was his son," she explained. "He lived downstairs to us, and never once did he try and see him. I never asked him for a cent of child support."

Questioned about Blake, the man she had lovingly described as her soul mate and Garnett's father, Lacey now admits she made him up.

"I invented Blake to protect my son from his father," she explained. "Garnett never knew anything about his father or Blake, and he never asked who his father was."

Lacey also refuted the prosecution's contention that Garnett did not need a G-tube.

"He could never eat properly," she said, "although he was getting better towards the end. How do they know? They weren't with him all the time like I was."

Asked about her reaction to Judge Neary's assertion that she suffers from Munchausen syndrome by proxy, Lacey expressed astonishment.

"I couldn't believe what he said at the sentencing," she told me. "He had no right. He's had no training as a psychiatrist."

At the end of our visit, Lacey repeated that she was certain she would not be in Bedford Hills Correctional Facility much longer.

"It's all so unreal, and I can't believe what's happened," she said. "I know I'm innocent, and I will be home in Florida soon."

One afternoon in late June 2015, Kimberly Philipson went over to Peggy Florence's house. The two neighbors were now back on speaking terms after their falling out during Lacey Spears's time in Clearwater.

"Lacey's grandmother was walking me to the back of her house, through Garnett's playroom," said Philipson, "and I was surprised to see all his toys still neatly arranged everywhere. There were so many toys. Everything was perfectly in place, ready for him to come home and start playing."

Philipson was so amazed to see all of Garnett's toys

still in his playroom that she stopped in her tracks to make sure she wasn't dreaming.

"It was creepy," she recalled, "and Miss Peggy must have seen the look on my face because when we walked outside she said, 'It chokes me up every time I walk through and see all his toys, but Lacey told me not to get rid of anything and to keep it the way it was.'"

Then Lacey's grandmother suddenly looked her neighbor right in the eye.

"And just so you know," Peggy Florence told her, "Lacey never laid a hand on Garnett."